Enterprise: Concepts and Issues

THE GLOBAL MANAGEMENT SERIES

Enterprise: Concepts and Issues

Norin Arshed and Mike Danson

(G) Goodfellow Publishers Ltd

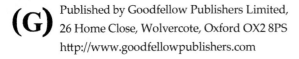

Published by Goodfellow Publishers Limited,
26 Home Close, Wolvercote, Oxford OX2 8PS
http://www.goodfellowpublishers.com

British Library Cataloguing in Publication Data: a catalogue record for this
title is available from the British Library.
Library of Congress Catalog Card Number: on file.

ISBN: 978-1-910158-75-3

 Design and typesetting by P.K. McBride, www.macbride.org.uk

Cover design by Cylinder

Printed by Baker & Taylor, www.baker-taylor.com

Contents

Acknowledgments

We are grateful to all those who helped shape the text especially our authoring team who deserve special mention. Conceiving, writing and rewriting each contribution has stretched some to the limit and all to deliver with humour and patience a valuable and coherent set of chapters. We welcome your individual and collective efforts in meeting the tight, if not impossible, deadlines. To our colleagues at Goodfellow Publishers, we remain indebted for their encouragement, support and advice.

NA and MD

Dedications

We would like to thank our colleagues who helped in writing this book.

NA and MD

Biographies

Norin Arshed is Programmes Director for the Leadership and Organisational Performance suite of MSc programmes in the Department of Business Management at Heriot-Watt University. She is an economist by background with professional experience both in the public and private sectors. Her work concentrates on enterprise policy, in particular, the role and contribution from those closely linked to the formulation process (ministers and civil servants), whilst also examining how enterprise policy is implemented (national, regional and local economic development agencies), and how entrepreneurs/SMEs experience and utilize such policy initiatives. Institutional theory is the theoretical lens used to highlight the dynamics of the enterprise policy process in her work.

Harveen Chugh is a consultant in entrepreneurship for start-ups and growing companies. She specialises in working with HE students and graduates to provide mentoring and coaching. She has consulted to the UK government on the Sirius graduate entrepreneurs programme and she was formerly a Lecturer in Entrepreneurship and Strategy at Royal Holloway University of London. Harveen gained her PhD in entrepreneurship from Imperial College London and has published research on entrepreneurial learning, feedback and university start-ups. As an ethnic minority female of Indian origin, Harveen champions diversity in entrepreneurship and supports organisations such as Girls Talk London and London Geekettes.

Mike Danson is Professor of Enterprise Policy at Heriot-Watt University and has worked widely on issues about urban and regional economic development, island and rural economies and enterprises, demographic change, volunteering, Gaelic, microbreweries and poverty. He has published 13 edited books and over 200 papers. He has advised parliaments, governments, and such organisations as the OECD, European Commission, Scottish Enterprise. Mike was recently awarded the prize for the best book in regional studies and graduated with the first DLitt from the University of the West of Scotland in 2012. He is Treasurer of the Academy of Social Sciences.

Lai Hong Ng is an Associate Professor in Marketing in the School of Management and Languages at Heriot-Watt University Malaysia. She has extensive experience in administration and teaching with a career that spans over 17 years across higher education institutions in Malaysia and UK. She teaches marketing and management courses to both undergraduate and post-graduate students. Her past research efforts have focused on services marketing, teaching and learning and student experience. Currently researching on developing learning spaces for educating Gen-Z in HEIs and the behaviour of interacting parties in service encounters – an interdisciplinary research borrowing literatures from social psychology.

Michelle Nguyen is a Programme Manager for International Trade and Investment promotion in the UK. She has previously advised and worked on projects for the Irish Government and the European Parliament. Michelle has a varied professional background in establishing new ventures, conducting international business, building client relationships and delivering corporate training. She has worked across blue chip companies, family-run enterprises and business incubation environments. Michelle holds a BA (Hons) in Economics and Social Studies from NUI Galway and an MBS in International Entrepreneurship Management from University of Limerick. Michelle's particular areas of interest are investigation of the environment required for success, the psychology of entrepreneurs and acting as a connector within industry.

Julie McFarlane is Assistant Professor for the School of Management & Languages at Heriot-Watt University, teaching areas in business, marketing and enterprise. She recently completed a PhD in Entrepreneurial Business Models in the Creative industries at the University of Strathclyde's Hunter Centre for Entrepreneurship. Prior to her PhD, Julie received a MSc (with Distinction) in Innovation, Commercialisation and Entrepreneurship from the University of Stirling as well as a BA (with Honours) in Business Studies and Marketing, and has over 10yrs experience working closely with entrepreneurs. Julie also has an interest in dynamic business models, specifically the process of entrepreneurship in the music industry.

Linda McGilvray has over 20 years' experience of working within the private, public and third sectors. As well as lecturing in social enterprise and business planning she has gained much of her professional experience researching economic and social issues for Scottish regeneration agencies. Linda has also worked in the social enterprise sector and managed a WISE project called *true GRIT* in Glasgow, which was dedicated to providing market and social research services. Lloyd, Patrick and Diarmuid were students in HW's Social Enterprise class during 2014-2015 and their contributions to the subject of social entrepreneurship were formative in the development of Chapter 5.

UmmeSalma Mujtaba is a Teaching Fellow in Management and International Business in the School of Management and Languages based at the Dubai Campus. She is also undergraduate year 1 and 2 coordinator at the School of Management and Languages.

Jaydeep Pancholi is a PhD student within the School of Management and Languages at Heriot-Watt University, Edinburgh. His PhD thesis is investigating business strategy within the context of conflict zones, reviewing stakeholder influences on strategic decision and conflict resolution. Prior to this Jaydeep gained a BA (hons) in International Business and Marketing at the University of Strathclyde, Glasgow, including an exchange at Nanyang Technological University, Singapore, studying courses in management and culture. This was followed by work at a leading automotive manufacture in corporate fleet. Jaydeep's academic interests are rooted in his extensive voluntary work in personal development and corporate sustainability while being a trainer for a global NGO.

Jane Queenan is an Associate Professor in the Department of Business Management, School of Management and Languages at Heriot-Watt University. She lectures in Entrepreneurship and Business Ethics. Jane has many years of experience in the field of business development and founded and managed two successful consultancy practices prior to entering academia.

John Sanders is an Associate Professor in Management in the School of Management and Languages at Heriot-Watt University. He teaches strategic management courses to both undergraduate and post-graduate students. In addition, he teaches a small business management course to final year undergraduate students. Strategic fit within a University setting was the subject of his PhD. His past research efforts have focused on Internet portals, website quality, social networks and the market reach of rural small firms in Scotland and New Zealand.

Yen Tran is an Associate Professor of Strategy, Innovation and Entrepreneurship. She completed her PhD at Copenhagen Business School (Denmark) and Stanford University (USA), obtained her MBA at Asian Institute of Technology (Thailand) and Ohio State University (USA) and her BBA at Hanoi Foreign Trade University (Vietnam). Her research has been internationally recognised at world-class conferences (the Academy of Management Conference) and published in world-class journals such as *R&D Management*, *Management International Review*, *Long Range Planning*, *International Business Review* and the *Academy of Management Best Paper Proceedings (USA)*. Her research area is within international entrepreneurship, capability development, knowledge management and new venture creation particularly in emerging markets. She also is an active member of the Academy of Management (USA).

Preface

Entrepreneurship throughout the world is awakening a revolution that is reforming and revitalising economies at all levels, with the establishment of both new ventures and the growth of existing businesses as crucibles for change. This rising recognition of entrepreneurship and entrepreneurs means they have become global phenomena over the last 25 years, whereby entrepreneurship is seen as a key driver of economic and social development. The entrepreneurial process underpinning these developments can be found in business start-ups, in growing enterprises and in multinational corporations and so the study of entrepreneurship has generated considerable interest from academics as well as policy makers and practitioners. To improve national competitiveness and promote resilience, governments are seeking to increase business start-up rates and improve the contribution of growing firms to employment and economic growth. For scholars, the importance of entrepreneurship to employment, innovation, productivity and income growth has led to increasing numbers of researchers investigating and contributing to the field.

This book introduces many of the terms, theories and practices in the fields of entrepreneurship and enterprise. It covers their origins and development and addresses their drivers, barriers and evolution into new areas of business and economic activity. Academics continue to debate and dispute what defines an entrepreneur, often using the terms self-employed, small business owner, small business owner/manager and entrepreneur interchangeably (Lundstrom and Stevenson, 2005). While the term 'entrepreneur' is French in origin, a literal meaning might translate as 'one who takes between' (Deakins, 1996). In the literature and practice fields today entrepreneurial behaviour has been extended beyond the individual running their own business into groups operating within larger companies. To understand how entrepreneurship is being applied across the economy, it is necessary to explore these different dimensions and these are offered in different chapters and studies reported here.

The confusion between entrepreneur, enterprise and small business confounds these definitional problems. Defining the term 'small business' is very difficult anyway, since there are conflicting ideas upon which factors to base the analysis as Storey (2002, p. 8) comments: 'there is no single, uniformly acceptable, definition of a small firm'. Definitions from the Bolton Report of 1971 are regarded by many to be of dubious value to a sector that has changed in complexion, composition, contribution and structure over the last few decades (Storey, 2002).

In more recent times, entrepreneurship has become a media favourite and is showcased in such spectacles as 'The Apprentice' and 'Dragon's Den' and individuals such as Mark Zuckenberg, Richard Branson and the likes of Jay Z are held in high esteem as enterprising celebrities. Despite this enhanced interest and profile, however, many would still claim that they do not know any entrepreneurs. Do you? Are any of your close relatives entrepreneurs, as family businesses are a significant part of the overall enterprising economy? Data on entrepreneurship, enterprises and SMEs (small and medium enterprises) have improved with the expansion of this sector of the economy, but the business structure does not fully reflect the diversity of society. So why might many women, young people, the unemployed and those living in social (rented) housing not have recognised that they knew an entrepreneur and why are they so under-represented amongst small business owners? These features of the 'entrepreneurial class' are examined in various chapters of this book to give some insights into the barriers, challenges and policies active in different and contrasting economies.

There is a significant degree of overlap between the characteristics of successful entrepreneurs and successful firms with leadership, creativity and innovation featuring in both academic studies and practitioner strategies. Each of these is introduced and analysed in this collection both in their entrepreneurship and wider economic and business contexts. Again there are benefits to both the individual and the company in research and practice from an appreciation of the transferability of the skills, attributes and behaviours underpinning these elemental factors.

Norin Arshed and Mike Danson

References

Deakins, D. (1999), *Entrepreneurship and Small Firms* (2nd ed.), McGraw-Hill, Maidenhead.

Lundstrom, A., & Stevenson, L. (2005). *Entrepreneurship Policy – Theory and Practices (ISEN International Studies in Entrepreneurship)*. Birkhäuser: Springer.

Storey, D. J. (1994). *Understanding the Small Business Sector*. Croatia: Thomson.

1 Understanding Entrepreneurship: An introduction

Mike Danson

The idea of 'enterprise' has entered the lexicon of economic development tools, active labour market policies, and employability skills for graduates, amongst other areas of public and private life in recent years. A quick look at the literature, however, shows a much narrower application of the term even as late as the 1980s and 1990s, when 'multinational enterprises' was the dominant use of 'enterprise' in business and economics texts. 'Entrepreneurship' and 'entrepreneur' have longer histories but these have tended also to accrue new powers as economies have restructured and developed in new ways. As with other sub-disciplines, though enterprise and entrepreneurship have spread gradually beyond their traditional social cores, their study, application and analysis have evolved over time to embrace a wide range of strategic, social, political and economic areas. This chapter introduces the concept of 'entrepreneurship' and offers a launching platform for the remainder of the book.

The definition

There are many definitions and lists of characteristics of 'entrepreneurship' and what it means to be 'an entrepreneur'. None is accepted by all, and examples of individuals who do not fit the stereotype or profile can also be found. Most commentators and scholars, however, will work with:

> ... the role of the entrepreneur: the Knightian approach, which highlights the risk-bearing and uncertainty-reducing role of entrepreneurs; and the Schumpeterian approach in which the entrepreneur is an innovator (Deakins and Freel, 2003, p9).

Timmons and Spinelli (2008), who have been highly influential in promoting the concept and application of entrepreneurship to the creation of new firms, identified the central themes or driving forces that dominate the dynamic entrepreneurial process as being:

☐ Opportunity driven

☐ Driven by a lead entrepreneur and an entrepreneurial team

☐ Resource parsimonious and creative

☐ Depending on the fit and balance among these

☐ Integrated and holistic.

If we unpick such working definitions, it can be seen they include the proposition that an entrepreneur is an individual – and so many studies focus on the personal characteristics, as we shall explore, although family businesses have always been a key part of the economy and so a focus of the research agenda. Also, however, the rise of not-for-profit businesses, which are run by entrepreneurs for a common or wider good, have attracted much attention and these are now an essential part of any consideration of where and how entrepreneurship is practised. Interestingly, the idea of the lone entrepreneur, with characteristics of risk taking, creativity, motivation to be their own boss and so forth, has been applied beyond the context of small and medium enterprises to much larger corporations where specialist managers operate within departments; this has led to interest in corporate entrepreneurship being linked to the core study of new, small and growing enterprises.

Within this brief introduction, it is apparent already that these terms of 'enterprise' and 'entrepreneurship' are fuzzy concepts which mean different things to different people, and are applied somewhat loosely in different contexts, disciplines and policy areas.

Do you know an entrepreneur?

In the mid-1990s, when the regional development agency for Scotland investigated why there was a lower rate of new business start-ups than in other parts of the UK, and indeed than much of the European Union as constituted at that time, they surveyed members of under-represented groups about their knowledge and attitudes to entrepreneurship and enterprise. However it was defined, and despite using prompts to try and make the concept clear, still over half of respondents claimed they did not know an entrepreneur. For most people in society, and in just about any economy in modern times, it might be thought they must surely be related to, know of or otherwise recognize someone in their community who could be considered as an entrepreneur, so this finding was surprising.

1

Even where it seems that there should be recognition and agreement over the use and meaning of the terms, such as in this survey, many had difficulties in understanding what and who is being referred to. This book therefore introduces entrepreneurship and enterprise from an academic perspective, based on theories and applications. It provides the basis for understanding the concepts, their origins and development, and how they have evolved and been applied. Knowledge and appreciation of the growing use of enterprise and entrepreneurship in wider forms is introduced in chapters on creativity, leadership, internationalization and other features which demonstrate the porous boundaries of the subject. Being able to integrate these various dimensions into analyses of individuals, firms, industries and economies, and to borrow from other disciplines to inform such work will enhance understanding.

Research on the role of SMEs and of new firms in the economy has revealed that regions and nations with high rates of start-ups also show high 'death' rates and, in aggregate, overall growth in the numbers of enterprises (Ashcroft and Love, 1996; Greene and Mole, p. 25-26). The significance of this churn, which is greater in the more dynamic cultural environments of the core regions of most economies, means that being aware of the drivers of exits, closures and failures of firms is essential if start-ups and entrepreneurship are to be understood more fully (Deakins and Freel, 2006, p. 5).

Growth of the firm through expansion into new markets and internationalization has been studied from the early days of interest in enterprise and multinational enterprises especially, but the different factors, features, constraints and opportunities faced by smaller companies requires a dedicated appreciation and discussion of these issues for new and growing businesses.

As larger operations are considered in entrepreneurship, with separate parts of the firm having their own managers, objectives and relationships, so the divorce of ownership and management leads to a need to consider the role of leadership within the company. An examination of different aspects of entrepreneurial leadership within the organization has therefore come to feature in wider considerations of all sizes of business. Managing risk is a key role and responsibility for those who and manage enterprises, regardless of size, sector or complexity, so that within the underlying theories on enterprise and entrepreneurship, rewards for taking risk is cited as crucial to understanding economic and personal motivations; together with the extension of entrepreneurship into larger firm environments, these demand consideration of the importance of business ethics in these contrasting contexts.

Although there is a tendency amongst some academic and business development agency practitioners genuinely to conflate the study and the application of entrepreneurship, this book is not, however, about how to start a business, raise finance, identify market opportunities, gain access to export markets, manage risk or to address any of the other features involved in being an entrepreneur or being enterprising. Rather it is to allow you to gain a grounded and informed grasp of the subject area so that you can take your new knowledge, skills and understanding and apply it in research and application. The remainder of this Introduction presents each of the chapters, to open up their aims, objectives and approach to understanding entrepreneurship.

Entrepreneurship

As is described in Chapters 2 and 3, the first scholarly discussions on 'entrepreneurship' and 'entrepreneurs' can be traced back over two centuries ago. The twentieth century could be said to be about the increasingly dominant role of massive corporations in economies, industries and markets, and so analyses and policies research have been focused on these major players also. Oligopolies operating across national and then international markets seemed to be on an inexorable rise in such globalized sectors as oil, cars, computers, and steel, as companies with massive monopoly power applied their production and marketing economies of scale to exert pressure on domestic markets progressively across the world. In some cases, natural monopolies were nationalized by the state to offer home businesses protection from super-profits being made and, in some cases, these state-owned firms entered international markets or international cartel agreements to create barriers to imports.

Despite this, from the early 1970s onwards there was a growing unease at the demise of the small and medium enterprise in the USA and UK, especially, in contrast to the continuing strength of the mittelstadt (SMEs) in Germany. The oil crises of that decade, the recession of the early 1980s, deregulation and privatization under Reaganism and Thatcherism led to and were led by major restructuring of the European and North American economies, with the USA and UK again leading many of the strategic and policy developments. As Keynesian interventionism gave way to laissez faire monetarism so there was a concomitant move towards a promotion of endogenous recovery and growth for communities, regions and sectors. And so the environment was set for increased global interest in entrepreneurship both by theorists and by institutions.

Chapter 2 explains, since the early 1980s this has generated "a remarkable renaissance in terms of the recognition of small firms' centrality as a necessary competitive instrument in the development of a modern, vibrant and progressive economy" (Beaver and Prince, 2004, p. 34). Entrepreneurs are recognized as now having a central role in economic development at all levels, and in the creation of income, wealth and evolutionary change. As well as official statistics and government bodies at national, regional and local levels, today there are organizations in the UK representing micro- and small enterprises, such as the Federation of Small Business, which reports that 99 per cent of the country's 5.2 million businesses are SMEs, accounting for 14.5 million people in employed positions (Federation of Small Business, 2015). As recorded in Chapter 2, commentators now argue that entrepreneurs have replaced the nationalized and large multinational enterprises as the driving force of economic restructuring. These developments are even more dramatic in some other parts of the world; for example in China and the transition countries of central and Eastern Europe, where their contributions to the transformation of their economies have been key. So as well as renewing and regenerating those economies adversely impacted by recessions and restructuring worldwide, they have been contributing to employment, cultural revolutions and economic, social and political stability.

Chapter 2 demonstrates that economists have often struggled with understanding the 'entrepreneur', despite their central position in the economy as described above. Therefore, an understanding and knowledge of the complex field of entrepreneurship is crucial, and this is offered through a critique of the history of the theory and literature, followed by an evaluation and analysis of their wider contributions to the distinctive economic theories of the entrepreneur.

Case study: Enterprise in Scotland

Scotland has long recognized that it has a lower rate of business start-ups than comparable economies so that it has been a crucible for innovations in understanding, analysing and promoting entrepreneurship (Danson, 1995, 1996; Deakins and Freel, 2006). In the mid-1990s, this led to a programme of research, commissioned by Scottish Enterprise, on the contribution of new enterprises and entrepreneurs to economic development, and the factors explaining the low levels of start-ups in Scotland. Comparative data, research and experiences from across the UK, European Union and US were called upon to improve the understanding of the processes involved. The findings were sometimes unsuspected, challenging the super-structure of business development agencies and their attitudes and behaviour towards indigenous potential entrepreneurs.

The research revealed no anti-enterprise or dependency culture, suggested as the cause of the poor rate of new businesses being formed, but rather the desire to set up as entrepreneur oneself was as strong elsewhere. The forensic analysis, however, demonstrated that many key intermediaries – bankers, accountants, business advisors and the staff of the development agencies were creating the barriers to disadvantaged groups becoming entrepreneurs. Stunted and narrow social networks, the anticipated negative impacts of failure on family life, and the lack of alternative opportunities after exit were also cited as major concerns of potential entrepreneurs (Scottish Enterprise, 1993: p. 24).

The research for Scottish Enterprise on entrepreneurship and business start-ups was followed by strategic interventions, culminating in the launch of the 'Business Birth Rate Strategy'. This was aimed particularly at broadening the cohort of the population who were actively seeking to start their own business, to approach the levels in other areas of the UK (Ashcroft and Love, 1996; Whittam and Kirk, 1996). The efforts to change the culture of enterprise are discussed in Chapter 11, with exploration of the many policies and initiatives across Scotland, the UK and beyond into the European Union. Many of these policies and instruments have aimed to incorporate support for more start-ups by women, the young and individuals from socially excluded groups, as these were identified, in the studies commissioned by Scottish Enterprise, as being less likely to establish a new firm (Danson, 1995, 1996); they are reviewed and examined further in Chapter 4.

Over the years, the Global Entrepreneurship Monitor (GEM) (published regularly but see Levie *et al.*, 2003 for an example of analysis) has provided further underpinning to the promotion of entrepreneurial activity by 'excluded' groups. As the business development landscape has evolved, so specific groups have been offered dedicated advice and assistance in establishing new firms. Often immigrant populations and non-white migrants into the UK and Europe are significantly more likely to behave entrepreneurially than other groups.

In a globalized and highly competitive world economy, we have seen the continuing dominance of national and international markets by transnational and multinational enterprises – furthered by the rise of common, single markets (such as the European Union and NAFTA, the North America Free Trade Agreement) and world trade agreements. However, as discussed earlier, some key smaller economies, including the Nordic countries and Singapore, have led the way in developing their economies through 'smart specialization', innovation and enterprise. Chapter 3 introduces the relationship between creativity and economic development, therefore, and recounts this in the context of the increasing recognition of the role and importance of creative activities. Increasingly over the last quarter of a century these concepts of creativity and innovation have been acknowledged in the fields of business and management and in the high level objectives of nations and the EU, as they recognize the need to gain forms of competitiveness. Just thinking of many of the changes in life across the world since 1990, particularly regarding developments in ITC in everyday and household activities, it is then apparent that many of these were introduced to the world by small companies – Nokia, Apple, Microsoft, Google, Amazon. The drivers, forms and entrepreneurship models underpinning these enterprises are considered in Chapter 3, with an exploration of how governments and agencies countries have come to accept that new markets and market growth are often only to be attained through creative and innovative solutions.

The creation and application of knowledge is core to many of these developments and, given that R&D and exploitation is so expensive in many sectors that it creates both barriers to entry and oligopoly powers, for new firms and SMEs to compete requires a high degree of enterprise and entrepreneurship. Studies into these and their relationships with growth have become increasingly important for economic development. To fully appreciate the role of creativity and innovation, it is necessary to understand the nature of entrepreneurship and, specifically, the creativity required to identify and exploit opportunities, and to acquire the necessary resources.

Chapter 3 provides an overview of these theories and issues and develops the discussion of who entrepreneurial individuals are, and what they do. The significance of dynamic processes is underlined with special attention given to theories of opportunity recognition. That leads onto examination of what entrepreneurs and innovators do, why they do it, where they do it, when they do it and of course how.

As noted in the text box on the relatively low enterprise birth rate in Scotland, research suggested that particular groups are less likely to start up a new business and so a better understanding of why this is the case and what barriers may be in their way should be useful in improving the rate of new firm formation overall. Studies from across the world, in both developing and developed countries, reveal that which groups suffer such exclusion and why can vary due to institutional, cultural, social, economic and other reasons. To explore and understand these, Chapter 4 considers diversity in terms of individuals of varied race, culture, gender, ethnicity, sexual orientation, social background, age, disability, political beliefs and other traits. Under the assumptions of neoclassical economic theories, free market systems should not tolerate or be hindered by discrimination or other impediments to individuals establishing and exploiting their own businesses. Extending this, diversity within the global population should be reflected in different propensities to undertake entrepreneurial activity as different preferences are revealed. However, within limits, entrepreneurship is relatively homogenous, but below aggregated data research has shown that diversity affects entrepreneurship (Audretsch *et al.*, 2008). Therefore, understanding diversity itself should allow a better appreciation of the motivations and challenges affecting entrepreneurs as a whole and within their diverse communities.

Given the usual groups in society recording lower rates of business start-up, this chapter examines the importance of diversity in entrepreneurship by focusing on women entrepreneurs, ethnic minority entrepreneurs, other minority entrepreneurs (including student and graduate entrepreneurs, lesbian, gay, bisexual and transgender (LGBT) entrepreneurs, older or grey entrepreneurs, and disabled entrepreneurs). As experienced in Scotland, this discussion leads onto a consideration of the implications for governments of all levels and government policies.

In terms of strategies and policies for entrepreneurship and enterprise (see Chapter 11), these analyses in different environments and landscapes should inform developments for change. Identifying and breaking down barriers to potential entrepreneurs in starting up and growing their businesses should be to the advantage of the individual and to the economy as a whole. Therefore, this chapter has an important role to play by increasing understanding of diversity, and this promises to be of value not only to entrepreneurs, who may face barriers to establishing and growing their own enterprise, but also to educators, researchers and policymakers.

In the restructuring of old industrial economies in the 1980s, away from a dependence on large branch plants of nationalized and multinational companies and towards indigenous enterprises, there were periods of very high unemployment and poverty. To fill the gaps created by these changes and the reliance on an endogenous economy that was slow in being established, many disadvantaged communities turned to new forms of business: social enterprises. Variously described as not-for-profit, social economy, third sector, voluntary sector, community enterprises etc., these have become an important if not critical employer and player in many neighbourhood, local and regional economies, and the role of their leaders and managers therefore needs to be considered. Chapter 5 introduces and explores social entrepreneurship, focusing on the similarities and differences between social entrepreneurship and such commercial activities as corporate social responsibility (CSR). Definitional issues abound in this sector so that some of the challenges facing academics and practitioners alike when attempting to define social enterprises and social entrepreneurs are examined.

In the same way that entrepreneurship can be considered as a practice, a process and a concept, so this chapter considers these in the context of social entrepreneurship. As social entrepreneurship is taken to describe the pursuit of an opportunity to deliver social value, so the term is considered within the wider genus of entrepreneur. The similarities between them are discussed from the vantage of their respective definitions. Comparisons of the parallels between the notion of the 'entrepreneurial firm', with its emphasis on being opportunity- and growth-focused and sustainable, and the distinguishing characteristic of social entrepreneurship as a social change agent, and ultimately as a creator of social value, are presented to set the scene for more detailed and expansive discussion of this form of entrepreneur.

Another case of the extension of the concept of 'entrepreneurship' from the individual person is found with corporations. As Chapter 6 argues, corporations of every size cannot be static, but must continually adapt and redefine themselves as they face competition from rivals and new players in the development and enhancement of new products, services, processes and technologies. In the long term, the barriers to entry that protect oligopolies and other large corporations break down, so that they need to be entrepreneurial to remain competitive. This chapter therefore establishes an understanding of corporate entrepreneurship and the approaches corporations can use as pathways to becoming sustainable and successful organizations. Corporate entrepreneurial actions are identified and evaluated in terms of their capacity to offer the path to sustainable competitive advantage and success in organizations of all types and sizes. The analysis suggests that time and investment are required in these processes, and the commitment to continual reinforcement by managers is vital to integrate the corporate entrepreneurial spirit into the mission, goals, strategies, structure, processes and values of the organization. In the exploration of corporate entrepreneurship, crucial terms and factors identified elsewhere in this collection are revealed: flexibility, speed, innovation and entrepreneurial leadership. A corporate entrepreneurial orientation is seen as an essential driver in the sustainability, growth and development of the firm, making the consideration of the crossovers between entrepreneurship and corporate leadership important in industry- and economy-wide studies.

A particular and very traditional form of enterprise, and so context for entrepreneurship, is the family firm. As Chapter 7 argues, these can be difficult to define and categorize, as they are active in many sectors and environments and take many forms. Nevertheless, common patterns and characteristics of working can be traced amongst family-owned firms and to do this effectively requires an understanding of these unique characteristics and how they develop. Research and experience reveals that, alongside all the usual traits and characteristics, these include the influence of family relationships, company culture and succession planning.

Inter-personal relationships within these firms means they tend to have enhanced and different levels and forms of communications than the norm, with naturally high levels of trust because of close family ties. However, the counter to these positive dimensions of social capital can be nepotism, with the exclusion of non-family members who have greater experience and qualifications for company positions taken by close relatives. Company culture can be different and nurtured over several generations in family firms, leading to better team building and working than in other forms of enterprise. Specific to the particular milieu of the family business, this often leads to the development of superior teamwork, a common vision and greater resilience than non-family businesses. The reasons and impacts of this are examined with examples in this chapter.

However, problems of path dependency can create problems for family firms and this is often considered as an issue of succession planning. As with any enterprise there is a need for forward planning but in a family business this can be confused and conflicted with reluctance to make difficult decisions, a close-ness between owners and managers – often across generations – and all this can lead to considerable relationship conflict. As with nepotism and internal culture, dissatisfaction and destructive competition within the firm can undermine its long term success and viability. This chapter discloses the remaining gaps in the comprehensive study of family businesses, which include the gender and ethnic minority dimensions, mirroring the concerns of Chapter 4.

In the early chapters, there is identification of the attributes and characteris-tics of entrepreneurs and of successful members of the species especially. One of the keys to success is suggested as leadership, and Chapter 8 concentrates on leadership styles and theories and, as with the other elements of this volume, it begins by defining leadership. In parallel with some other analyses here, it considers the intersection of entrepreneurship and leadership by incorporating entrepreneurial leadership specifically. The discussion reflects the different major styles in this field and then offers an approach that might answer the question 'What type of leadership actions and behaviours are appropriate?' with the phrase 'It depends on the circumstances.' There is often a tendency in the media and popular discourse around entrepreneurs and entrepreneur-ship to over-emphasise the leadership role and so to identify and privilege the 'great man'; we just to have think of shows such as *The Apprentice*. The academic approach has applied theories, such as trait studies, followed by the behavioural school of thought, which assumes that leadership capability can be learned, rather than being inherent. To understand leadership in the entrepreneurship context, this led to the proposition that either 'transactional leadership' where leaders and followers are in some type of exchange relationship in order to get needs met, or 'transformational leadership', which serves to change the status quo by appealing to followers' values and their sense of higher purpose, were the two options available.

Subsequently, entrepreneurial leadership has been favoured as representing those identifiable traits of entrepreneurial leaders, including being risk averse, proactive and innovative. Building on the discussions in Chapters 2 and 3, the entrepreneurial dimension of leaders focuses on innovativeness through the search for creative and meaningful solutions to operational problems and needs. Again picking up those earlier explorations, risk-taking is considered as involving the willingness to commit resources to opportunities, while proactiveness is concerned with execution, and assisting to make actions materialize through appropriate means, which typically includes the efforts of others. In this way, the exercise of effective entrepreneurial leadership is seen as being fulfilled within an array of exciting activities and new creative developments.

For many start-ups and SMEs, satisficing behaviour is their main driver with no particular interest or ambition to grow. However, for other entrepreneurs and businesses, long term aspirations are to develop and grow, eventually internationally. To explore this growth-oriented enterprise, Chapter 9 looks at internationalization and globalization. Business development agencies often have policies and support programmes based on ideas of stages of growth with an expectation that some firms will seek to develop towards internationalization as a way to expand into new markets, achieve economies of scale and gain higher profits. In extremis, globalization allows not only the international expansion of multinational enterprises but also the evolving success of early internationalized firms or young international start-ups, which internationalized and succeeded in multiple foreign markets at birth or early in their operation. Limited resources, lack of knowledge, the need for appreciably higher working capital, and so forth are all obstacles to rapid or unproblematic growth into foreign markets. This chapter focuses on these early internationalizing firms and examines theories and examples of how successful firms excel with their performance in competitive global markets. As an entry into this discourse, and similar to the coverage of other forms of business and entrepreneurs, essential definitions underpin an understanding of globalization influences, the emergence of early internationalized firms or global start-ups. The theoretical foundations and motivations of international entrepreneurship are then used to introduce an examination of the characteristics and traits of an international entrepreneur. Finally, with examples from developing and developed economies, the chapter discusses what international entrepreneurial capabilities are required for starting an international venture.

As pointed out at the outset of this Introduction, regional and metropolitan economies with the highest rates of business start-up and entrepreneurship also have the highest levels of churn, and therefore of business failure (Ashcroft and Love, 1996). In considering the international research and the findings of the GEM surveys over the years, it is apparent also that attitudes to business failure and exit vary by culture and society. Even where the objective of a textbook, programme or agency is to start and run a successful business, it is important to understand why about 10 per cent of all firms in the US fail each year, according to the U.S. Small Business Administration, while in the UK the rate is similar, with 20 per cent failing in their first year and 30 per cent within the first three years. Chapter 10 assesses the theories, causes and reasons for business exit and failure. It explores the meaning and importance of business failure followed by why firms fail and the effect this can have on the entrepreneur. Given the costs – financial, opportunity and psychic – to the entrepreneur and their family and associates, and to the public purse where state support is offered, it is a priority for potential and existing entrepreneurs and for governments that there is a good understanding of these challenges and drivers. By a better appreciation of the effectiveness of theories and policies to address failure, it should be possible to improve responses. The chapter also discusses how to avoid such failures and provides an insight into some famous failures.

In the chapters on the growing importance of entrepreneurship in creating income and employment, on driving and being driven by innovation, and in providing opportunities for productivity enhancement and income growth, it has been clear that market and other failures provide a rationale for government interventions. This has led to an interest in enterprise policy at all levels from community to EU. Enterprise policies are discussed and explored in Chapter 11. Strategies and policies are becoming ubiquitous in developed, developing and transitional economies, often with the aim of meeting economic and social challenges in difficult neighbourhoods, in highly competitive sectors and where there are other high barriers to entry. Local business development agencies through national organizations up to and with supra-national bodies such as the EU are involved in forming, implementing and delivering such support for new and existing entrepreneurs.

The chapter considers how acknowledging the importance of entrepreneurs and SMEs drives the attention and significance being paid to enterprise policy. To define, understand and review enterprise policy, it addresses such issues as the nature and form of enterprise policy, the economic rationale for undertaking it, its evolution into such a core element of economic strategy, and the main instruments of enterprise policy. Examples of effective and successful approaches are offered, as well as lessons for their transfer to other contexts.

The final chapter in this volume addresses the principles of ethical business practice and explores their application in greater depth within the broad environment of modern business management. This examination of business ethics is included as a way of considering business management decision making that is substantially different from other areas of business management and entrepreneurship theory. Consistent with the discussions on social enterprises, social entrepreneurship and corporate social responsibility in Chapter 5, the discourse here stretches our understanding away from asking about what a business should do in order to achieve a particular objective, but rather asks about what a business should do – what might constitute good behaviour. Again, mirroring the discussions in Chapter 5, the discussions in Chapter 12 allow us to contrast the fundamental aims and modus operandi of social enterprises with the aim of private businesses generally which is to make profit. In pursuing this examination of what constitutes good behaviour within the framework of business ethics, it encourages an exploration of how good ethical practice contributes to commercial success.

References

Ashcroft, B. and Love, J. (1996) Employment change and new firm formation in UK counties, 1981-9 in M. Danson (ed.) *Small Firm Formation and Regional Economic Development*, Routledge, London, 17-35.

Danson, M. (1995) New firm formation and regional economic development: An introduction and review of the Scottish experience, *Small Business Economics*, **7**(2), 81-87.

Danson, M. (ed.) (1996) *Small Firm Formation and Regional Economic Development*, Routledge, London.

Deakins, D. and Freel, M. (2006) *Entrepreneurship and Small Firms*, 4th edition, McGraw-Hill, Maidenhead.

Greene, F. and Mole, K. (2006) Defining and measuring the small business, S. Carter, and D. Jones-Evans, (eds.) *Enterprise and Small Business. Principles, Practice and Policy*, 2nd edition, Harlow: Prentice Hall.

Levie J. Brown W. and Cooper S. (2003) *Global Entrepreneurship Monitor Scotland 2003*, Hunter Centre, University of Strathclyde.

Scottish Enterprise (1993) *Scotland's Business Birth Rate*, Scottish Enterprise, Glasgow.

Scottish Enterprise (2003) *Business Birth Rate Strategy*, Scottish Enterprise, Glasgow.

Timmons, J. and Spinelli, S. (2008) *New Venture Creation Entrepreneurship for the 21st Century*, 8th ed., international ed, New York: McGraw-Hill.

Whittam, G. and Kirk, C. (1996) The business birth rate, real services and networking: strategic options in M. Danson (ed.) *Small Firm Formation and Regional Economic Development*, Routledge, London, 132-143.

2 Economic Theories of Entrepreneurship

Julie McFarlane

What is entrepreneurship? Since the turn of the century, there has been increased global interest in entrepreneurship both by individual theorists and by institutions. This is significant because over the last quarter of a century there has been a remarkable renaissance in terms of the recognition of small firms' "centrality as a necessary competitive instrument in the development of a modern, vibrant and progressive economy" (Beaver and Prince, 2004, p. 34). The economics literature acknowledges the central role of entrepreneurs in economic development, the creation of wealth and evolutionary change. In the United Kingdom alone, over 5.2 million businesses are operating as of 2015; of those, 99% are SMEs, accounting for 14.5 million people in employed positions (Federation of Small Business, 2015). The literature suggests that it is entrepreneurs who are the driving force of such a revolution, in the form of an economic trend that is transforming and in some cases renewing economies worldwide, contributing not only to employment but also to economic, social and political stability. Therefore, it is vital to develop an understanding of the complex field of entrepreneurship by drawing on the early entrepreneurship literature, and by evaluating and understanding the wider contributions to the now-established distinctive economic theories of the entrepreneur.

An entrepreneurial definition

In the past, scholars have wondered, either "implicitly or explicitly", why anyone should study entrepreneurship (Shane and Venkataraman, 2000, p. 219). The phenomenon itself has been described as a "slippery concept", in that it is hard to work into a formal analysis. According to this view, "data are difficult to obtain, theory is underdeveloped, and findings to date are the same as those obtained in other areas of business" (Shane and Venkataraman, 2000, p. 219). The relatively recent transformation in entrepreneurship research has come about because a body of knowledge has developed over the past few years, and in response, entrepreneurship theorists are now able to offer new and exciting reasons as to why scholars "should" study the topic (Bygrave, 2003, p. 2). However, to date, the phenomenon has only become established as a broad label under which "a hodgepodge of research is housed" (Shane and Venkataraman, 2000, p. 217), and the largest obstacle to creating a fuller understanding of the phenomenon has been the difficulty in arriving at a consensus in its definition. As a result, researchers have had trouble identifying the distinctive contribution of the field, thereby undermining its economic legitimacy (Shane and Venkataraman, 2000; and Bygrave, 2003).

In fact, over a long period of time economics literature had relatively little to say about entrepreneurship. Surprisingly it is now the social sciences that tend to deal directly with the contemporary economic reality of the entrepreneur (Rocha, 2012).

Essentially entrepreneurship is an economic phenomenon involving "a nexus of two phenomena: the presence of lucrative opportunities and the presence of enterprising individuals" (Shane and Venkataraman, 2000, p. 218): entrepreneurs prioritise the creation of wealth rather than its transfer.

Over the years scholars have provided numerous definitions of entrepreneurs each of which has differed in various respects. To date, most have defined the field solely in terms of:

☐ Who the entrepreneur is (Delmar, 2006)

☐ What they do (Venkataraman, 1997)

☐ Why they do the things they do (Davidsson, 2008)

☐ How they do the things they do (Garnter, 1985)

☐ Where they do it (Welter, 2011).

Some define entrepreneurship in terms of enterprising dispositions (Delmar, 2006), others look at it from a behavioural perspective (McClelland, 1961), while the majority focus on the processes (Moroz and Hindle, 2012), and the outcomes of entrepreneurial activities (Dimov 2011). Yet for many, the most striking characteristic of the phenomenon is its diversity (Gartner, 1985).

While the definitions presented above are at best incomplete it is important to recognize their distinctive contributions, each citing their own distinct set of "meaningful patterns" to understand the mystique of entrepreneurship.

Exercise

How would you define entrepreneurship? Note down your own definition.

The history of economic thought on the entrepreneur

In the opening sections of this chapter, the difficulty in defining entrepreneurship was discussed. We now turn to the entrepreneur themselves. Entrepreneurial strategies are not a twentieth-century phenomenon. When Marco Polo established trade routes to the Far East, he demonstrated the risk-taking behaviour we associate with entrepreneurship today (Osborne, 1995, p. 4) (Figure 2.1).

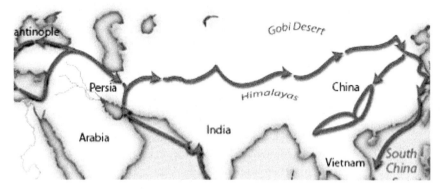

Figure 2.1: Marco Polo's trade routes

Source: aventalearning.com/content168staging/2008AmHistA/unit1/html/section_3_page_7.html

The 'fit' this explorer found between his skills and the environmental opportunity is a perfect illustration of entrepreneurial strategy, and in particular it is relevant to understanding entrepreneurship, with its increasing global scope (Osborne, 1995, p. 4). According to Hisrich, Peters and Shepherd (2005, p. 8), the "ability to innovate and create can be observed throughout history; although the fundamental tools may have changed the ability has been present in every civilization". For example, there are numerous examples of entrepreneurial behaviour dating as far back as Biblical times (for example, Jacob), through the Middle Ages (e.g. the merchant Ghini) to the Renaissance (e.g. the painter Carlo Crivelli) (Bolton and Thompson, 2000).

Exercise

Can you think of any other examples? Note down and justify five examples of entrepreneurial activity dating back fifty years.

The first proper noun for an entrepreneur emerged from the seventeenth-century French verb *entreprendre* (to undertake). The entrepreneur is, therefore, the 'undertaker', that is, someone who undertakes to make things happen (Kirby, 2003). This definition emphasises that entrepreneurs exercise a high degree of initiative and are willing to take a higher than average degree of risk, although such considerations can also be said to cover a wide range of occupations.

However, the true evolution of entrepreneurship was strongly influenced by a few key economists and analysts who are highlighted in Table 2.1, each of whom sought to provide a different role for the entrepreneur in society.

Date	Author	Concept
1755	Cantillon	Introduced the concept of entrepreneurs from *entreprendre* ('ability to take charge')
1803, 1817	Say	Emphasised the ability of the entrepreneur to 'marshal' resources in order to respond to unfulfilled opportunities
1871	Menger	Noted the ability of entrepreneurs to distinguish between 'economic goods' - those with a market or exchange value - and all others
1893	Ely and Hess	Attributed to entrepreneurs the ability to take integrated action in the enterprise as a whole, combining roles in capital, labour, enterprise and entrepreneur
1911, 1928	Schumpeter	Envisioned that entrepreneurs proactively 'created' opportunity using 'innovative combinations' which often included 'creative destruction' of passive or lethargic economic markets
1921	Knight	Suggested that entrepreneurs were concerned with 'efficiency' in economic factors by continually reducing waste, increasing savings and thereby creating value, implicitly understanding the opportunity-risk-award relationship
1948, 1952, 1967	Hayek	Continued the Austrian tradition of analytical entrepreneurs giving them capabilities of discovery and action, recognising the existence of information asymmetry which they could exploit
1973, 1979, 1997, 1999	Kirzner	Attributed to entrepreneurs a sense of 'alertness' to identify opportunities and exploit them accordingly
1974	Drucker	Attributed to entrepreneurs the capacity to 'foresee' market trends and make a timely response
1975, 1984, 1985	Shapero	Attributed 'judgement' ability to entrepreneurs, to identify 'credible opportunities' depending on two critical antecedents - perceptions of 'desirability' and 'feasibility' from both personal and social viewpoints

Table 2.1: Evolving entrepreneurs

The crucial role of the entrepreneur in economic theory was first identified by Richard Cantillon (1755), who identified that shifts in "demand and supply in a market create opportunities for buying cheaply and selling at a higher price and that this sort of arbitrage would bring equilibrium to competitive market" (Rocha, 2012, p. 4). He was the first to identify those who take advantage of these unrealized profit opportunities as "entrepreneurs" (Landström, 2005);

and for Cantillion (1755) there was no distinction between the entrepreneur and the capitalist.

The capitalist: An individual who has invested their capital in a business enterprise. A good exemplar of this is Sir Philip Green the Chairman of the Arcadia Group, which includes retailers Topshop, Topman, Wallis, Evans, Burton, Miss Selfridge, Dorothy Perkins and Outfit.

Hébert and Link (1989) observed that the taxonomy of entrepreneurial economic theories can be "condensed into three major schools of traditions (Figure 2.2) – Chicago (Knight, 1921), German (Schumpeter, 1934), and Austrian traditions (Kirzner 1973 and Baumol, 1968) – each one tracing its origin to Richard Cantillon" (Rocha, 2012). Within each of these schools are the contributions of classical and neo-classical economists who have shared and debated their opinions over time; however, one thing missing from Herbert and Link's (1989) summary is the fourth tradition which has also played a part in the debate - the British school of thought.

According to Bygrave (2003, p. 1), it was economic theorist **Joseph Schumpeter** (1934), who "gave us the modern definition of an entrepreneur as an individual who shakes the foundations of the existing economic order by introducing new products and services, and or exploiting new ways of doing things" (Bygrave, 2003, p. 1). This view posits the entrepreneur as the source of disequilibrium in the economy. However, Schumpteter had some opposition where he attributed this to periods of "market efficiency impacted by periods of upheaval" that allowed economic actors to disturb the market equilibrium through innovation and in order to earn an entrepreneurial profit.

Israel Kirzner (1973) "believed opportunities to be in existence even in the absence of new information", contending that individuals actually create it through recognition of chaos, and those who are most alert will utilise resources to exploit entrepreneurial opportunities (Eckhardt and Shane, 2003, p. 341). **Frank Knight** (1921) took this further by advancing the concept stating "the entrepreneur was ready to take action when outcomes were uncertain, an individual with the confidence, and who is venturesome enough to make judgments about an uncertain future", although this is not done by chance but by minimising uncertainty (Hisrich *et al.*, 2005, p. 17).

Figure 2.2: Key economic schools of thought

The British School

According to Kirby (2003, p. 1), "the British school, epitomized by the writings of
Adam Smith (1723-1790) and David Ricardo (1772-1823), conflated the function of
the entrepreneur with that of the capitalist and profits were the reward for risking
capital". The concept was taken further by Jeremy Bentham (1748-1832), who argued
that "entrepreneurs possessed the inclination, technical knowledge and capital
power to create wealth" (Kirby, 2003, p. 12).

The American School or Chicago School

Similar thoughts were expressed in America through the work of Amasa Walker
(1799-1875) and, subsequently, his son Francis A. Walker (1840-1897), who both
saw the entrepreneur as "an individual with foresight, and a facility for organization,
administration, energy and leadership" (Kirby, 2003, p. 12). Frank Knight (1921)
took this further by advancing the concept of risk. Knight "sympathised with
Austrian economics" (Khalil, 2007, p. 14), identifying a distinction between insurable
and uninsurable risk (2003, p. 15). For him (Deakins and Freel, 2006, p. 6-7), "the
entrepreneur was ready to take action when outcomes were uncertain, an individual
with the confidence, and who is venturesome enough to make judgments about an
uncertain future", although this is not done by chance but by minimising uncertainty
(Hisrich *et al.*, 2005, p. 17).

The German School

Around the same time, the German school emerged through Von Thunen (1785-
1850), who saw the entrepreneur as "risk taker and innovator, and their return is
the reward for uninsurable risk", while in the twentieth century, Shackle (1966)
conceptualised the entrepreneur as creative and imaginative, allowing them to
imagine opportunities for profit which others are unable to see.

The Austrian School

In contrast with the above schools, the Classical and Austrian views of
entrepreneurship are emotional, "self-actional", and are focused on purposeful,
human action as opposed to mechanistic processes (Kirby, 2003, p. 12). Carl
Menger (1840-1921) suggested that "entrepreneurial activity is focused with
obtaining information in order to make decisions that give rise to economic change",
(Smith, 1990); however for Izreal Kirzner (1973), the entrepreneur does not create
disequilibrium, but rather "brings order, and is distinguished from others by greater
'alertness', allowing them to see opportunities others cannot" (Khalil, 2006, p.
14). Kirzner (1973) stated that individuals do not search for opportunities because
"opportunity; by definition is unknown until discovered"; and, after all, one cannot
search for something that one does not know exists.

■ Summaries and limitations

Kirzner

☐ Entrepreneur is alert to profitable opportunities for exchange

☐ Identifies suppliers and customers and acts as an intermediary (no necessity to own resources and profit arises from intermediary function)

☐ Entrepreneur has additional knowledge which is not possessed by others (the role of information is very important)

☐ Anyone could potentially possess the additional knowledge and be alert to opportunities for exchange and trade.

Now while Steve Jobs or Bill Gates fit nicely into this, for Kirzner (1973) how can one search for that which one does not know exists? In this view, the entrepreneur is someone who is alert through additional knowledge, not possessed by others. Yet this discounts those examples of businesses created through hobbies or even chance encounters.

Knight

☐ The entrepreneur is an individual who is prepared to undertake risk – an uninsurable risk – and the reward, profit, is the return for bearing uncertainty.

☐ Entrepreneur is a calculated risk taker

☐ Opportunity for profit arises out of uncertainty surrounding change

☐ Responsibility for one's own actions

Here of course Richard Branson or Donald Trump would fit nicely as would many other risk takers, yet again this discounts social enterprises or lifestyle firms.

Schumpeter

☐ The entrepreneur "destroys the existing economic order"

☐ They introduce "new products and services, by creating new forms of organization, or by exploiting new raw materials."

☐ They are responsible for "creative destruction"

☐ The entrepreneur is a "special person"

☐ The entrepreneur is an "innovator"

☐ Develops new "technology"

Now while James Dyson or Mark Zuckerberg may fit nicely into this, it also discounts anyone who chooses to start an online business.

More recently there has been a variety (Kuratko *et al.*, 2015) of shades in between the views of Schumpeter, Kirzner and Knight, including Baumol's (1993) spectrum of productive, unproductive, and destructive forms of entrepreneurship (Figure 2.3).

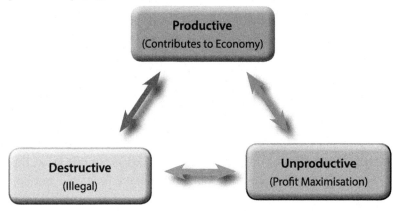

Figure 2.3: Baumol's (1993) spectrum of entrepreneurship

It is important to note that each economic theory makes certain assumptions about individual decisions and the conditions under which decisions are made. Even so, the works of key economists such as Knight, Schumpeter, Kirzner and Baumol have become some of the most influential articles in the debate on the importance of entrepreneurship for economic development and growth.

Exercise

Which of the economic theorists outlined above do you agree with? Why? Note down your answers.

In fact, it can be argued that a number of views of entrepreneurship have over-simplified the economic process by presenting it as a clocklike mechanism, and the economic literature until the early 19th century largely overlooked the need for specialised individuals "to perform the discovery, coordination, promotion and risk-bearing functions" (Rocha, 2012, p. 3) associated with running a business. Only recently did "Small is beautiful" become the catchphrase in business (Rocha, 2012).

The entrepreneur today: Economic hero or a man of myth

Today, we have witnessed how many other theorists in a number of disciplines have begun to pay increasing attention to the entrepreneur, in terms of not just their economic role but their role in society. Yet even to state the entrepreneur is one of the most "intriguing and elusive characters to constitute the subject of analysis" (Baumol, 1968, p. 64).

More poetically, it has been said that:

> "He has been hunted by many individuals using various trapping devices, but no one so far has succeeded in capturing him. All who claim to have caught sight of him report that he is enormous, but disagree on his particulars."

(A.A. Milne, in Kirby, 2003, p. 11)

Theorists over the years have likened entrepreneurs in society today with that of the mysterious Heffalump creature from the A. A. Milne *Winne the Pooh* tales.

Exercise

Why do think theorists have over the years likened the entrepreneur to the Heffalump? Think about this and then select five 'Heffalumps' (entrepreneurs). How different are their particulars?

However, while the entrepreneur is an individual who is enveloped with a creative mystique which no one quite understands or is able to deliberately emulate, it has been suggested that a typical entrepreneur is characterised by their ability to take risks (see discussion of Knight, 1921 above). Littunen (2000) argues they must amount to more than that and proposes that they must be innovative, have a strong grasp of how the market functions, and, crucially, have all the necessary technical skills, manufacturing know-how, marketing skills, management skills, and the ability to acquire resources (Casson, 2005).

Since the turn of the millennium several ec onomists have more fully recognized the role of entrepreneurship and the entrepreneur within economic theory. As mentioned above, scholars have presented many definitions (see Figure 2.4) each differing in a multitude of dimensions.

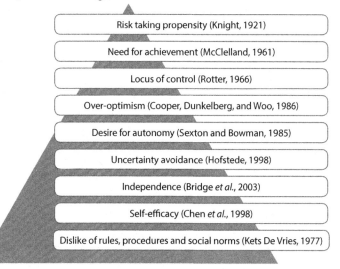

Figure 2.4: Entrepreneurial types

Deakins and Freel (2003, p. 17), define the entrepreneur as a risk-taker but "not a gambler". They are highly self-motivated according to Burns (2001), and driven by their strong inner need for achievement (McClelland, 1961). They are epitomised by the statement "what happens to me is my own doing" (Burns, 2001). They have a strong desire to go it alone, resenting restraints, "they want to break down barriers, placing merit on independent thought and action" (Bridge *et al.*, 2003, p. 67). Entrepreneurs want to be in control, they have a higher need for autonomy and a great fear of external controls; they value individualism and freedom and have a dislike for rules, procedures and social norms (Kets De Vries, 1977).

More recently, theorists have begun to research the fit of individuals to entrepreneurial activity (Sarasvathy, 2003, p. 205) by evaluating the role cognition plays in the discovery of entrepreneurial opportunities (Kaish and Gilad, 1991; Shaver and Scott, 1991, and Busenitz and Barney, 1996), where the entrepreneur is cast as a bundle of traits or heuristics and biases. Here, the entrepreneur takes centre stage (Sarasvathy, 2003, p. 2), with scholars seeking to explain how these cognitive forces influence the decisions they make, attributing the ability to discover and exploit entrepreneurial opportunities to individual differences in perceptions of success. Consequently, those who decide to exploit entrepreneurial opportunities (Shane and Venkataraman, 2000, p. 224) typically overestimate their chances of success in a potentially unrealistic way (Palich and Bagby, 1995), leading them to act first and analyse later (Busenitz and Barney, 1997). Several researchers have argued that this is down to individual differences in the willingness to bear risk (Knight, 1921), once the potential opportunity has been discovered, which in turn shapes the individual's judgement of whether or not exploitation is possible (Khilstrom and Laffont, 1979; Knight, 1921).

In this view, enduring human attributes will lead some people and not others to choose entrepreneurship. Those entrepreneurs who exhibit such traits are more likely to exploit opportunities, because exploitation requires people to act in the face of scepticism (Chen, Greene and Crick, 1998). For Drucker (1985), this involves risk, because the potential entrepreneurs invest time, effort, and money before the return is known. Researchers propose that such actions are down to a greater taste for uncertainty, and argue that those with a greater taste for the unknown are more likely to 'choose' to become entrepreneurs. Thus, potential entrepreneurs either have the right traits, or they don't. And if they don't, they are urged to cultivate them.

The entrepreneur: Consider how these traits manifest in successful entrepreneurs such as Sir Richard Branson and Bill Gates. Both entrepreneurs exhibited a steely determination and an ability to recover from setbacks.

However, over the years, the general concept of 'risk' has been simplified and broken down. Bird (1989) simplifies the division of risks into five types:

1 Economic risk

2 Social risks

3 Career development risks

4 Psychological risks

5 Health risks.

Rresearch suggests the concept can be broken down further to include specific sub-categories such as:

☐ Financial risk

☐ Physical risk

☐ Social risk

☐ Professional risk

☐ Performance risk

☐ Opportunity cost risk

☐ Time risk.

Exercise

Each one of these risks is clearly potentially relevant to the entrepreneur. But how? Research and note down examples of each risk and what it has to do with entrepreneurship.

According to Gustafsson (2006), entrepreneurial decision making is more a matter of reducing uncertainty in certain situations than it is about personality or 'innate' abilities, as in both situations the opposite would occur. For this author, in 'low uncertainty' situations the expert entrepreneur relies on analysis to reduce the risk, whereas in 'high uncertainty' situations the expert relies on intuitive decision making, taking the less planned approach, and basing decisions on contingencies (Sarasvathy, 2003).

According to Bolton and Thompson (2005, p. 83), much ambiguity exists across scholars' opinions about 'who' entrepreneurs are, which is why drawing an accurate picture of the individual entrepreneur as a person is almost impossible. Look at Anita Roddick and Richard Branson. The biggest differences between the two would probably be with their business goals; for example, Anita Roddick set out to build an ethical company in the Body Shop, while Richard Branson set out to make his own decisions. Scholars trying to tie the most common psychological traits of entrepreneurs with the opportunities they discover and exploit have thus far failed to arrive at any definitive conclusions (Gartner, 1985). The most important issue here appears to be the fit between the process and other key elements of entrepreneurship, rather than between an individual or individuals and an idea. Overall, the conflicting findings suggest that no true entrepreneurial profile exists. Rather Shane (2000) chooses to explain entrepreneurship by instead identifying the reasons why individuals enter into it.

Exercise

Select one entrepreneur that fits the description for each one of the character traits discussed above. Note down your responses.

Why do entrepreneurs do it?

As suggested in the previous discussion, for a long time economics literature had relatively little to say about entrepreneurship (Cosgel, 1996). Mainstream economics, particularly the theory of the firm, ignored the role of the individual until quite recently. Deakins and Freel (2003, p. 13) found in a review of the literature that traits of entrepreneurs discussed by economic theories ignore crucial issues such as gender, age, social class and education, all of which can have bearing on the propensity of an individual to embark on entrepreneurial activity (2003, p 14). Entrepreneurs are no different from people in general according to Delmar (2006, p. 12), but this view does not offer any explanation as to why certain individuals choose to undertake an entrepreneurial career (2006, p. 12). The answer, in his view, lies in the fact that situations are looked upon differently by different people, depending on their own experiences, and importantly, the traits discussed above cannot account for that (2006, p. 12).

Personality characteristics are formed by the interplay between individuals and their environment, according to Littunen (2000, p. 296); the author adds that life situations and experiences play a central role in becoming an entrepreneur, and suggests that this may lead to a change in someone's life which is profound enough to have an effect on their personality (2000, p. 296). According to Gibb and Ritchie (1982; cited in Littunen, 2000, p. 297), entrepreneurship can be wholly understood by the type of situation encountered, while the know-how of the entrepreneur is heightened by their ability to recognize and react to change (Gartner 1985, cited in Littunen 2000, p. 298). However, as all entrepreneurs are different, they will inevitably have unique personal experiences. It follows that because all individuals view the world differently, a situation which is deemed an opportunity by one may be seen as a problem by another (Kirby, 2003, p. 117).

Scholars have argued that the main objectives for most entrepreneurs are profit and growth, while others have suggested that personal motives are far more important. Alstete's (2002) review of literature surrounding the area reveals various 'push' and 'pull' factors as motivators for business start-up (Figure 2.5).

Push	Pull
Redundancy	Independence
Unemployment	Being one's own boss
Frustration with previous job	Using creative skills
Need to earn a reasonable living	Doing enjoyable work
Support family	Making a lot of money

Figure 2.5: The drivers of business start-up

Exercise

Can you think of any examples of entrepreneurs who were either 'pushed' or 'pulled' into entrepreneurship?

Paige and Littrel (2002, p. 314) found a desire for independence, the seeking of a good work/life balance and personal happiness, and the gratification that comes from personal expression, to be of value. For example musicians like Beyoncé and artists are driven by both a need to earn a living and a desire to create. Some researchers have pointed to passion as an explanation for the "goals that control and guide desires, thoughts, plans, and behaviours and that persist over time, regardless of costs, external obstacles, and moral objections" (Frijda, 2005, p. 512). The individual's passion for their craft activates a sense of "pleasure and promise", because they are motivated by a love of what they are doing. This passion can "enhance mental activity, and provide meaning to everyday work" (Brannback *et al.*, 2006, p. 3), and it is said to foster individual drive, the desire to achieve, a willingness to work long hours, and to maintain courage and persistence in the face of obstacles.

Cox and Jennings (1995) found successful entrepreneurs to be intrinsically motivated by interest in, and enjoyment of, their work and the sense of achievement it provides. This can be identified in high profile entrepreneurs, such as Tony Robbins or the late Steve Jobs. Meanwhile Smith (1967) put forward a distinction between the craftsman and the opportunist:

☐ The craftsman – motivated by intrinsic rewards such as autonomy and who is driven by a need for independence, for example Gerry Swartz, Canada's 24th richest man.

☐ The opportunist – who is focused on the functional activities associated with management and motivated by the prospect of growth, for example Richard Branson.

Timmons and Spinelli (2008) further distinguished between lifestyle and high-growth entrepreneurs, in that the former category are content to maintain a comfortable standard of living, while the latter are driven by the achievement of a high level of success/economic gain. Bhave (1994) suggests both "internally and externally stimulated" motives. The latter characteristic is more goal-oriented; here "the potential entrepreneur(s) begins actively searching for opportunities, typically selecting several alternate ideas that are considered and evaluated ('opportunity filtration') before one is chosen" (Davidsson, 2008, p.8). The internally stimulated process is the opposite, though according to some studies, it is also just as common (Handy, 2004). In this case, "...the individual has no prior intention to go into business, yet experienced or were introduced to needs that could not be fulfilled. Finding a solution, the individual becomes aware of others with the same problem, and in turn enters the entrepreneurial process" (Davidsson, 2008, p. 8).

Exercise

Can you think of any examples of lifestyle or high-growth entrepreneurs?

But opportunities do not come pre-packaged (Venkataraman, 1997), and why individuals decide to exploit or even create them is far from straightforward. While it is most often conceptualised as an outcome, opportunity can also be seen as an unfolding process. Bhave (1994, p. 230) suggests that the strongest trigger is often when "the prospective entrepreneurs [experience], or [are] introduced to, needs that [can]not be fulfilled by others". For example, James Dyson created his cyclone technology to solve a problem. Seeing an opportunity, the entrepreneur takes the necessary action to capitalise upon it (Bolton and Thompson, 2000). This implies a match between the market, on one hand, and the knowledge, skills and competencies of the entrepreneur on the other. Entrepreneurial motivation may be intrinsic, extrinsic or both; the entrepreneur may be pushed by an internal stimulus, or pulled by the incentive of achieving their end goal. Beyond this:

☐ Enculturation,

☐ Prior experience

☐ Education

☐ Support of family, friends

All help to determine an individual's propensity to enter the entrepreneurship.

It is however important to remember that even when individuals decide to enter entrepreneurship, there are numerous instances of aspiring entrepreneurs failing to identify a variety of opportunities, or identifying the wrong ones (Singh 2001), for example the Blackberry. Moreover, entrepreneurship literature is full of stories of entrepreneurs searching for one thing and finding another; for example when Arthur Gensler, owner of Gensler Design (a small architecture firm), met the CEO of JetBlue on his flight and designed an airport for him (http://fortune.com/2015/06/02/gensler-architecture-jetblue/). As Dew (2009) explains, "entrepreneurship is a series of random collisions", and while entrepreneurs may start with a systematic plan of action in one area, by luck, accident or chance they may be just as likely to end up in another.

Thus, while much entrepreneurship research suggests that entrepreneurs are motivated by the risk-reward motive and the general prospect of financial reward, studies of entrepreneurship indicate that more entrepreneurs are motivated by intrinsic rather than extrinsic rewards. From the review, it is apparent that individuals can and will enter entrepreneurship without prior intention, but it is also evident that they do not always occur through serendipitous discovery, as some have suggested. For the most part, the research suggests that individuals choose to enter entrepreneurship through "a mix of individual experience, network connections… learning from others, and blind variation" (Aldrich, 1999, p. 333). The most significant factor is the individual's motivations, which "may be the spark that transforms a latent intention into real action and therefore, the missing link between intentions and action" (Carsrud and Brännback, 2011, p. 12).

Entrepreneurship in the 21st century: Conclusions

While there is still a high degree of fragmentation in the entrepreneurship field with respect to current theories, very different questions are now being addressed. Even so, according to Rocha (2012), "the boundaries of the entrepreneurship field remain highly permeable". There is still strong interest in the individual entrepreneur, the firm, the environment in which they operate, the processes they use and their impacts on industries, regions and the economy as a whole. But it appears the importance of the entrepreneur in the real world is becoming more and more difficult to ignore (Wennekers and Thurik, 1999).

From the above discussion, it is clear that the debate surrounding the entrepreneur as an economic hero is ongoing. The entrepreneur has a special place in society thanks to the early theorist Richard Cantillon; indeed, they occupy a position "which is most emphasized yet least understood by economists (Kanbur, 1980; Montanye, 2006)" (Rocha, 2012, p. 27). The recognition of the roles played by entrepreneurs has arrived thanks to the contribution of some important economists over the years such as Cantillon, Say and Walker, Von Thunen, Kirzner, Schumpeter and Baumol, and has led to the rebirth of this figure within the field of economics. Now, in the 21st century, the economics literature is increasingly anxious to understand the importance of the entrepreneur, the firm and the environment. Some of the first attempts to do so were concerned with the identification of the reasons behind the decision to engage in entrepreneurship. However, more recently the field has moved towards placing increasing importance on entrepreneurship as one of the key explanatory factors of economic growth and development. In addition, while there has been much discussion about the entrepreneur and his/her roles in the economics literature, the field is still young and emergent. While we are more aware of the *who, what, where, when, why,* and *how* of entrepreneurship and the entrepreneurial process, the context of entrepreneurship in relation to economic theory is still in need of substantial further attention, and while there is much to be thankful for from economists to date, the field at present is one of growing academic interest (Rocha, 2012).

Exemplar paper

Rocha, V. C. (2012). *The entrepreneur in economic theory: from an invisible man toward a new research field* (No. 459). Universidade do Porto, Faculdade de Economia do Porto.

Summary

The Rocha paper analyses the evolution of economic thought on entrepreneurship, and in particular the author focuses on the path through which the entrepreneur (re)entered economic theory over the 20th century, leading to the new and increasingly independent research field of the Economics of Entrepreneurship. The paper outlines all of the key economic theories of entrepreneurship, both past and present.

Findings

The authors present key theorists in the domain of economic entrepreneurship as well as a detailed discussion of important journals. They believe that the field still remains fragmented however there is still great concern in economics for theories of the individual, the firm and the environment in entrepreneurship.

■ Additional sources for reading – Who to read

William B. Gartner is a world-renowned Professor of Entrepreneurial Leadership and over the last 25 years has written a number of articles on entrepreneurship theory and new venture creation. Gartner's (1985) views on entrepreneurship have been hugely influential in terms of education and research, however with his own ties to industry Gartner is also able to bridge the gap between theory and practice in a seamless manner. He was one of the first to conduct a nationwide study of nascent entrepreneurs and to create a framework that highlights how entrepreneurs identify opportunities, acquire resources in order to solve problems, and take action to successfully launch new ventures.

References

Aldrich, H.E. (1999) *Organizations Evolving*. Thousand Oaks, CA: Sage Publications.

Alstete, J.W. (2002) On becoming an entrepreneur an evolving typology. International *Journal of Entrepreneurial Behaviour & Research*, **8**(4), 222-234

Baumol, W. J. (1968) Entrepreneurship in economic theory. *American Economic Review* **58**(2): 64-71.

Baumol, W. J. (1993) *Entrepreneurship, Management and the Structure of Payoffs*. Cambridge, MA and London, England: MIT Press.

Beaver, G., & Prince, C. (2004) Management, strategy and policy in the UK small business sector: a critical review. *Journal of Small Business and Enterprise Development*, **11**(1), pp. 34-49.

Bhave, M. (1994) A process model of entrepreneurial venture creation. *Journal of Business Venturing*, **9**(3), 223-242.

Bird, B. (1989), *Entrepreneurial Behavior*, Glenview, IL: Scott, Foresman & Co.

Bolton, B. & Thompson, J. (2000) *Talent, Temperament, Technique*. Oxford: Butterworth-Heinemann.

Bridge, S., O'Neill, K., and Cromie, S. (2003) *Understanding Enterprise, Entrepreneurship and Small Business*. 2nd Ed, UK: Palgrave Macmillan, pp. 52-95, p. 509.

Burns, P., (2001) *Entrepreneurship and Small Business*. New York: Palgrave.

Bygrave, W. (1989) The entrepreneurship paradigm (II): Chaos and catastrophes among quantum jumps? *Entrepreneurship Theory and Practice*, **14**(2), 7-30.

Bygrave, W. (2003) The entrepreneurial process. In: W. Bygrave & A. Zacharakis, eds. *The Portable MBA in Entrepreneurship*. 3rd ed. New York: John Wiley and Sons.

Cantillon, R. (1931, original 1755) *Essai sur la nature du commerce en general*. Edited and translated by H. Higgs, London: McMillan.

Carsrud, A. & Brännback, M. (2011) Entrepreneurial motivations: what do we still need to know? *Journal of Small Business Management*, **49**(1), 9-26.

Carter, S., & Shaw, E. (2006). Womens's Business Ownership: Recent Research and Policy Developments (pp. 1-96). DTI.

Casson, M. (2005) Entrepreneurship and the theory of the firm. *Journal of Economic Behavior and Organization* **58**: 327-348.

Chen, C.C., Greene, P.G., & Crick, A. 1998. Does entrepreneurial self-efficacy distinguish entrepreneurs from managers? *Journal of Business Venturing*, **13**(4): 295-315.

Cosgel, M. M. (1996) Metaphors, stories, and the entrepreneur in economics. *History of Political Economy* **28**(1), 57-76.

Cox, C. & Jennings, R. (1995) The foundations of success: the development and characteristics of British entrepreneurs and intrapreneurs. *Leadership & Organization Development Journal,* **16**(7), 4-9.

Davidsson, P. (2008) *The Entrepreneurship Research Challenge.* Cheltenham, UK: Edward Elgar Publishing.

Deakins, D. and Freel, M. (2003), *Entrepreneurship and Small Firms,* Maidenhead{ McGraw-Hill.

Delmar, F. (2006) The psychology of the entrepreneur. In: 2nd, ed. *Enterprise and Small Business: Principles, Practice and Policy.* Harlow, Essex: Pearson Education, pp. 152-175.

Dimov, D. (2011) Entrepreneurial opportunities. In: S. Carter & D. Jones-Evans, eds. *Enterprise and Small Business: Principles, Practice and Policy.* 3rd ed. Oxford: Financial Times/Prentice Hall, pp. 129-150

Drucker, P.F. (1985). Entrepreneurial strategies. *California Management Review,* **27**(2), 9-25.

Eckhardt, J. & Shane, S. (2003) Opportunities and Entrepreneurship. *Journal of Management,* **29**(3), 333-349.

Federation of Small Business, (2015) www.fsb.org.uk/stats Frijda, N. (2005) Emotion experience. *Cognition and Emotion,* **19**(4), 473-497.

Gartner, W. (1985) A Conceptual Framework for Describing the Phenomenon of New Venture Creation. *The Academy of Management Review,* **10**(4), 696-706.

Gustafsson, V. (2006) *Entrepreneurial Decision-making: Individuals, Tasks and Cognitions.* Edward Elgar Publishing.

Hisrich, R.D., Peters, M.P., Shepherd, D.A. (2005) *Entrepreneurship,* 6th Edition, USA: McGraw Hill Irwin, p. 6.

Hébert, R. F., Link, A. N. (1989) In search of the meaning of entrepreneurship. *Small Business Economics* **1**, 39-49.

Kaish, S., & Gilad, B,. 1991. Characteristics of opportunities search of entrepreneurs verses executives: sources, interests and general alertness. *Journal of Business Venturing,* **6**(1), 45-61.

Kanbur, S. M. (1980) A note on risk taking, entrepreneurship and Schumpeter. *History of Political Economy* **12** (4), 489-498.

Kets de Vries, M. F. R. (1977), The entrepreneurial personality: a person at the crossroads, *Journal of Management Studies* (Feb.), 34-57.

Khalil, E.L. (2007). Entrepreneurship and economic theory. In M. Weber (Ed.), *Handbook of Whiteheadian Process Thought,* Frankfurt: Verlag. pp. 145-160.

Kihlstrom, R.E., and Laffont, J.J. (1979). A general equilibrium entrepreneurial theory of firm formation based on risk aversion. *Journal of Political Economy*, **87**(4), 719-748.

Kirby, D.A. (2003) *Entrepreneurship*, UK: McGraw Hill, pp. 1-206.

Kirzner, I. (1973) *Competition and Entrepreneurship*. Chicago: University of Chicago Press.

Knight, F. (1921) *Risk, Uncertainty and Profit*. New York: Houghtom Mifflin.

Kuratko, D. F., Morris, M. H., & Schindehutte, M. (2015) Understanding the dynamics of entrepreneurship through framework approaches. *Small Business Economics*, **45**(1), 1-13.

Landström, H. (2005) *Pioneers in Entrepreneurship and Small Business Research*. International Studies in Entrepreneurship Series, Volume 8, Springer.

Littunen, H. (2000) Entrepreneurship and the characteristics of the entrepreneurial personality. *International Journal of Entrepreneurial Behaviour and Development*, **6**(6), 295-310.

McClelland, D. (1961) *The Achieving Society*. New York: The Free Press.

Montanye, J. A. (2006) Entrepreneurship. *The Independent Review*, **10** (4): 549-571.

Moroz, P. & Hindle, K. (2012) Entrepreneurship as a Process: Toward Harmonizing Multiple Perspectives. *Entrepreneurship Theory and Practice*, **36**(4), pp. 781-818.

Osborne, RL,. 1995. The essence of entrepreneurial success, *Management Decision*, **33**(7), 4-9.

Paige, R. & Littrel, M. (2002) Craft retailers' criteria for success and associated business strategies. *Journal of Small Business Management*, **40**(4), pp. 314-332.

Rocha, V. C. (2012). *The entrepreneur in economic theory: from an invisible man toward a new research field* (No. 459). Universidade do Porto, Faculdade de Economia do Porto.

Sarasvathy, S. (2003) Entrepreneurship as a Science of the Artificial. *Journal of Economic Psychology*, **24**(2), 203-220.

Schumpeter, J. (1934) *The Theory of Economic Development*. Cambridge, Mass: Harvard University Press.

Singh, R. (2001) A comment on developing the field of entrepreneurship through the study of opportunity recognition and exploitation. *Academy of Management Review*, **26**(1), 10-12.

Shane, S,. 2000. Prior knowledge and the discovery of entrepreneurial opportunities. *Organization Science*, **11**(4), 448-469.

Shane, S. & Venkataraman, S. (2000) The Promise of Entrepreneurship as a Field of Research. *Academy of Management Review*, **25**(1), 217-226.

2

Shaver, K. & Scott, L. (1991) Person, process, and choice: the psychology of new venture creation. *Entrepreneurship Theory and Practice*, **16**(2), 23-42.

Smith, N. (1967) *The Entrepreneur and His Firm: The Relationship Between Type of Man and Type of Company*. East Lansing, Michigan: Michigan State University Press.

Timmons, J. & Spinelli, S. (2008) *New Venture Creation: Entrepreneurship for the 21st Century*. 8th ed. Boston: McGraw-Hill/Irwin.

Venkataraman, S. (1997). The distinctive domain of entrepreneurship research: An editor's perspective. In J. Katz & R. Brockhaus (Eds.), *Advances in Entrepreneurship, Firm Emergence, and Growth*, vol. 3:119-138. Greenwich, CT: JAI Press.

Welter, F. (2011) Contextualizing entrepreneurship — conceptual challenges and ways forward. *Entrepreneurship Theory and Practice*, **35**(1), 165–184.

Wennekers, S., Thurik, R. (1999) Linking entrepreneurship and economic growth. *Small Business Economics* **13**, 27-55.

3 Creativity, Innovation and Entrepreneurship

Julie McFarlane

Over the past few years the relationship between creativity and economic development has received increasing interest from a number of different fields of study, in parallel with increasing recognition of the role and importance of creative activities. Since the 1990s, creativity and innovation have achieved acceptance in the fields of business and management in the form of acknowledgement that new markets, or even market growth, may only be attained via creative and innovative solutions. Studies of entrepreneurs and entrepreneurship and growth have become the prime catalysts for the identification and promotion of innovative knowledge industries, whose economic importance has become increasingly significant. Thus, in order to fully appreciate the role of creativity and innovation, it is first vital to understand the nature of entrepreneurship and, specifically, the creativity required to identify and exploit opportunities, and to acquire the necessary resources.

Creativity defined

In the past, the act of being creative meant to "unleash, harness, and empower potential from whatever source" (Landry, 2005, p. 53). The traditional view also states that "the artist is a channel for a superior power, creativity a gift from the gods, and the imagination a divine spark" (Throsby, 2001, p. 94). To borrow an overview from Hisrich, Peters and Shepherd (2005, p. 8), the "ability to innovate and create can be observed throughout history; although the fundamental tools may have changed the ability has been present in every civilization".

Today, creativity is defined as "…the ability or quality displayed when solving hitherto unsolved problems, when developing original and novel solutions to problems others have solved differently, or when developing original and novel… products" (Parkhurst, 1999, p. 18). This could, for example, mean new processes to help us do something better, or ideas for new ways to use existing products. It could also mean new services to supply to new or existing customers and, of course, it can mean new ways of thinking about things, encompassing.

Flexibility: Willing to look at an issue from many angles, not set in our ways
Originality: Attempts to find non-typical responses to problems
No-judgment: Not rejecting a potential solution without giving it appropriate consideration

---

This shift in theory leads to a move away from Feldman's (1979, p. 660) elitist view that creativity is only for the gifted.

The **elitist** view sees creativity as an individual spiritual experience; an innate ability that cannot be harnessed. In the **developmental** view, creativity is in us all, not a select few, and is more a problem-solving process that can be learned, practised and applied by anyone.

Instead, creativity is seen as a process, not an event, and as something that can be harnessed and supported. Creativity is not a minority phenomenon, but can be developed in anyone, as it involves engaging in a problem-solving process more than expressing innate, special ability. In other words, it may be out of the ordinary but it can be learned, practised and applied by anyone. Thus what was once considered the work of the artist-genius became democratised. Today, we all aspire to be creative in some respect. Even so, the value of individual skill and talent in innovation must still be recognized, and should be cultivated more intensely than ever before.

Edward de Bono (2008), a theorist of creativity, noted that the process of creativity does not just happen in a flash of inspiration. Individuals, entrepreneurs, teams and business don't just sit waiting for the "lightbulb moment"; instead, he argues that they approach their problem systematically. He developed "The Six Thinking Hats" technique to aid this process. The basic premise is for an individual or project team to learn how to separate thinking into six clear functions and roles by "wearing one hat at a time" when considering a problem. Each role is identified with a symbolic thinking hat in a different colour. By mentally wearing and switching hats, teams can easily focus or redirect their thoughts, conversation, or meeting. At any one time, everyone will wear the same colour of hat, or in other words, everyone will look at the problem at hand from only one perspective, which at any given time is the perspective indicated by the hat being worn (see Figure 3.1).

For example, the blue hat differs from the thinking represented by the other hats because it is involved with directing the thinking process itself. The blue hat is used whenever the next hat is to be used. Usually, this hat will be used in the following types of circumstances:

1 At the outset of a discussion

Let's decide what we want to think about and which hats will we use?

2 At a midpoint to restate the thinking goal

I think we are getting away from what we want to talk about. Can someone redirect the conversation?

3 At the end, to summarise what thinking has been done

Think of one sentence to sum up today's activities

Adapted from: De Bono, E. (2008) *Six Frames For Thinking about Information*. London: Vermilion. p. 19).

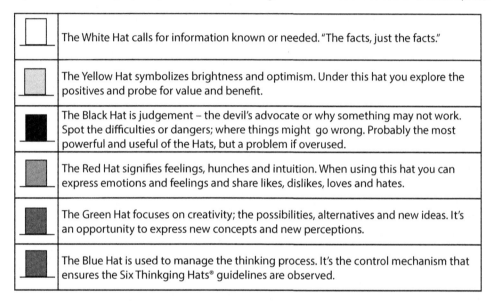

	The White Hat calls for information known or needed. "The facts, just the facts."
	The Yellow Hat symbolizes brightness and optimism. Under this hat you explore the positives and probe for value and benefit.
	The Black Hat is judgement – the devil's advocate or why something may not work. Spot the difficulties or dangers; where things might go wrong. Probably the most powerful and useful of the Hats, but a problem if overused.
	The Red Hat signifies feelings, hunches and intuition. When using this hat you can express emotions and feelings and share likes, dislikes, loves and hates.
	The Green Hat focuses on creativity; the possibilities, alternatives and new ideas. It's an opportunity to express new concepts and new perceptions.
	The Blue Hat is used to manage the thinking process. It's the control mechanism that ensures the Six Thinkging Hats® guidelines are observed.

Figure 3.1: De Bono's Six Thinking Hats (2008)

Adapted from: De Bono, E. (2008), *Six Frames For Thinking about Information*. London: Vermilion.

The hats themselves can be used singly at any point in thinking, but the blue hat facilitates the discussion. The rest of the hats are used to direct and switch thinking. They are used to question in different ways, as De Bono explains:

Design sequence example

For example, the **yellow hat** (representing sunny optimism) followed by the **black hat** (caution), may ne used to assess a new idea. The **black hat** (caution) followed by the **green hat** (new ideas) may also be used to improve a design. Also, the **red** and **white** hats are best for comparing facts and opinion, and the **black**, **yellow** and **green** are best used when comparing and synthesising ideas.

Adapted from: De Bono, E. (2008), *Six Frames For Thinking about Information*. London: Vermilion.

Exercise

Using the design sequence shown above come up with a business idea. Making use of each hat, assess the viability of the idea. Note down your findings.

Figure 3.2: Questions relating to the Six Thinking Hats

Adapted from: De Bono, E. (2008), *Six Frames For Thinking about Information*. London: Vermilion.

De Bono's 'Six Thinking Hats' technique has had a wide range of applications in industry, from management training to new product development stages, and has become a highly regarded creative problem solving activity. It helps teams to generate knowledge and awareness of a certain problem area, and also encourages them to learn more about the problem as a team, as well as assisting them in researching possible solutions and incubating their ideas in moments of reflection by asking questions at each stage (see Figure 3.2).

How creative thought can turn into innovation

Over recent years there has been fierce debate over the concept of creativity, along with considerable discussion of how creative thought can be transformed into creative action and innovation. Fox (2002) suggests that creativity can change the way we do things in modern times. In understanding how this can happen, a clear understanding of what it means to innovate is required (Goffin and Mitchell, 2005). To innovate, according to the *New Oxford Dictionary* (2004, p. 942), means to be able to: "Make changes in something established, especially by introducing new methods, ideas, or products". According to the UK government, "innovation is the process by which new ideas are successfully exploited to create economic, social and environmental value" (BIS 2011, p.7). In the mid-twentieth century, economist Joseph Schumpeter (1950) pioneered the categorization of innovation as the creation of something 'new' that creates and adds value for those who interact with, or consume, it. Something 'new' can also mean the updating of something which already exists in order to take advantage of a specific segment or a newly-identified or emerging market.

Ultimately, innovation can be divided into two categories: functional, and design-driven. The former category includes products' functional elements: does it work? Does it meet customer needs? For example, the Apple iPhone operating system is part of the functional design of the device, while the easy-to-use form is a remnant of the design element. Design-driven innovations focus on the symbolic nature of the product. Certain important questions are inherent in the design: what does it mean to the consumer? How do they feel when they use the product? Ultimately, innovation must add value in the key consumer areas of price, quality, and functionality, but it also has to fulfil a number of intangible requirements.

Another seminal theorist in the field, Christensen (1997), identified two types of innovations: *disruptive* innovations and *sustaining* innovations. The former involve a new value proposition by which new markets are created. In such instances, individuals or business organizations seize upon basic inventions and transform them into economic innovations, thereby disequilibrating and altering the existing market structure, then waiting until the process eventually settles down before the next wave of innovation begins. In contrast, the latter concept of 'sustaining' innovations is best thought of as improvements to existing products, processes or markets.

Examples

A prime exemplar of a 'disruptive' innovation would be the impact Apple's iTunes had on the rest of the music industry. Apple observed the impact and capabilities of MP3 technology and quickly moved to design the first generation iPod, and following the success of the file sharing site Napster, they launched the first legal online music service, iTunes, in April 2003 (Vaccaro and Cohn, 2004, p. 48). Apple didn't just innovate with regard to the way music was played – they also had a huge impact on the way music was listened to by huge sections of the public. The result was wide-ranging changes in how music was produced, manufactured and distributed, along with an inevitable impact on overall profits. With each year that passed, further advancements in technology meant that sales both of downloads and physical products fell. With the introduction of streaming capabilities and music genome software such as Pandora and iTunes genius, patterns of music consumption have now become as fragmented as the industry itself.

The latter concept, 'sustaining' innovations, are best thought of as improvements to existing products, processes or markets. We see many examples of such innovations on a daily basis; however consumers never see many of these sustaining innovations. They include, for example, organisational process improvement in terms of making supply chains more efficient, as Spanish retailer Zara have managed to do in order to react far more quickly and efficiently to changing consumer demands or new trends. Other examples could include making the organisation more streamlined, diversifying operations and divestment activities. Taking a resource-based view (Penrose, 1959) of the organisation with a focus on utilising its core competencies, the search for new techniques to improve business processes has subsequently grown, both internally and externally (Poolton and Ismail, 2000, p. 795).

Exercise

Can you think of any other disruptive or sustaining innovations? Note them down and then think about why you have defined them in this way.

In terms of the impact of innovation on the small firm, small firms usually focus on sustaining innovations more than on disruptive ones. One of the main pioneers of a clear concept of entrepreneurship, Schumpeter (1934) distinguished inventions from an entrepreneur's innovations by explaining that entrepreneurs innovate not simply by working out how best to use inventions, but also by introducing new means of production, new products, and new forms of organization (see Figure 3.3). He argued that innovations demand as much skill and daring as does the process of invention itself.

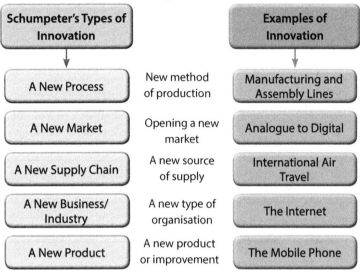

Figure 3.3: Schumpeter's five types of innovation

Very few businesses have the potential to alter economies, and in doing so, to initiate the Schumpeterian 'gale of destruction'. Most small firms will utilise their core competencies and focus on improvements to products, processes or markets. They may, for example, create a new product in an existing market, such as Skechers, who introduced their Breathable shoe after Geox had launched years before. Or, as Google have done, firms may be able to create an entirely new market for themselves. Innovation can either be radical or incremental; in some cases it can even be both, and even small changes can impact the economy. Yet, it is clear that innovation is clearly multi-dimensional and should be thought of as a process rather than as an activity.

Exercise

Note down another example for each of Schumpeter's five types of innovation.

Some researchers still focus on the individualistic nature of innovation (Chell, 2001), while others, such as Goffin (2005), suggest that innovation is about working as part of a team. As Amazon founder Jeff Bezos has suggested, it is "people who are our greatest asset", and in terms of the inception and implementation of innovation, it is down to people and the context in which innovation is harnessed. However, there are two opposing views of innovation, and on how organizations should innovate: *closed* and *open* innovation (see Figure 3.4). The former suggests that successful innovation requires control and ownership of the innovation or its intellectual property (IP). In this view, a company should control the creation and management of ideas, retain ownership of R&D activities, or perhaps integrate new product development (NPD) cycles. Here, innovation is performed in a closed and self-sufficient way. The latter is based on the idea that, in a global world, "no company is an island"and instead they should tap into external resources, for example by buying or licensing processes or inventions (i.e. patents) from other companies.

Closed Innovation Principles	Open Innovation Principles
Most of the smart people in our field work for us	Not all the smart people work for us, so owe must find and tap into the knowledge and expertise of bright individuals outside our company
To profit from R&D, we must discover, develop and ship ourselves	External R&D can create significant value; internal R&D is needed to claim some portion of that value
If we discover it, we will get it to market first	We don't have to originate the research in order to profit from it
If we are the 1st to commercialise we will win	Building a better business model is better than getting to market first
If we create the most and the best ideas in the industry, we will win	If we make the best use of internal and external ideas, we will win
We should control our intellectual property (IP) so that our competitors don't profit from our ideas	We should profit from others' use of our IP, and we should buy others' IP whenever it advances our own business model

Figure 3.4: Principles of Open and Closed Innovation

Source: Adapted from Chesbrough, H. W., 2006. *Open innovation: The new imperative for creating and profiting from technology.* Harvard Business Press.

While following the concept of closed innovation has assisted companies in attaining competitive advantage during most of the 20th century, today the increasing mobility of knowledge workers (Florida, 2002), the expansion of venture capital, and the increased availability of technology and out-sourcing options has meant innovation can no longer be considered in isolation and instead is also about integration and networking.

Moreover, while small and large organizations are encouraged to innovate to enhance their competitive advantage, being innovative is believed to depend on the stakeholders of the organization, and their diversity is vital to engendering a creative environment (Hyland and Beckett, 2005, p. 352). Innovation is 'invariably a team game' (Trott, 2005, p. 11) and often innovation management is about the people you employ, and work alongside, so when organizations foster the right conditions, innovative behaviour will be likely to flourish.

To sum up, while we usually think of innovations as new products or processes with the power to transform how we live, often innovation refers to customization and specialization through the harnessing of creativity and knowledge. The business organization should always aim to follow strategic plans that facilitate good conditions both for individual creativity and for organizational efficiency. Innovation is a complex phenomenon, and any person or organization wishing to innovate must understand that new innovations are only as good as the next ones. Further, innovation can be radical or incremental in nature, but as we have discussed here, it is also multi-dimensional and should be thought of as a process rather than an activity. Finally, not all creative thought is ultimately actioned and not all ideas are creative, nor will all such thought and ideas necessarily facilitate an opportunity.

Opportunity identification

There is a widely-held misconception that the secret to being a successful entrepreneur is to come up with a truly original idea. The reality is somewhat different, as opportunity recognition and discovery always "carry an element of surprise" (Davidsson, 2008, p. 8). As Bygrave (203, p.14) succinctly puts it:

> almost any idea an entrepreneur has, will more likely than have occurred to someone else, even the most revolutionary thoughts in the history of mankind occurred to more than one person almost simultaneously.

It has been said that "ideas are a dime a dozen" (Bygrave, 2003), but "developing that idea, honing the right resources, implementing them, and building a successful business around them" are the most important aspects of entrepreneurship (Kirby, 2003, p. 64). Most people in their lifetime have an idea that could form the basis for establishing their own business but, in reality, few do so (Burns, 2001, p. 71). Therefore, it is important not only to understand *how* these opportunities come into existence but also *why* these particular opportunities have been discovered (Shane and Venkataraman, 2000).

The Oxford English Dictionary (in Sarasvathy *et al.*, 2003, p. 142) defines opportunity as "a time, juncture, or condition of things favourable to an end or purpose, or admitting of something being done or effected". In the entrepreneurship literature, Casson (1982, in Shane and Venkataraman, 2000, p. 220) defines opportunities as "those situations where new goods, services, raw materials, and organizing methods are introduced and sold at greater than their cost of production". For Singh (1999, p. 11), an opportunity is "a feasible, profit-seeking, would-be venture that provides an innovative new product or service to the market". However, it is important to recognize that an entrepreneurial opportunity is just that – an opportunity to do something (see Figure 3.5):

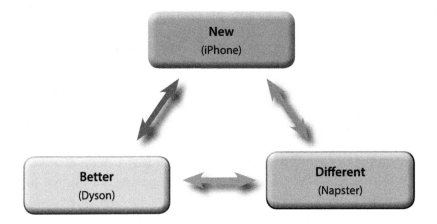

Figure 3.5: An opportunity is?

The choice of mode depends on the nature of the organization, the opportunity, and all things favourable to its achievement (Venkataraman and Sarasvathy, 2000, p. 654).

Exercise

Can you think of an example of an entrepreneurial opportunity that is a) new, b) different, c) better?

However, if opportunity, by definition, is unknown until it is discovered or created, then how can someone search for something they do not know exists? And, if it were known to exist, would the market not already have taken advantage of it?

How and why particular opportunities are discovered is usually determined by a complex mix of factors. While it is most often conceptualised as an outcome, an opportunity can also be seen as an unfolding process. As Dimov (2011, p. 133) explains, opportunities are "situated expressions of prospective entrepreneurs' motivation, knowledge, and cognitive and learning abilities". Previous research has shown that individuals differ in their ability to identify entrepreneurial opportunities, to perceive particular market changes, and to know how to create specific products or services. One reason for this is that information is imperfectly distributed, with the result that "no two people share all of the same information at the same time" (Shane and Venkataraman, 2000, p. 221).

Most prior research suggests that opportunity creation or discovery is idiosyncratic (Venkataraman, 1997), and that it results from a combination of factors (see Figure 3.6):

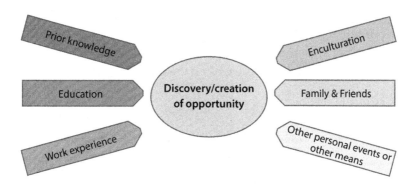

Figure 3.6: Factors influencing the creation or discovery of opportunities

All these factors influence the entrepreneur's ability to comprehend, extrapolate, interpret, and apply new information in ways which those lacking such abilities cannot. According to Venkataraman (1997), each person's prior knowledge creates a "knowledge corridor" which allows them to recognize certain opportunities, but not necessarily others (Shane, 2000, p. 452). Aldrich (2001, p. 133) agrees, suggesting that potential opportunities "ultimately derive from a mix of individual experience, network connections, learning from others, and blind variation", which "can be of immeasurable help", and adds that often, many would-be entrepreneurs forego alertness in favour of utilising contacts in their chosen industry, thus making them more able to spot gaps others have missed (Burns, 2001, p. 75).

Exercise

Think about each of the above factors and how each impact the types of opportunities entrepreneurs create or discover?

As entrepreneurial opportunities come in a variety of forms, the search involves more than simply defining the ideas, as understanding the acts and the entrepreneurial activities themselves is also vital. Davidsson (2008) suggests that the literature generally points to a somewhat egocentric systematic search in relation to the creation or discovery of opportunities. Kirzner (1973) held that no optimal solution exists with regard to how best to search an unbounded domain, leaving alertness as the only alternative for many aspiring entrepreneurs. In this view, "the individual chooses among acts while nature metaphorically 'chooses' among alternative states" (Hirshleifer and Riley, 1979, p. 1377). Yet, since the discovery of entrepreneurial opportunities is not an optimization process by which people make mechanical calculations (Baumol, 1993), most potential entrepreneurs must discover these opportunities through other means (Sarasvathy, 2000). Bhave (1994, p. 230) suggests a trigger when "the prospective individuals [experience], or [are] introduced to, needs that

[can]not be fulfilled by others". In this explanation, the entrepreneur sees an opportunity then takes the necessary action to capitalise upon it. This implies a match between the market on the one hand, and the knowledge, skills and competencies of the entrepreneur on the other (see Figure 3.7).

Figure 3.7: Context factors influencing the creation or discovery of opportunities

For Shane and Venkataraman (2000, p. 220), this is because "different people possess different beliefs (be it luck, a hunch, superior intuition, or information they possess), about either current markets or what possible new markets could be created in the future". Meanwhile, for Burns (2001, p. 75), most potential entrepreneurs "base their ideas on prior experience, or through a hobby, often feeling undervalued in current employment – they have an idea but cannot persuade others to take it on board, thus exploiting it to their own advantage". But opportunities do not come pre-packaged, and the opportunity recognition process is not straightforward. The literature usually recommends that entrepreneurs systematically search for opportunities, yet some have suggested that this is impossible since an opportunity, by definition, is always unknown until it is discovered or created. Aspiring entrepreneurs must therefore be alert.

It is evident that entrepreneurial opportunities do not always occur through serendipitous discovery, as some have suggested (Von Stamm, 2005). Most research suggests that prior knowledge, work experience, education, personal experience, networks and other factors may all play a part, either on their own or in various combinations. As identified above, the discovery of entrepreneurial opportunities is rarely, if ever, down to a flash of inspiration or pure luck; rather, it involves the conscientious exploitation of resources which are already to hand or can somehow be found. The decision to undertake the next stage of the entrepreneurial process is not a simple one, and potential entrepreneurs must not only distinguish between the various types of information they possess, but also trade off the risks and benefits of investing in specific activities (Fiet and Patel, 2008).

Of course, not all ideas become money-making opportunities. There have been numerous instances of aspiring entrepreneurs failing to identify a variety of opportunities, or identifying the wrong ones, a good example being the infamous Sinclair C5. Moreover, as Singh (2001) explains, entrepreneurs may succeed in spotting a great opportunity but then fail to act upon it in the best possible way. Good planning is needed which involves (see Figure 3.8);

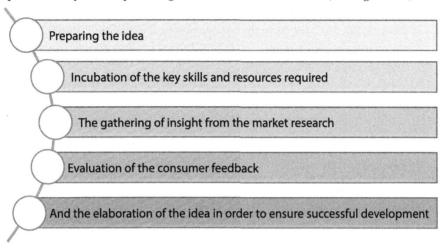

Figure 3.8: Planning stages

In addition, domain-relevant skills, intrinsic (internal) motivation or a drive to create, and the process of creation are all given prominence as important factors in the subject literature (Venkataraman and Sarasvathy, 2000, p. 658).

With the above discussion in mind, entrepreneurship obviously involves elements of both luck and planning, as the idea by itself is clearly insufficient, and only becomes successful at the exploitation stage when it promises an effective strategic position. In other words, ideas are vital in entrepreneurship, but are useless on their own (Bolton and Thompson, 2005, p. 82). It is therefore up to the individual not only to discover the opportunity and decide to exploit it but also to make things happen after the initial decision has been made. As has been suggested by some of the authors discussed in this chapter, entrepreneurs see or realise where there is an opportunity, engage in the necessary activities and make things happen (Bolton and Thompson, 2005, p. 86). This process implies a match between the market and the knowledge, skills and competencies offered by the entrepreneurial venture. The ideas themselves must be created and then implemented in an attempt to fulfil the organization's initial objectives. This is a metaphorical process, continually evolving as and when required. In some cases, as has previously been suggested, the initial concept or idea will evolve, as might the direction of the venture.

Even though a great amount of skill is often needed to spot a potential entrepreneurial opportunity, it usually takes even more to implement the idea successfully. Regardless of any viewpoint, "a true entrepreneur is someone who knows the right people, can pick a good team (Horovitz, 1997), act quickly and make it all happen" (Nolan Bushnell; in Bolton and Thompson, 2005, p. 13). Entrepreneurs can be found in every walk of life, yet as Bhave (2003) suggests, numerous ideas have occurred in similar forms in the minds of many different people, yet few will have the inclination or the ability to exploit them, nor will they have the skills necessary to build them up into something of value (Bolton and Thompson, 2005, p. 34).

Exercise

Below is a list of different opportunity types. Identify a current enterprise that fulfils one of these opportunity types.

- New products/services
- Solutions to existing problems
- New consumer markets
- New industries
- Experience industries
- New operating/manufacturing process
- New supply chain

Steps of creative thought in turning ideas into innovations

Opportunities are not like raindrops – they do not fall at our feet. Entrepreneurs *seek* out or *develop* opportunities, while from time to time something might just happen which allows an entrepreneur to move forward. If they sit and wait for an opportunity to appear, they will probably never succeed. Drucker (2002) suggested internal and external change would open up opportunities for innovation (see Figure 3.9).

Internal	External
1 The unexpected - can we react to change?	1 Changes in demographics – age, income health, etc.
2 Incongruity – can we cope with the difference between what we thought would happen and what actually happened? This could create an opportunity.	2 Changes in perception, mood, meaning – can we react to changes in fashion, culture, attitudes?
3 Inadequacy in underlying processes – can existing processes and procedures be improved?	3 New knowledge – science and industry affect our products and processes.
4 Changes in our industry and our market – can we respond positively?	

Figure 3.9: Drucker's (2002) Opportunity scan

Adapted from: Drucker, P. F. (2002). The discipline of innovation. *Harvard Business Review*, **80**(8), 95-100.

Turning an idea into an innovative opportunity requires more than simply defining innovation; an understanding of how innovation is achieved is also needed. It is clear that innovation is complex and does not occur by accident; as has been discussed, it is a process initiated through planning and strategy.

Akio Morita of Sony once stated that:

> Ordinary people cannot innovate all of the time
> (Goffin and Mitchell, 2005, p. 265)

It is tempting to believe that entrepreneurs are able to identify or 'craft' opportunities that other people miss even though the information which generates the idea is theoretically there for all to see. They are not, however, 'magicians'; rather, they are creators first and implementers second, and both types of abilities are heavily involved in the iterative process (Bolton and Thompson, 2005, p. 16). Therefore, while it is important to recognize that the person-centric view has a place within entrepreneurship research, it is more valuable to gain an in-depth understanding of the processes they use and the activities they undertake (Bolton and Thompson, 2005, p. 14).

The majority of innovations are harnessed through an individual's idea and an organization's supportive structure and culture. Successful innovation is a 'multi-actor' process requiring integration from areas both internal and external to the process, and is increasingly facilitated by technological developments and IT-based networking. Creativity alone is therefore insufficient for true innovation as it can come up with ideas, but will not necessarily be able to reap the benefits. Today, creativity is defined as a personal problem-solving process of a non-routine kind, which can be learned, practised and successfully applied by anyone.

Many of the greatest opportunities for innovation began as ways to solve a problem. According to Lumpkin and Lichtenstein (2005) there are five stages to creative problem solving (see Figure 3.10).

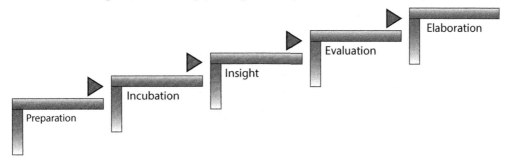

Figure 3.10: Stages in creative problem solving

Adapted from: Lumpkin, G. T., and Lichtenstein, B. B. (2005). The role of organizational learning in the opportunity-recognition process. *Entrepreneurship Theory and Practice*, **29**(4), p. 458.

The stages shown in Figure 3.10 are flexible, however they can be said to form a toolkit for organizations' innovation development processes. In organizations, ideas are usually prepared in a brainstorming session and are then internalised and refined before being taken to the market to test. Once the idea has been disseminated either to customers or the test market, the insights gained are usually evaluated internally before any changes are made prior to commercialization. However, this is a simplified version of the creative process which in reality is much more complex and often ad-hoc in organizations, due to the constantly changing business environment.

While some observers still argue in favour of the 'hero', in the form of an individual with the drive to make an idea reality, in fact the secret to success is far more about having "the nerve, energy, passion, commitment and skill to build a business, than it is about a great idea" (Barrow *et al.*, 2005, p. 16). Importantly, there is obviously an element of both luck and planning in the make-up of success in many cases, as the idea alone is inadequate, and only becomes successful at the exploitation stage. Therefore, it is up to the individual not only to discover the opportunity and decide to exploit it but also to make things happen after the initial decision has been made.

As Davidsson (2006) states, this process is iterative and, like discovery, exploitation too relies on revision and new insights. Those who hope to make it happen must revisit and revise the original idea (Bolton and Thompson, 2005, p. 304). An enterprise and its resources give new life to the opportunity by developing it to the point at which it can be shown to potential investors and customers. Perhaps this won't be the final product, or perhaps prototypes will be required, but its value proposition and intent should be apparent to all. Once this process has ended, the opportunity then needs to be exploited and established within the marketplace.

If the initial exploitation is successful, this will create its own unique challenges – and in turn generate a new set of demands. The original venture will have to change, and will need constant refinement and improvement to sustain that change. The organization or venture will need to take into account the characteristics of the market within which they are operating, and the opportunities available to them, as well, of course, as the resources they have, and those which they will need to acquire to achieve realization, while also keeping an eye on their competitors. Ultimately, the venture needs to find a new position in the market where it can still be seen to provide something of value for the user (Bolton and Thompson, 2005, p. 87).

Conclusion

This chapter has provided an overview of the presence of creativity and innovation and in light of the current theory, we have discussed who entrepreneurial individuals are, and what they do. We have developed an understanding of the current theories of opportunity recognition, and explained that the process itself is not linear but instead that it is dynamic. The discussion has also indicated that consideration and understanding not only of who the entrepreneurs or innovators are, but also of what they do, why they do it, where they do it, when they do it and of course how, are of greater importance in understanding entrepreneurs and innovation than simply focusing on who they are.

3

Exemplar paper

Fillis, I. (2002) An Andalusian Dog or a Rising Star? Creativity and the Marketing/ Entrepreneurship Interface. *Journal of Marketing Research*, **18**(1), 379-395.

Summary

This paper discusses the origins of the study of creativity, from social psychology to the business discipline. Creativity is viewed as a key competency at the marketing/entrepreneurship interface, linked with related issues such as innovation, vision, leadership and motivation. The benefits of developing creative competencies are presented and linked to a knowledge entrepreneur's set of 21st century business skills.

Findings

A model of creativity as competitive advantage is developed, built from sets of internal and external factors which impinge upon the firm and managerial performance. Finally, a series of recommendations for both marketing practitioners and academics are made, focusing on the need to challenge convention in order to progress ideas, products and services into the new century.

Additional sources for reading – Who to read

Professor Per Davidsson is well known for his extensive research on the start-up and growth of small firms, as well as the societal well-being and job creation effects of those activities. In addition to many books, book chapters and research reports, he has published over 50 peer reviewed articles in, for example, the *Strategic Management Journal, Regional Studies*, the *Journal of Management Studies, Entrepreneurship Theory & Practice, Entrepreneurship and Regional Development*, and *Journal of Business Venturing*, including the most cited articles ever published by the latter two journals.

References

Aldrich, H.E. (1999) *Organizations Evolving*. Thousand Oaks, CA: Sage Publications.

Barrow, C., Burke, G., Molian, D. & Brown, R., (2005). *Enterprise Development: The Challenges of Starting, Growing and Selling Businesses.* UK: Thomson, pp. 1-51.

Baumol, W., (1990). Entrepreneurship: productive, unproductive, and destructive. *Journal of Political Economy*, **98**(5), pp. 893-921.

BIS, (2011). *Innovation Report. Innovation, Research and Growth,* London: The Stationery Office (TSO). Available at: https://www.gov.uk/government/uploads/system/uploads/attachment_data/file/293635/bis-14-p188-innovation-report-2014-revised.pdf [Accessed 09 August 2015].

Bhave, M., (1994). A process model of entrepreneurial venture creation. *Journal of Business Venturing*, **9**(3), pp. 223-242.

Bolton, B. & Thompson, J. (2000) *Talent, Temperament, Technique*. Oxford: Butterworth-Heinemann.

Burns, P., (2001). *Entrepreneurship and Small Business*, N.Y.: Palgrave, pp. 1-97.

Bygrave, W.D., (2003). The entrepreneurial process. In: W. Bygrave & A. Zacharakis, eds. *The portable MBA in entrepreneurship*. 3rd ed. New York: John Wiley and Sons Publishing.

Chell, E., (2001). *Entrepreneurship: Globalization, Innovation and Development*. UK: Thomson, pp. 225-248.

Chesbrough, H. W., (2006). *Open innovation: The new imperative for creating and profiting from technology*. Boston: Harvard Business Press.

Christensen, C. M., (1997). *The Innovator's Dilemma When New Technologies Cause Great Firms to Fail*. Cambridge, MA: Harvard Business School Press.

Davidsson, P., 2006. The entrepreneurial process. In: S. Carter and D. Jones-Evans, eds. *Enterprise and Small Business: Principles, Practice and Policy*. 2nd ed. Financial Times/Prentice Hall: Hanslow.

Davidsson, P., (2008). *The Entrepreneurship Research Challenge*. Cheltenham, UK: Edward Elgar Publishing.

De Bono, E., (2008). *Six Frames for Thinking about Information*. London: Vermilion.

Dimov, D., (2011). Entrepreneurial opportunities. In: S. Carter & D. Jones-Evans, eds. *Enterprise and Small Business: Principles, Practice and Policy*. 3rd ed. Oxford: Financial Times/Prentice Hall, pp. 129-150

Drucker, P.F., (2002). The Discipline of Innovation. *Harvard Business Review* **80**(8), 95-100.

Feldman, D., (1979). Toward a non-elitist conception of giftedness. *Phi Delta Kappan*, **60**(9), pp. 660-663.

Fiet, J. O. and Patel, P. C., (2008). Entrepreneurial discovery as constrained, systematic search. *Small Business Economics.* **30**, 215-299.

Fox, M., (2002). Creativity: *Where the Divine and the Human Meet.* 1st ed. New York: Tarcher/Putnam

Goffin, K and Michell, R., (2005). *Innovation Management: Strategy and Implementation Using the Pentathlon Framework.* London: Palgrave McMillan.

Hirshleifer, J., & Riley, J. G., (1979). The analytics of uncertainty and information-an expository survey. *Journal of Economic Literature,* 1375-1421.

Hisrich, R.D., Peters, M.P. & Shepherd, D.A., (2005). *Entrepreneurship.* 6th Edition, USA: McGraw Hill Irwin, p. 6.

Horovitz, (1997) MISSING p 47

Hyland, P., and Beckett, R., (2005). Engendering an innovative culture and maintaining operational balance. *Journal of Small Business and Enterprise Development,* **12**(3), pp. 336-35.

Kirby, D.A., (2003). *Entrepreneurship.* UK: McGraw Hill, pp. 1-206.

Landry, C., (2005). Lineages of the creative city. In: S. Franke & E. Verhhagen, eds. *Creativity and the City: How the Creative Economy is Changingthe City.* Rotterdam: NAI Publishing, pp. 42-55.

Lumpkin, G. T., & Lichtenstein, B. B., (2005). The role of organizational learning in the opportunity-recognition process. *Entrepreneurship Theory and Practice,* **29**(4), 451-472.

Parkhurst, H. B., (1999). Confusion, lack of consensus, and the definition of creativity as a construct. *The Journal of Creative Behavior,* **33**(1), 1-21.

Penrose, E., (1959). *The Theory of the Firm.* Oxford: Basil Blackwell.

Poolton, J., & Ismail, H., (2000). New developments in innovation. *Journal of Managerial Psychology,* **15**(8), 795 – 811

Sarasvathy, S., (2000). Report on the seminar on research perspectives in entrepreneurship. *Journal of Business Venturing,* **15**(1), pp. 1-57.

Sarasvathy, S., Dew, N., Velamuri, S.R. & Venkataraman, S., (2003). Three Views of Entrepreneurial Opportunity. In: Z. J. Acs & D. B. Audretsch, eds. *Handbook of entrepreneurship research: an interdisciplinary survey and introduction. Vol. 1.* New York: Springer, pp. 141-160.

Schumpeter, J.A., (1934). *The Theory of Economic Development.* Cambridge, Mass: Harvard University Press.

Schumpeter, J. A., (1950). *Capitalism, Socialism, and Democracy.* 3rd ed. New York: Harper.

Shane, S., (2000). Prior knowledge and the discovery of entrepreneurial opportunities. *Organization Science,* **11**(4), pp. 448-466.

Shane, S. & Venkataraman, S., (2000). The promise of entrepreneurship as a field of research. *Academy of Management Review*, **25**(1), pp. 217-226.

Singh (1999), MISSING p. 43

Singh, R., (2001). A comment on developing the field of entrepreneurship through the study of opportunity recognition and exploitation. *Academy of Management Review*, **26**(1), pp. 10-12.

The New Oxford Dictionary. (2004). 3rd ed. Oxford, UK: Oxford University Press

Throsby, D., (2001). *Economics and Culture.* Cambridge: Cambridge University Press

Trott, P., (2001). The role of market research in the development of new products. European *Journal of Innovation Management.* **4**(3). pp. 117-125.

Vaccaro, V. & Cohn, D., (2004). The evolution of business models and marketing strategies in the music industry. *International Journal on Media Management*, **6**(1-2), pp. 46-58.

Venkataraman, S., (1997). The distinctive domain of entrepreneurship research: an editor's perspective. In: *Advances in entrepreneurship, firm emergence and growth.* Greenwich, CT: JAI Press, pp. 119–138.

Venkataraman, S. & Sarasvathy, S., (2000). Strategy and entrepreneurship: outlines of an untold story. In: M. Hitt, R. Freeman & J. Harrison, eds. *The Handbook of Strategic Management*. Oxford: Blackwell Publishing, pp. 650-658.

Von Stamm, B., (2005). *Managing Innovation, Design and Creativity*. 2nd ed. UK: Wiley, p. xi.

4 Diversity in Entrepreneurship

Harveen Chugh and Michelle Nguyen

Diversity refers to groups of individuals of varied race, culture, gender, ethnicity, sexual orientation, social background, age, disability, political beliefs and other traits. In theory, diversity within the global population should be reflected in entrepreneurial activity, yet entrepreneurship is relatively homogenous. Research has shown that diversity affects entrepreneurship (Audretsch *et al.*, 2008). Understanding diversity further allows us to recognize the motivations and challenges affecting entrepreneurs. Moreover, as we grow a new generation of entrepreneurs, we must identify and break down barriers to support them in their journey towards success. Increased understanding of diversity is not only of value to entrepreneurs, but also to educators, researchers and policymakers. This chapter examines the importance of diversity in entrepreneurship focusing on:

☐ Women entrepreneurs;

☐ Ethnic minority entrepreneurs;

☐ 'Other' minority entrepreneurs including:

■ Student and graduate entrepreneurs;

■ Lesbian, gay, bisexual and transgender (LGBT) entrepreneurs;

■ Grey entrepreneurs;

■ Disabled entrepreneurs);

☐ Implications for government/government policies.

Women entrepreneurs

In 2012, 126 million women reportedly were starting or running their own business in 67 economies around the world (Kelley *et al.*, 2013). Women-led businesses comprise approximately one third of businesses globally and 29% of the self-employed population in the UK, contributing £75 billion in Gross Value Added annually (BIS, 2013). In the US, historically the leader in female entrepreneurship, one out of ten businesses are women-led, which is the highest in any developed economy (Kelley *et al.*, 2014). Although women are one of the fastest growing entrepreneurial populations internationally (Brush *et al.*, 2009; Carter and Shaw, 2006), men remain twice as likely as women to start a business (Marlow *et al.*, 2012). Hughes *et al.* (2012) gathered and analysed the research direction and approach to women's entrepreneurship since the 1980s. Having established that gender was an important discourse in entrepreneurship with significant individual and contextual components, they found research tends to focus on the identification and deconstruction of barriers facing nascent and active women entrepreneurs.

Case study: The Diana project

The Diana Project was founded in 1999 and was a milestone towards global understanding of women entrepreneurs. The project was set up as a research foundation to build awareness and expectations of women business owners and the growth of their firms. Their research focuses on investigating the factors that lead to growth for women entrepreneurs and their contribution to economies around the world.

Source: http://www.dianaproject.org.

Bruni *et al.* (2004, p.15) examine the five thematic research areas of female entrepreneurs:

1 **The 'breeding grounds' of female entrepreneurship** – women-led businesses tend to be disproportionally service-oriented (Carter *et al.*, 2015), have low capital requirements for entry, are focused on traditionally female-oriented sectors, require less skill and provide low value add (Carter and Shaw 2006). Table 4.1, from the UK Office of National Statistics (ONS, 2014) displays the gender imbalance within industry with male-oriented work being skilled trades, while women exceed men in caring, and administrative occupations. Science, engineering and technology are most notably dominated by men (Marlow and McAdam, 2012).

Major occupation group	Men		Women	
	Thousands	Per cent	Thousands	Per cent
Managers, directors and senior officials	493	15.8	246	17.0
Professional occupations	498	15.9	251	17.3
Associate professional and technical occupations	415	13.3	258	17.8
Administrative and secretarial occupations	32	1.0	111	7.7
Skilled trades occupations	1,112	35.6	109	7.5
Caring, leisure and other service occupations	39	1.2	272	18.8
Sales and customer service occupations	59	1.9	46	3.1
Process, plant and machine operatives	313	10.0	29	2.0
Elementary occupations	159	5.1	127	8.7
Total	3,123	100.0	1,450	100.0

Table 4.1: Number of people self-employed by gender and major occupational group 2014
Source: ONS (2014).

2 **Patterns of female entrepreneurship** - typologies of the female entrepreneur are most commonly described within the context of life course and role within the family rather than from a rational business perspective (Davis and Shaver, 2012). Not only does this undermine women in business, women themselves fail to recognize the legitimacy of their work (Carter *et al.*, 2015; Marlow and McAdam, 2012) viewing it as a temporary solution (Marlow *et al.*, 2012) and undervaluing it as a whole (Shinnar *et al.*, 2012). This humility could be viewed as retaliation to the strongly masculine construct of the entrepreneur (Bruni *et al.*, 2004).

3 **The barriers against female entrepreneurship** – consists of three components:

☐ *Socio-cultural barriers* – the social construct of women as mother and homemaker undermines the credibility of women in the workplace. Evidence continually shows greater impacts on business for women entrepreneurs with children than for men, who are largely unaffected by fatherhood status (Davis and Shaver, 2012). In cultures where women are strongly defined by their role in the home these barriers are even more pronounced (Carter *et al.*, 2015). However, Powell and Eddleston (2013) found that family offered substantial support for women entrepreneurs, enriching both their business and personal lives.

☐ *Access to networks* – women have less access to formal networks which affects their access to knowledge. They have different kinds of networks to men and rely more on the informal networks of family and friends (Watson, 2012), which reduces their perceptibility of industry opportunities and trends (Brush *et al.*, 2009). Carter and Shaw (2006) report that although women can be highly active networkers, they often spend time making weak ties that establish credibility, but are less useful to business performance.

☐ *Access to capital* – women-led businesses start with a third less financial capital, lower capital-to-debt ratios and are less likely to use equity or venture capital (Carter and Shaw, 2006). Failure to access financial resources is attributed to three distinct problems (Carter *et al.*, 2015): (1) structural dissimilarities in business profiles; (2) supply-side discrimination in accessing seed and growth capital (Wu and Chua, 2012); and (3) demand-side risk-aversion – women are less inclined to request loans, (Marlow and Carter 2006) and tend to request less capital than men (Carter and Shaw 2006).

Case study: Arianna Huffington

Arianna Huffington is the co-founder, President and Editor-in-Chief of The Huffington Post Media Group. The Greek born author of fourteen books, launched *The Huffington Post* as a news and blog site that quickly became one of the most widely-read online news sources. She came to prominence during the 1990s as a political figure, supporting her then politician husband Michael Huffington, expanding her network from politics, to media, entertainment and commerce.

In 2011, AOL acquired The Huffington Post for US$315 million with Arianna remaining in control of the expanded media group. She has been named in *Time Magazine's* list of the world's 100 most influential people and the *Forbes* Most Powerful Women list.

Source: http://www.huffingtonpost.co.uk

4   **The motivations of women entrepreneurs** – can be divided into push and pull factors and are largely centred on mainstream reasons for entering self-employment. Motivations behind business start-up have implications for ownership and control, resource acquisition, team formation and growth intentions (Davis and Shaver, 2012).

☐ *Pull* factors include supplementing income, ease of access criteria and a desire for flexibility. Women are significantly more likely than men to cite family reasons for becoming self-employed (Carter *et al.*, 2015).

☐ *Push* factors include striving for independence and autonomy, professional self-fulfilment, supplementing income, socio-economic mobility or to fulfil a social mission. Women are more likely to come into self-employment out of necessity than men (Singer *et al.*, 2015).

5   **The 'enterprise culture' of women entrepreneurs** – suggests that women are more likely to take an evolutionary approach to business planning and a consensus approach to leadership. Women-led businesses can take longer at gestation, exhibit lower performance, remain small and exit early (Carter *et al.*, 2015). Women are more likely to employ and utilise family members' support within their businesses leading to positive business outcomes (Powell and Eddleston, 2013). Despite what are often perceived as shortcomings in management style, Kalnins and Williams (2014) found that female businesses tend to out-survive male businesses.

Exercise

Review the following article: Kalnins, A. and Williams, M. (2014) 'When do female-owned businesses out-survive male-owned businesses? A disaggregated approach by industry and geography', *Journal of Business Venturing*, **29**(6), 822-835.

1   Did you agree with the two initial hypotheses?

2   Do you see a pattern emerge within the sectors where female-led businesses out-survived male-led businesses?

3   Previous research indicates that women are more likely to exit their businesses early. How do you reconcile the findings in this report with previous findings? (See for example Carter *et al.*, 2015).

Ethnic minority entrepreneurs

Ethnic entrepreneurship is a "set of connections and regular patterns of interaction among people sharing common national background or migration experiences" (Waldinger *et al.*, 1990, p.33). The term 'immigrant entrepreneur' is often used as an alternative to ethnic entrepreneur, capturing those that have migrated (Volery, 2007), while ethnic groups may also be born native. Immigrant entrepreneurship may be defined as "the self-employment efforts by individuals that voluntarily migrate to a different country and engage in business ownership" (Chaganti *et al.*, 2008, p.115). Several different ethnic groups now exist in different countries providing an important route for national economic growth (Assudani, 2009). In the US, for example, there has been high migration of entrepreneurs in computing, information technology and the internet industries (Chaganti *et al.*, 2008). The UK Small Business Survey (2014) shows that 7% (over 367,000) of SME (small-medium enterprise) business employers are led by minority ethnic groups, (with an ethnic minority in sole control of the business or a management team with at least half of the members from an ethnic minority). The size of this contribution to the UK economy was estimated at £25-32 billion per year (Carter, 2015), having rapidly multiplied in the last 40-50 years

(Ram and Jones, 2008). As well as small business activity, there is also strong indication that ethnic minorities are starting up new businesses. For example, 35% of the UK Government Start Up Loans scheme has been taken up by ethnic minority entrepreneurs (Department for Communities and Local Government, 2013) indicating a strong economic contribution in the coming years.

Case study: UK government

The UK government department for Trade & Investment (UKTI) has two entrepreneurship programmes that invite foreign entrepreneurs to the UK: the Global Entrepreneur Programme, for high growth international technology businesses that can establish a UK headquarters; and the Sirius Programme, which invites global graduate entrepreneurs to relocate and start-up a UK business on a 12-month programme with financial, business and visa support provided.

Source: UK Trade & Investment website http://www.ukti.gov.uk

■ Motivations

Some ethnic cultures have been found to be more likely to engage in entrepreneurship than others (Volery, 2007) and their performance to also vary across different ethnic groups (Masurel *et al.*, 2002). Push factors for ethnic entrepreneurs may include economic disadvantage and challenges in gaining employment, such as racial discrimination when seeking employment (Estrin *et al.*, 2008; Ram and Jones, 2008). In the US, for example, Edelman *et al.* (2010) found black entrepreneurs are 50% more likely to start up a business than white entrepreneurs, though to be less successful than white-owned businesses. Pull factors may include market opportunity and increased alertness in the move from country of origin to resident market (Kirzner, 1979; Estrin *et al.*, 2008). Similarly, Chaganti *et al.* (2008) found ethnic-immigrant entrepreneurs had a strong propensity to seek and pursue entrepreneurial opportunities, while entrepreneurs who share ethnicity with venture capitalists are more likely to receive investment for their business (Bengtsson and Hsu, 2015).

Case study: Rekha Mehr

Rekha Mehr is a British-born Indian entrepreneur. In 2012, she founded Pistachio Rose, a boutique bakery for Indian-inspired cakes, with the aim of changing the perception of Indian sweets in the UK market. The cakes were successfully sold in the prestigious Fortnum & Mason Bakery department. Rekha since founded Moonrekha in 2013 providing consultancy, pitch training and food retail expertise to entrepreneurs.

■ Challenges

Despite the significance of the contribution that ethnic minority entrepreneurs make to the economy, they still face a number of challenges that impede their success potential (Robb, 2002). First, financial resource is a challenge simply by virtue of their status as ethnic (Bengtsson and Hsu, 2015). Specific challenges they face include lack of access to finance due to poor credit scorings, a lack of formal savings, poor financial track record and collateral shortages (Department for Communities and Local Government, 2013). Second, narrow market segments, particularly service and retail industries with lower entry barriers than others (Sürgevil and Özbilgin, 2010). Third, inexperience in starting a growth oriented venture and the requisite skills and knowledge to do so (Wickham, 2006). Higher education is a crucial enabler, though the role of entrepreneurial learning in the process has largely been overlooked (Estrin *et al.*, 2008; Wang and Chugh, 2014). Technology has the capability to increase internationalization in ethnic entrepreneurship (Estrin *et al.*, 2008) and international networks can provide competitive advantages to immigrant business owners for export (Neville *et al.*, 2014). Last, language barriers are self-explanatory in that difficulty in speaking the main language in the residing country can have an impact on the ability to do business.

Case study: Mohamed Al Fayed

Mohamed Al Fayed is an Egyptian-born entrepreneur who migrated to the UK in the 1960s. He previously held ownership in the UK department stores House of Fraser and Harrods. He reportedly sold Harrods to Qatar Holdings in 2010 for £1.5 billion. He also held ownership in Fulham Football Club from 1997-2013 and he currently owns the luxurious Hotel Ritz Paris among other companies.

Sources: http://news.bbc.co.uk/1/hi/business/8669657.stm and http://edition.cnn.com/2013/07/12/sport/football/fulham-al-fayed-khan/

Exercise

Select an ethnic or immigrant entrepreneur of your choice. Analyse their motivations and challenges.

'Other' entrepreneurs

We have focused on two of the largest groups of diverse entrepreneurs so far – women entrepreneurs and ethnic minority entrepreneurs. In this section, we cover four smaller groups of diverse entrepreneurs.

■ Graduate entrepreneurs

There were approximately 12 million graduates in the UK (e.g. ONS, 2013). We focus on Higher Education (HE) in the UK and define graduate entrepreneurship as engagement by a HE graduate into self-employment or new venture creation within two years after graduation. Research on the types of business that graduate entrepreneurs can build has found they are more likely to have higher qualifications, intellectual property and high growth potential (Pickernell *et al.*, 2011). University support has played a crucial role in enabling the transition to graduate entrepreneurship (Astebro *et al.*, 2012) and there has been a strong link between entrepreneurship programmes and increased entrepreneurial intentions (Souitaris *et al.*, 2007). The biggest challenges for graduate entrepreneurs are a lack of business skills and access to finance (McLarty, 2005).

■ Lesbian, gay, bisexual and transgender entrepreneurs

Little is known about the lesbian, gay, bisexual and transgender (LGBT) entrepreneurs, (having an alternative sexual orientation and/or self-identity to assumed contemporary heteronormativity (Galloway, 2007)). Census data (ONS, 2011) showed 94% of the UK population self-identified as heterosexual, 1.5% declared themselves as gay, lesbian or bisexual, leaving 4.5% as unknown. Within the workplace, it is estimated that 34% of gays in the UK and 41% in the US are closeted (Browne, 2014). Gay entrepreneurs report stronger pull factors towards entrepreneurship and there is also evidence of push factors such as corporate discrimination (Galloway, 2012; Gedro, 2010). LGBT entrepreneurs perceive that self-employment would be easier than employment, with more opportunity to be treated equally and be open about their sexuality (Galloway, 2012). Challenges reported by gay entrepreneurs include homophobic investors, suppliers or customers, and the reluctance of well-known companies to publicise their ties to the gay community (Schindehutte *et al.*, 2005).

■ 'Grey' entrepreneurs

The emergence of the 'grey' entrepreneur, sometimes referred to as silver, senior, older, or third age, is timely and gaining momentum. The United Nations (2015) report that the 60+ population is set to reach 25% globally and 40% in the UK by 2050. Botham and Graves (2009) define 55 as the critical age, after which entrepreneurial activity and success decline. Although less likely to have a formal education qualification, grey entrepreneurs benefit from great levels of technical, industrial and management experience along with superior personal networks and a strong financial asset base (Weber and Schaper, 2004). Pull factors into self-employment include reduced work stress, flexibility to reduce work hours, reduced physical effort, reduced managerial responsibilities and greater freedom through financial security (Johnson and Kawachi 2007, Maestas and Zissimopoulos, 2010). Push factors are lack of quality jobs, negative impacts on wages, pensions and health benefits, accommodation of health conditions, declining energy levels and the reluctance of employers to hire and retain older workers (Maestas and Zissimopoulos, 2010; Pick *et al.*, 2015).

4

■ Disabled entrepreneurs

Disability is defined as an impairment that causes a sustained limitation on daily activities (World Health Organization / World Bank, 2011). Contrary to perception, disability is more often a temporary state which many will experience at some point in their lives and more likely with age (Jones, 2011). Push factors for disabled entrepreneurs include employment discrimination and limited employment opportunities (Blanck *et al.*, 2000, Schur 2003). Despite adversity, there are higher rates of self-employment among disabled people than able-bodied people in both Europe and the USA (Schur, 2003). Self-employment can provide autonomy, flexibility in work tasks, pacing, hours, location and an alternative route to accomplishment (Jones and Latreille, 2011) as well as a potential rehabilitation vocational tool (Arnold and Seekins, 2002). Common barriers reported by disabled entrepreneurs are the lack of access to start-up capital, loss of social welfare benefits, lack of knowledge, skills and confidence along with limited aspirations (Jones 2011, Jones and Latreille, 2011, Blank *et al.*, 2000). Consumer discrimination for goods and services produced by disabled business owners can also affect demand (Jones and Latreille, 2011).

Exercise

Compare and contrast the motivations, challenges and success potential of graduate, LGBT, grey and disabled entrepreneurs. From your analysis, are you able to rank the groups in any particular order of importance?

Implications for government/government policies

In this section, we discuss the policy implications of our findings for diverse entrepreneurs.

■ Women entrepreneurs

For women entrepreneurs, policy could take three approaches; first , mentoring and coaching programmes to build skills are found to be useful business supports with high rates of uptake (Brush and Cooper, 2012). These ensure women entrepreneurs have strong role models and perceive their entrepreneurial activity with greater value. Entrepreneurship training courses prepare women and should be promoted for women at all stages of the entrepreneurial process. Second, access to capital for women entrepreneurs could be improved by alleviating some of the risk components of lending for both lenders and borrowers. Third, governments should provide support mechanisms to enable them to balance family life as well as run their own business through childcare and carer supports.

■ Ethnic minority entrepreneurs

For ethnic entrepreneurs, realising their contribution to national economies along with their heterogeneity makes a 'one size fits all' policy difficult. Carter (2015) suggests targeted and local policy initiatives may be more successful. Implications are also for governments to consider the openness of their immigration policies and visa access for entrepreneurs. Encouraging entrepreneurs to stay when the formal support (e.g. financial, mentoring or visa) runs out remains a challenge. Help to build a sustainable business, awareness of continued support and embeddedness into the local ecosystem can all increase their likelihood of staying and converting to citizenship.

Tip: For more information on different government start-up schemes, see:

- Sirius Programme (UK): http://www.siriusprogramme.com
- Start-up Chile: http://www.startupchile.org/
- French Tech Ticket: http://www.frenchtechticket.paris/
- Italia Startup Visa http://italiastartupvisa.mise.gov.it/

■ Graduate entrepreneurs

For graduate entrepreneurs, while there is now a strong provision of entrepreneurship education at HE level, the focus needs to be driven more towards economic outcome (O'Connor, 2013). There is also a danger that graduates are unable to support themselves financially and are pushed towards full-time employment. Support could enable them to utilise this window of opportunity and engage in start-up activity. Living expenses, financial support or the provision of desk space could entice them. The UK Trade & Investment Sirius Programme (2013-2015) focused on attracting international entrepreneurs, but a domestic scheme for UK graduates administered by universities could fill the gap in the ecosystem.

■ LGBT entrepreneurs

For LGBT entrepreneurs, while it would be easy to state policy could help them to be more open about their sexuality, this is a far broader and personal issue than one we could address. Entrepreneurs with strong television or media profiles could help to break down stereotypes encouraging the LGBT community to engage in entrepreneurial activity more openly.

■ 'Grey' entrepreneurs

Older entrepreneurs and business people have a lot to share with the business community, which could be through mentorship. For grey entrepreneurs who may be putting their savings towards their business, tax breaks on applying their savings towards their business could be provided. A government-backed investment fund for the 55+ could also fuel entrepreneurial activity among this group. Information technology skills will be crucial for grey entrepreneurs to participate in business formation and management.

■ Disabled entrepreneurs

For disabled entrepreneurs, policy could focus on the provision of education to increase their business and/or technology skills. With the recent increase of co-working spaces in the UK and Europe, it is also important to ensure these facilities consider the needs of disabled entrepreneurs. As the loss of welfare benefits is a disincentive for the engagement of the disabled into entrepreneurship in the UK, this policy should also be reconsidered.

Conclusions

The aim of this chapter was to increase our understanding of diversity so we can better recognize the motivations and challenges affecting entrepreneurs. We focused on six diverse groups and acknowledge that there are overlaps, whereby individuals identify with multiple groups and face similar or compounded challenges. Common themes emerge of traditional pull factors, unique push factors and barriers spanning across groups with varying levels of intensity. We also discussed implications for governments and policy that can help alleviate some of these. Given that some of the challenges transcend more than one group, such as education, access to finance and adapting to technology, it would be ideal to have policies in place that target both the individual entrepreneur and the context in which they operate. Addressing the distinct challenges, rather than the criteria or label through which they are simply perceived as a diverse entrepreneur could be the key to unlocking the vast potential of these groups.

Further reading

Audretsch D. B., Dohse, D. and Niebuhr, A. (2008). *Cultural diversity and entrepreneurship: A regional analysis for Germany.* Centre for Economic Policy Research discussion paper (DP6945). Available at: http://www.cepr.org/active/publications/discussion_papers/dp.php?dpno=6945 [Accessed 09 September 2015].

Carter, S. and Shaw, E. (2006). *Women's Business Ownership: Recent Research and Policy Developments: Report to the Small Business Service* Small Business Service. Available at: https://www.strath.ac.uk/media/departments/huntercentre/research/researchreports/file38338.pdf [Accessed 09 September 2015].

Carter, S., Mwaura, S., Ram, M., Trehan, K. and Jones, T. (2015). *Barriers to ethnic minority and women's enterprise: existing evidence, policy tensions and unsettled questions.* International Small Business Journal. (In Press). Available through the University of Strathclyde Library website http://strathprints.strath.ac.uk/49565/ [Accessed on 09 September 2015].

Dana, L-P. (2007). *Handbook of Research on Ethnic Minority Entrepreneurship: A Co-Evolutionary View on Resource Management.* Cheltenham, UK: Edward Elgar.

Foo, M. D. and Wong, P. K. and Ong, A. (2005). Do others think you have a viable business idea? Team diversity and judges' evaluation of ideas in a business plan competition. *Journal of Business Venturing,* **20**(3), 385-402.

Kitching, J. (2014) *Entrepreneurship and Self-employment by People with Disabilities.* [pdf] OECD Project on Inclusive Entrepreneurship. Available at: http://www.oecd.org/cfe/leed/background-report-people-disabilities.pdf [Accessed 09 September 2015].

Ram, M. and Jones, T. (2008). Ethnic minority business: Review of research and policy. *Government and Policy (Environment and Planning 'C'),* **26**(2), 352-374.

References

Arnold, N. and Seekins, T. (2002). Self-employment: A process for use by vocational rehabilitation agencies. *Journal of Vocational Rehabilitation, 17*, 107-13.

Assudani, R. (2009). Ethnic entrepreneurship: The distinct role of ties. *Journal of Small Business & Entrepreneurship*, **22**(2), 197-205.

Astebro, T., Bazzazian, N. and Braguinsky, S. (2012). Startups by recent university graduates and their faculty: Implications for university entrepreneurship policy. *Research Policy*, **41**, 663-677.

Audretsch D. B., Dohse, D. and Niebuhr, A. (2008). *Cultural diversity and entrepreneurship: A regional analysis for Germany*. Centre for Economic Policy Research discussion paper (DP6945). Available at: http://www.cepr.org/active/publications/discussion_papers/dp.php?dpno=6945 [Accessed 09 September 2015].

Bengtsson, O. and Hsu, D. H. (2015). Ethnic matching in the U.S. venture capital market. *Journal of Business Venturing* **30**(2), 338-354.

BIS. (2013*) Business population estimates for the UK and regions 2013*. Department for Business, Innovation and Skills. Available at: https://www.gov.uk/government/uploads/system/uploads/attachment_data/file/254552/13-92-business-population-estimates-2013-stats-release-4.pdf [Accessed on 09 September 2015].

Blanck, P. D., Sandler, L. A., Schmeling, J. L. and Schartz, H. A. (2000). Emerging workforce of entrepreneurs with disabilities: preliminary study of entrepreneurship in Iowa. *Iowa Law Review*, **85**, 1583-1668.

Botham, R., and Graves A. (2009). *The grey economy: How third age entrepreneurs are contributing to growth*. NESTA. Available at: https://www.nesta.org.uk/sites/default/files/the_grey_economy.pdf [Accessed 09 September 2015].

Browne, J. (2014). *The Glass Closet: why coming out is good for business.* New York: Harper Collins.

Bruni, A., Gherardi, S. and Poggio, B. (2004). *Gender and Entrepreneurship: An ethnographic approach.* New York: Routledge.

Brush C. and Cooper S. (2012). Female entrepreneurship and economic development: An international perspective. *Entrepreneurship & Regional Development: An International Journal*, **24**(1-2), 1-6.

Brush, C. G, de Bruin, A. and Welter, F. (2009). A gender-aware framework for women's entrepreneurship. *International Journal of Gender and Entrepreneurship*, **1**, 8-24.

Carter, S. (2015). *ESRC evidence briefing. Supporting ethnic minority and female entrepreneurs*. Available at: http://www.esrc.ac.uk/_images/supporting-ethnic-minority-and-female-entrepreneurs_tcm8-33735.pdf [Accessed 09 September 2015].

Carter, S. and Shaw, E. (2006). *Women's Business Ownership: Recent Research and Policy Developments: Report to the Small Business Service* Small Business Service. Available at: https://www.strath.ac.uk/media/departments/huntercentre/research/researchreports/file38338.pdf [Accessed 09 September 2015].

Carter, S., Mwaura, S., Ram, M., Trehan, K. and Jones, T. (2015). *Barriers to ethnic minority and women's enterprise: existing evidence, policy tensions and unsettled questions.* International Small Business Journal. (In Press). Available through the University of Strathclyde Library website http://strathprints.strath.ac.uk/49565/ [Accessed on 09 September 2015].

Chaganti, R. S., Watts, A. D., Chaganti, R. and Zimmerman-Treichel, M. (2008). Ethnic-immigrants in founding teams: Effects on prospector strategy and performance in new Internet ventures. *Journal of Business Venturing*, **23**(1), 112-139.

Davis, A. E. and Shaver, K. G. (2012). Understanding gendered variations in business growth intentions across the life course. *Entrepreneurship Theory and Practice*, **36**(3), 495-512.

Department for Communities and Local Government. (2013). *Ethnic minority businesses and access to finance.* Available at: https://www.gov.uk/government/uploads/system/uploads/attachment_data/file/225762/EMBs_and_Access_to_Finance.pdf [Accessed 09 September 2015].

Edelman, L. F., Brush, C. G., Manolova, T. S. and Greene, P. G. (2010). Start-up motivations and growth intentions of minority nascent entrepreneurs. *Journal of Small Business Management*, **48**, 174-196.

Estrin, S., Meyer, K. E. and Bytchkova, M. (2008). Entrepreneurship in transition economies. In: Casson, M., Yeung, B., Basu, A. and Wadeson, N. (eds.) *The Oxford Handbook of Entrepreneurship*, Oxford: Oxford University Press. Ch.27.

Galloway, L. (2012). The experiences of male gay business owners in the UK. *International Small Business Journal*, **30**(8), 890-906.

Galloway, L. (2007). Entrepreneurship and the gay minority: Why the silence? *Entrepreneurship and Innovation*, **8**(4), 271-280.

Gedro, J. (2010). The lavender ceiling atop the global closet: Human resource development and lesbian expatriates. *Human Resource Development Review*, **9**, 267-268.

Hughes, K. D., Jennings, J. E., Brush, C., Carter, S. and Welter, F. (2012). Extending women's entrepreneurship research in new directions. *Entrepreneurship Theory and Practice*, **36**(3), 429-442.

Johnson, R.W., and Kawachi, J. (2007). *Job changes at older ages: Effects on wages, benefits, and other job attributes.* Centre for Retirement Research at Boston College. Available at http://crr.bc.edu/wp-content/uploads/2007/02/wp_2007-4-508.pdf [Accessed 09 September 2015].

Jones, M. (2011). Disability, employment and earnings: an examination of heterogeneity. *Applied Economics*, **43**(4), 1001-1017.

Jones, M.K. and Latreille, P.L. (2005). *Disability and self-employment: Evidence from the UK LFS*. University of Wales, Swansea. Available at: http://www.researchgate.net/profile/Melanie_Jones5/publication/228354698_Disability_and_self-employment_evidence_from_the_UK_LFS/links/02e7e51cc0764b5044000000.pdf [Accessed 09 September 2015].

Kalnins, A. and Williams, M. (2014). When do female-owned businesses out-survive male-owned businesses? A disaggregated approach by industry and geography. *Journal of Business Venturing*, **29**(6), 822-835.

Kelley, D. J., Brush, C. G., Greene, P.G. and Litovsky, Y. (2013). *Global entrepreneurship monitor: 2012 women's report*. Global Entrepreneurship Research Association. Available at: http://www.babson.edu/Academics/centers/blank-center/global-research/gem/Documents/GEM%202012%20Womens%20Report.pdf [Accessed 09 September 2015].

Kelley, D.J., Ali, A, Brush, C., Corbett, A.C., Lyons, T., Majbouri, M. and Rogoff, E.G. (2014). *Global entrepreneurship monitor: 2013 United States report*. Global Entrepreneurship Research Association. Available at: http://www.babson.edu/Academics/centers/blank-center/global-research/gem/Documents/GEM%20USA%202013.pdf [Accessed 09 September 2015].

Kirzner, I. M. (1979). *Perception, Opportunity, and Profit: Studies in The Theory of Entrepreneurship*. Chicago: University of Chicago Press.

Maestas, N. and Zissimopoulos, J. (2010). How longer work lives ease the crunch of population aging. *Journal of Economic Perspectives*, **24**(1), 139-60.

Marlow, S. and McAdam, M. (2012). Analyzing the influence of gender upon high-technology venturing within the context of business incubation. *Entrepreneurship Theory and Practice*, **36**(4), 655-676.

Marlow, S. and Carter, S. (2006) If you don't ask you don't get! Self-employment and finance. Paper presented at the Warwick Business School Small Firms Finance Conference, May.

Marlow, S., Hart, M., Levie, J. and Shamsul, M. K. (2012). *Women in enterprise: a different perspective*. RBS Group. Available at: http://www.rbs.com/content/dam/rbs/Documents/Sustainability/Women-in-Enterprise.pdf [Accessed 09 September 2015].

Masurel, E., Nijkamp, P., Tastan, M. and Vindigni, G. (2002). Motivations and performance conditions for ethnic entrepreneurship. *Growth and Change*, **33**, 238-260.

McLarty, R. (2005). Entrepreneurship among graduates: towards a measured response. *Journal of Management Development*, **24**(3), 223-238.

Neville, F., Orser, B., Riding, A. and Jung, O. (2014). Do young firms owned by recent immigrants outperform other young firms? *Journal of Business Venturing*, **29**(1), 55-71.

O'Connor, A. (2013). A conceptual framework for entrepreneurship education policy: Meeting government and economic purposes. *Journal of Business Venturing*, **28**(4), 546-563.

ONS. (2011). *Integrated household survey April 2010 to March 2011: Experimental statistics.* The Office of National Statistics. Available at: http://www.ons.gov.uk/ons/dcp171778_227150.pdf [Accessed 09 September 2015].

ONS. (2013). *Full report - graduates in the UK labour market 2013.* The Office of National Statistics. Available at: http://www.ons.gov.uk/ons/dcp171776_337841.pdf [Accessed 09 September 2015].

ONS. (2014). *Self-employed workers in the UK – 2014.* The Office of National Statistics. Available at: http://www.ons.gov.uk/ons/dcp171776_374941.pdf [Accessed 09 September 2015].

Pick, D., Weber, P., Hennekam, S. (2015*).* Challenges of older self-employed workers in creative industries*. Management Decision*, **53**(4), 876-891.

Pickernell, D., Packham, G., Jones, P., Miller, C. and Brychan, T. (2011). Graduate entrepreneurs are different: they access more resources? *International Journal of Entrepreneurial Behavior & Research*, **17**(2), 183-202.

Powell, G. N. and Eddleston, K. A. (2013). Linking family-to-business enrichment and support to entrepreneurial success: Do female and male entrepreneurs experience different outcomes? *Journal of Business Venturing,* **28**(2), 261-280.

Ram, M. and Jones, T. (2008*).* Ethnic minority business: Review of research and policy. *Government and Policy (Environment and Planning 'C')*, **26**(2), 352-374.

Robb, A. M. (2002). Entrepreneurial performance by women and minorities: The case of new firms. *Journal of Developmental Entrepreneurship*, **7**(4): 383-397.

Schindehutte, M., Morris, M. and Allen, J. (2005). Homosexuality and entrepreneurship: Implications of gay identity for the venture creation experience. *The International Journal of Entrepreneurship and Innovation,* **6**(1), 27-40.

Schur, L. (2003). Barriers or opportunities? The causes of contingent and part-time work among people with disabilities. *Industrial Relations: A Journal of Economy and Society*, **42**(4), 589-622.

Shinnar, R. S., Giacomin, O. and Janssen, F. (2012). Entrepreneurial perceptions and intentions: The role of gender and culture. *Entrepreneurship Theory and Practice*, **36**(3), 465-493.

Singer, Slavica, E. Amoros, and D. Moska. (2015) GEM 2014 Global Report. Global Entrepreneurship Research Centre. Available at: http://www.babson.edu/Academics/centers/blank-center/global-research/gem/Documents/GEM%20 2014%20Global%20Report.pdf [Accessed 09 September 2015].

Small Business Survey. (2014). *Small Business Survey 2014: SME employers.* BIS Research Paper Number 214. Available at: https://www.gov.uk/government/uploads/system/uploads/attachment_data/file/414963/bis-15-151-small-business-survey-2014-sme-employers_v1.pdf [Accessed 09 September 2015].

Souitaris, V., Zerbinati, S. and Al-Laham, A. (2007). Do entrepreneurship programmes raise entrepreneurial intention of science and engineering students? The effect of learning, inspiration and resources. *Journal of Business Venturing,* **22**(4), 566-591.

Sürgevil, O. and Özbilgin, M. (2010). High technology entrepreneurs: equality, diversity and inclusion, in A. Malach-Pines and M. F. Özbilgin (eds), *Handbook of Research on High-Technology Entrepreneurs,* Cheltenham, UK & Northampton, MA, USA: Edward Elgar. Ch.17.

United Nations (2015). *World population prospects: The 2015 revision* The United Nations. Available at: http://esa.un.org/unpd/wpp/Publications/Files/Key_Findings_WPP_2015.pdf [Accessed 09 September 2015].

Volery, T. (2007). Ethnic entrepreneurship: a theoretical framework. In L-P. Dana (ed.). *Handbook of research on ethnic minority entrepreneurship,* Cheltenham: Edward Elgar.

Waldinger R. D., Aldrich, H. E., Ward, R. (Eds) (1990). *Ethnic Entrepreneurs: Immigrant Business in Industrial Societies.* Newbury Park, CA: Sage Publications.

Wang, C. and Chugh, H. (2013). Entrepreneurial learning: Past research and future challenges. *International Journal of Management Reviews,* **16**(1), 24-61.

Watson, J. (2012). Networking: Gender differences and the association with firm performance. *International Small Business Journal,* **30**, 536-558.

Weber, P. and Schaper, M. (2004). Understanding the grey entrepreneur. *Journal of Enterprising Culture,* **12**(2), 147-164.

Wickham, P. A. (2006). *Strategic entrepreneurship.* England: Pearson Education.

World Health Organization / World Bank. (2011). *World Report on Disability,* [online]. The World Health Organization. Available at: http://www.who.int/disabilities/world_report/2011/en/index.html [Accessed 09 September 2015].

Wu, Z. and Chua, J. H. (2012). Second-order gender effects: The case of U.S. small business borrowing cost. *Entrepreneurship Theory and Practice,* **36**(3), 443-463.

5 Social Entrepreneurship

Linda McGilvray, with contributions from Lloyd Parker, Patrick Quinn and Diarmuid Cowan

The *Big Issue* case study (page 74) illustrates various aspects of social entrepreneurship (SE). A social entrepreneur, John Bird, identified an opportunity to meet an unmet need and marshalled the resources to create a venture to meet that demand. In 2015 the *Big Issue* generated sales revenue of over £30.6M; it employed 2,000 vendors, sold 85,000 copies per week in the UK (www.thebigissue.org.uk), and has inspired street newspapers in 120 countries world-wide (www.thebigissue.com). Similarly, Grameen Bank, specialising in micro-finance to the poor and founded in 1983 by Muhammed Yunus in Bangladesh, has over 8.349 million borrowers and is a global success story (http://www.grameen-info.org/about-us/). In this respect there might seem to be little difference between John Bird and entrepreneurs like Mark Zuckerberg of Facebook. This has led some theorists to propose that social entrepreneurship is a branch of entrepreneurship (Sassmannshausen and Volkmann, 2013). It could be suggested that social entrepreneurship represents a new form of entrepreneurship where personal wealth is not a driver of entrepreneurial activity; rather, the drivers are the personal needs of the beneficiaries and the creation of social value. For example, *Big Issue*'s UK website reported that between 2013 and 2014 it successfully met the needs of 5,852 homeless people and delivered life-changing outcomes to them. (http://www.bigissue.org.uk/about-us/service-outcomes-2014). Likewise, Grameen Bank has been formative in the economic and social development of 9.4 million of the world's poor through its Micro Finance Institutional Partners (www.grameenfoundation.org, 2015).

This new and exciting subject of social entrepreneurship has established centres of learning at Stanford University, The University of Birmingham, and Glasgow Caledonian University, which has the Yunus Centre, named after the Nobel Prize-winning SE Mohammed Yunus. Significantly, social entrepreneurship is not confined to universities; governments are also giving it increased attention (Zeyen *et al.*, 2013) and have tried to encourage the practice through economic and social policy initiatives, examples of which are President Obama's launch of the Office of Social Innovation (www.genesysworks.org, 2015) and the UK's Social Investment Roadmap (Gov.uk, 2014). With social entrepreneurship holding an increasingly important stake in the UK economy, indicated by 4.2% of the UK population involved in socially entrepreneurial activity (SEFORIS, 2014), discussion about its practice is essential to scholars and practitioners alike.

This chapter will consider social entrepreneurship and will focus on the similarities and differences between social entrepreneurship and such commercial activities as corporate social responsibility (CSR). It will also spotlight some of the challenges facing academics and practitioners alike when attempting to define SE.

Case study: Big Issue

John Bird was a founder of the *Big Issue*, a magazine set up in 1991 to deal with the impact of homelessness. The magazine is sold by homeless people, who buy it from the publisher and sell it to consumers. The price of the publication is split between the *Big Issue* magazine, which is a social enterprise (a not-for-personal-profit business), and the vendor. The organization's funding comes from income earned from sales of the magazine and from advertising revenue, just like many other publications (http://www.bigissue.org.uk/news/2014/october/6/setting-record-straight). Generating profit is a goal, but surpluses are used for social benefit rather than for private gain. In other words, profits from the *Big Issue* are used to generate social value. The social aim of the *Big Issue* is to counter the effects of homelessness and to deal with social exclusion, which is defined as a state of deprivation, characterised by a lack of social and economic opportunities. John Bird seized the opportunity to use a traditional business model to create positive outcomes for homeless people, without thought of personal financial gain. A candid account by John Bird about his motivation to social entrepreneurship and the inception of the *Big Issue* can be viewed at https://www.youtube.com/watch?v=XTc2Cq6f2BQ.

Defining social entrepreneurship

Entrepreneurship can be considered a practice, a process and a concept, and social entrepreneurship is no different. Social entrepreneurship is the term used to describe the pursuit of an opportunity to deliver social value. According to Dees (2001:p. 2), "social entrepreneurs are one species of the genus entrepreneur", and the two terms are indeed closely related. The similarities between them are clear from their respective definitions. Timmons & Spinelli (1994) put forward the notion of the entrepreneurial firm, which is, amongst other things, opportunity- and growth-focused and sustainable, which is remarkably similar to Dees' definition of SE. The distinguishing characteristic of social entrepreneurship revealed by analysing Timmons' and Dees' definitions is the role of the SE as a social change agent, and ultimately as a creator of social value.

Timmons (1994: p. 6)	Dees (2001: p. 4)
Definition of entrepreneurship	Definition of social entrepreneurship
"creating and seizing an opportunity and pursuing it regardless of the resources currently controlled…it is a human creative act…it usually requires a vision…it involves building a team…of sensing opportunities and finding and marshalling resources and ensuring the venture does not run out of money.	"Social entrepreneurs play the role of change agents in the social sector, by: - Adopting a mission to create and sustain social value - Recognizing and relentlessly pursuing new opportunities to serve that mission; - Engaging in a process of continuous innovation, adaptation, and learning; - Acting boldly without being limited by resources currently in hand; and - Exhibiting a heightened sense of accountability to the constituencies served and for the outcomes created."

Table 5.1: Comparison of definitions of entrepreneurship and social entrepreneurship

Most notable theories of entrepreneurship, including Knight (1921), Schumpeter (1942), Kirzner (1979), Meredith *et al.* (1982), and Timmons and Spinelli (2007), theorise entrepreneurship in ways that sit comfortably with SE. Notably, the creation of the *Big Issue* by John Bird shows that social entrepreneurs exhibit some or all of the character traits mentioned by theorists like Knight, Kirzner, and Meredith and Neck, as well as having an opportunity focus and the ability to effect significant social and economic change, mentioned by Timmons and Spinelli and Schumpeter.

This has led theorists such as Kraus *et al.* (2014) to posit that a key challenge affecting the study of social entrepreneurship is distinguishing it from other types of commercial and charitable activity.

Exercise

Research the Grameen bank and review its activities. How does its business model differ from a typical high street bank?

When does entrepreneurship become social entrepreneurship?

The simplest way to understand the differences between social entrepreneurship and entrepreneurship is to consider the practice of social entrepreneurship. This is best achieved by looking at social entrepreneurs and examining some of the characteristics of the organizations they have founded.

The table below lists four well-known social entrepreneurs and their organizations and identifies two characteristics common to each.

SE	Firm	Social purpose/social need	Social value created
John Bird	The Big Issue	Homelessness and social exclusion	Economic and social benefits to homeless people
Tim Smit	Eden Project	Sustainability and environmental conservation/education	Local wealth, employment and educational outcomes
Jamie Oliver	Fifteen	Youth unemployment	Economic and social advantage, jobs and awareness of youth issues
Mohammed Yunus	Grameen Bank	Alleviation of poverty through the provision of affordable credit	Economic wealth, stability, social advantage

Table 5.2: Social entrepreneurs' defining characteristics

The SEs in Table 5.2 have created commercial ventures to execute a social mission and to create social value. Table 5.3 illustrates the industry sector each firm belongs to and how each organization is funded. Typically, SEs use traditional business models to achieve their aims and the examples presented show that SE is not restricted to a specific industry or sector, having application in business-to-business as well as consumer markets. Social entrepreneurs in general fund their ventures through sales revenue, but not exclusively so, as we will see when we consider Victoria Hale.

Firm	Type of firm	Customer type	Funding
The Big Issue	Magazine publisher	Private consumers	Sales - Trading Income (TI)
Eden Project	Visitor attraction	Private consumers	Sales (TI)
Fifteen	Restaurant	Private consumers	Sales (TI)
Grameen Bank	Financial services	Private consumers and business	Sales (TI)

Table 5.3: SE organizations by industry sector, type of market and funding

Another question to emerge from the analysis is what is the difference between a social entrepreneur and social entrepreneurship? The terms are often used interchangeably, but the easiest way to differentiate them is to say the social entrepreneur practices social entrepreneurship, while the practice of social entrepreneurship extends beyond the activity of a single entrepreneur to encompass organizations such as Kibble Enterprises and communities like Mull Community Enterprise. Both of these organizations have grown to encompass a portfolio of businesses designed to deliver social benefit, and although a single entrepreneur cannot be identified, an entrepreneurial orientation is evident. Figure 5.1 makes some of the differences between the two explicit.

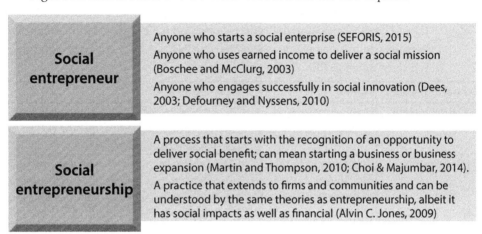

5

Figure 5.1: The difference between social entrepreneur and social entrepreneurship

Exercise

Research the Big Issue and identify the social problems it seeks to deal with. Based on your research, how successful has it been in meeting its aims? Use recent statistics and narratives to support your answer.

Social entrepreneurship: The problem of definition

Dacin *et al.*, in their 2010 paper on the problem of definition, discuss 37 theorists' definitions of SE. Defourny and Nyssens (2010) attempt to add clarity to the discussion by distinguishing two schools of thought:

1 The earned income school

2 Tthe social innovation school of thought.

Earned income theory proponents (Yunus and Weber, 2011; Boschee and McClurg, 2003) set pre-qualifying conditions for SE. To be considered a social entrepreneur or socially entrepreneurial, the venture must be 100% self-sufficient from earned income, and its income cannot be derived in whole or part from income streams commonly used in social entrepreneurship (and by SEs), such as grants and donations. The application of earned income theories to the definition of SE is strongly contested by theorists like Dees (2007).

Proponents of social innovation theories, such as Dees (2007) and Leadbetter (1997), propose more idealised definitions, suggesting that social entrepreneurs and socially entrepreneurial organizations exist on a spectrum from entirely charitable (100% dependent on fundraising and donations) to completely commercial (100% reliant on earned income).This greatly widens the definition of SE, as it encompasses those who fit general 'entrepreneurial characteristics', such as those discussed previously, and use these in pursuit of social objectives. The two opposing definitions are noted in Table 5.4. The evident disparity between definitions can leave scholars searching for a common language from which to develop SE's theoretical basis.

School of thought	Author	Definition of SE
Social innovation	Austin *et al.* (2007) J. Gregory Dees (2001)	An innovative, social value-creating activity that can occur within or across the non-profit, business, or government sector.
Earned income	Boschee and McClurg (2003) Yunus and Weber (2010)	Any person, in any sector, who uses earned income strategies to pursue a social objective. Social entrepreneurship entails self-sufficiency from earned income.

Table 5.4: Two opposing definitions of social entrepreneurship

The earned income school of thought supports the view that only social businesses can be socially entrepreneurial. Yunus' (2006) definition of a social business is a non-loss, non-dividend company that prohibits non-mission-aligned profit distribution. This limiting of profit distribution is consistent with definitions of social entrepreneurship, as social entrepreneurship is concerned with using profit to further mission-specific activities. However, the earned income school of thought is strongly contested. In the view of Volkmann *et al.* (2012), SE is not a synonym for social business. Instead, they state that the concept of social business is more restrictive than SE.

Nonetheless, there are similarities between them. The first of these relates to their common aim, which is to serve a social mission (Martin and Thomson, 2010). Another similarity is that profits from social businesses are reinvested to allow the businesses to serve the social mission in a sustainable manner and to allow for subsequent growth (Yunus, 2006). Pursuing new opportunities and seeking growth are key characteristics of entrepreneurship and, insofar as a social business demonstrates these characteristics, it is entrepreneurial. Despite this, social businesses are not entrepreneurial solely by virtue of having a social mission and having achieved self-sufficiency, in the same way that not all organizations or people who start businesses are entrepreneurial. Instead a social business, as defined by Yunus, is a particular type of social enterprise, which is 100% funded through commercial revenue.

An example of a social business is One Difference. Duncan Goose started One Difference, a social business that sells bottled water in the UK and uses profits to provide clean water and other vital services in African counties (One Difference, 2015). The business is 100% trade funded and non-profit distributing.

Restricting the use of theories of social entrepreneurship to a small segment of businesses within the social enterprise sector, which are social businesses, is too narrow an interpretation. The narrow economic space social business occupies and the manner in which social value has to be created, namely from profit generated from earned income, means it cannot be a synonym for social entrepreneurship.

This can be illustrated by considering the case of Victoria Hale a former winner of the Schwab Foundation for Social Entrepreneurship's Social and Economic Innovation Award (Skoll Foundation, 2015).

5

Case study: Institute for One World Health

In 2000 Victoria Hale established the world's first not-for-profit pharmaceutical company, the Institute for One World Health. The firm's social objective was to alleviate suffering in India caused by a disease called kala-azar in Hindi, a parasitic infection spread by sand-flies that affects over one million people per year in its various forms (http://www.patient.co.uk/doctor/leishmaniasis). Although a broad-spectrum antibiotic, paromomycin, had been produced that would treat the disease, it had gone out of production. Despite acute need for the product, its production was not economically viable for firms seeking to generate profit from its manufacture. Clearly, the market had failed. There wasn't a capitalist (for personal or shareholder profit) solution to ensuring those in the greatest need could obtain it. Indeed, its market constituted some of the poorest populations on earth (India, Bangladesh and the Sudan) and was unattractive to profit seekers. Victoria Hale saw this as an opportunity for a different type of approach that was not based on private profit models of business, but instead brought together a range of resources to ensure the production and distribution of paromomycin to those in the greatest need. The venture was funded by donations, fundraising, and partnering arrangements. The stated social mission was "The Institute for One World Health Develops Safe, Effective, and Affordable New Medicines for People with Infectious Diseases in the Developing World" (http://www.bvgh.org, 2015). It focuses on delivering health care to those with the greatest need and to creating social value, rather than prioritising personal wealth creation.

Victoria Hale has since left the Institute for One World Health to develop another socially entrepreneurial venture, Medicines 360, which uses a range of funding options including sales to secure attainment of its social mission.

Whether we gravitate towards the social innovation school of thought or the earned income school, both acknowledge the role of a social mission and social value in SE. This indicates a need for a more inclusive definition, one which is less divisive and allows a more holistic perspective approach to SE, such as that offered by Pearce (2007: p. 191): "Any activity which uses entrepreneurial skills and techniques for social purposes."

Exercise

Consider Dees' definition of social entrepreneurship from Table 5.3 and those from Table 5.4 and watch Victoria Hale's moving narrative of the origins of the Institute for One World Health (https://www.youtube.com/watch?v=GMyqugXlMqA). Do you think that Victoria Hale is a social entrepreneur? What are the implications of applying the earned income theory of SE to Victoria Hale and One World Health?

Where does the social entrepreneurial business model fit within the economy?

The previous section introduced the concept of social enterprise and positioned social businesses within it. To fully understand the nature of social entrepreneurship and social business and their relationship with social enterprise, it is necessary to identify where the socially entrepreneurial business model fits within the economy

Figure 5.2: The three sectors of the economy .
Source: Pearce (2007: p. 25).

Traditionally, three areas (Figure 5.2) are identified within the economy (Pearce, 2007):

1 The private sector, which is focused on earned income models and is profit driven;

2 The public sector, which is paid for through taxes and focuses on providing public services;

3 The third sector, which is composed of charitable enterprises and voluntary sector organizations, as well as social enterprises, sustained through a variety of income streams including grants, donations and earned income. This sector is independent of the state and is not driven by shareholder value or the pursuit of personal wealth. Companies in this sector might be called not-for-personal-profit enterprises.

Figure 5.3: The third sector of the economy
Source: Compiled from Pearce, 2007 and Deakins and Friel (2012).

Pearce draws a distinction between various types of Third Sector enterprises (Figure 5.3) and highlights a sub-segment that he calls the social economy. Firms in the social economy use trading income to pursue their social mission and can function very much like private sector firms, but are not concerned with the generation of private income for individuals. The role of earned income theory as a means of classifying firms in the third sector is a valuable one in this context. It serves to differentiate charities and other types of third sector organizations, which are predominantly reliant on grants and donations from organizations with income derived from trading. Companies with more than 50% of funds from grants and donations are considered part of the social economy but constitute non-trading, not-for-profit enterprises within the social economy. Charities like Oxfam and Amnesty International are good examples of this. As a rule of thumb social enterprises typically derive 50% or more of their income from trading (Pearce, 2007; Young, 2006; SEFORIS 2014).

The *Big Issue* is an excellent example of a social enterprise and it is also a social business, like One Water: they are key players in the social economy, generating 100% of their income from sales, and are also a part of the wider Third Sector. By the same token, The Institute for One World Health is not a social enterprise and does not belong to the social economy, because it does not trade, but it is a Third Sector organization.

However, social entrepreneurship is not confined to the third sector segment of the economy and it extends its influence to all sectors (Deakins and Friel, 2012; Defourny and Nyssens, 2010; Birch and Whittam, 2009). This is a view shared by Volkmann *et al.* (2011): the social economy can be seen as narrower than social entrepreneurship. The existence of social entrepreneurship within the private sector is supported by Austin *et al.* (2007), who termed it 'corporate social entrepreneurship' (cited in Nicholls, 2010). Similarly, the public sector was responsible for initiating a number of WISE (work integration social enterprises) schemes in the late 90s and early part of the 21st century. Companies like True GRIT, a research and information company based within a local development company in Glasgow, worked on a commercial basis to provide research to local companies, whilst offering training and work to people excluded from the workforce for a variety of reasons. This was an entrepreneurial venture that used a mix of earned income and grant funding to support its social mission, which centred on creating employment opportunities.

Having established that social entrepreneurship can exist across all sectors of the economy, it seems that social entrepreneurship cannot be pigeonholed or identified through its association with a particular economic segment. SE offers a different approach to business.

Exercise

Research One Water and one WISE project and identify the differences between them. In what circumstances might a SE enterprise be unable to achieve self-sufficiency from earned income? Hint: Search for 'Work Integration Social Enterprise' on a search engine of your choice.

SE, CSR and social business models

Another area of commercial activity often confused with social entrepreneurship is corporate social responsibility (CSR). It is a broad concept and is commonly considered to be concerned with the ways in which a firm exceeds its minimum obligations to stakeholders, specified through regulation (Johnson, Scholes and Whittington, 2009). There are a number of perspectives of corporate social responsibility, ranging from the extreme laissez-faire approach to the shaper-of-society angle.

Some of the problems related to defining social entrepreneurship involve clarifying why it differs from other types of business activity or forms. For example, Richard Branson extending Virgin's activity to social mission-based activities might suggest that social entrepreneurship and CSR are similar. Christine Volkmann (2012: p. 36), UNESCO Chair for Entrepreneurship and Intercultural Management, asserts that "social entrepreneurship is not.. a new form of corporate responsibility." Devinney (2009) states that CSR can be conceptualised narrowly, where the organization has little obligation to society, and more expansively, where corporations serve as instruments of public policy. The narrow view of CSR is reflective of Freidman's (1970) perspective that the only social responsibility of a business is to maximise shareholder returns.

On the other hand, broader conceptualizations of CSR appear very similar to social entrepreneurship. CSR from the shaper of society perspective – for example, the Body Shop's position on animal testing and Jamie Oliver's position on healthy eating – is more reflective of Devinney's (2009) expansive view of CSR in which firms are active participants in society, integrating social aims into the business realm. From this perspective the primary objective of the corporation is to serve a social mission, the same primary objective of social entrepreneurship from both the innovation and earned income schools of thought. In addition to these similarities between the concepts, Devinney (2009) also claims corporations are valid instruments for social entrepreneurship, primarily basing this claim on the ability of corporations to experiment and gauge social demands of conflicting constituencies without having to adhere to transparency requirements. CSR from this perspective unleashes the entrepreneurial self-interest of investors, firms and managers to solve social problems.

Despite these similarities, there are a number of issues with CSR in its current form, which restricts social entrepreneurship from being a new form of CSR. The first relates to Volkmann *et al.*'s (2012) statement that social entrepreneurship cannot be a new form of CSR, as the primary mission of corporations is to generate profits and maximize shareholder returns. This primary goal of profit maximization differs significantly from the primary goal of social entrepreneurship from both the earned income and school of innovation perspectives of social entrepreneurship, which is to serve a social mission. Volkmann *et al.*'s (2012) point can be illustrated in the case of Toyota, who introduced a hybrid car to the market based on an identification of market demand for hybrid vehicles (Reinhardt, Yao and Egawa, 2006). Whether or not Toyota had intended to help save the planet is immaterial; Toyota developed the hybrid technology in response to an opportunity in the business environment and sold the car into the market where there was demand (Devinney, 2009).

Despite the shaper of society perspective of CSR sharing the same primary goal of a social mission with social entrepreneurship, the manner in which the social mission can be served in CSR is broader than in definitions from the earned income and social innovation perspectives of social entrepreneurship. CSR from the shaper of society angle does not have to include an element of trade, although it can, so it does not sit with the school of earned income perspective of social entrepreneurship, which requires an element of trade by definition. Similarly, CSR from the shaper of society perspective does not have to be entrepreneurial. CSR in this broad sense is a wider concept than social entrepreneurship.

Besides, there is a healthy scepticism about some aspects of CSR. Devinney (2010) presents an example of the McGellar Corporation successfully using CSR as a back door to change the basis of industry competition in their favour and of using public means to advance a private agenda. There is also the view that CSR is little more than the icing on a rotten cake (Pearce, 2003) and that companies with the poorest history of CSR are its strongest advocates. This is the case for Nestlé (Porter and Kramer, 2006, 2011) and for BP, with its recent and tragic consequences of breaches of health and safety procedures

Social value and the impact of social entrepreneurship

So far considerable emphasis has been placed on the creation of social value, along with social mission, as the sine qua non of social entrepreneurship, but what is social value and how do we identify and measure it?

Grönroos (2011: p. 242) posits two views of value, one based on the notion of cost benefit analysis on the part of the buyer, and also his own definition that:

> "[v]alue for customers means that they, after having been assisted by the provision of resources or interactive processes, are or feel better off than before."

Grönroos further contends that an organization's success in terms of delivering value can be measured in monetary terms. Measuring success in purely economic terms of supply and demand is easily achieved through a number of methods like return on investment (ROI); turnover, and net and gross profit margins; however, how can the value created through a venture like the *Big Issue* be identified and measured? Social value is a more complex concept than economic value and shares many of the same definitional problems associated with an emergent discipline like social entrepreneurship. Social value can be considered the combination of impacts in three key areas, commonly referred to as the triple bottom line: people, planet and profit.

Before looking further at this concept it is worth drawing a parallel between social value and shared value, the preferred term amongst private sector advocates of the approach. Porter and Kramer (2011: p. 3) describe shared value:

> "The concept of shared value resets the boundaries of capitalism. By better connecting shared value to societal improvement, it opens up many ways to serve new needs, gain efficiency, create differentiation and expand new markets."

Whether or not shared value is considered a new and virtuous reconceptualization of capitalism, it fails to capture the notion of social value, as the shared value model subordinates social value creation to little more than a strategic means of improving organizational position and success across a range of traditional performance measures. This is in contrast with social entrepreneurship, where social value is an end in itself (Agafonou, 2014; Santos, 2012) rather than merely a means of improving commercial performance. Pearce's (2003) definition of social entrepreneurship emphasises the hegemony of social mission and the role of traditional business models and entrepreneurial techniques in the fulfilment thereof.

Social value or social impact can be determined according to two broad approaches, one mainly quantitative, called *Social Return on Investment* (SROI), and the other mainly qualitative, called the *social audit*. The former demands that social impacts are quantified in monetary terms and a ratio produced that shows how much social value is created by each £1 invested. SROI broadly equates with its counterpart from traditional accountancy. The second approach, the social audit, is a methodology that reviews all areas of mission-related activity across a range of performance areas against which success can be gauged. Whichever approach is endorsed, and each comes with its own methodological/ epistemological problems, they both review three central areas of impact:

- ☐ **Economic** – improving the economic situation of individuals allows them to pay taxes and to buy services and products that support the market economy more generally, thereby improving socio-economic conditions, creating successful markets, and countering social exclusion. This is true of the *Big Issue*, the Grameen Bank, and Fifteen (Pearce, 2003; Brooks, 2009).

- ☐ **Social improvement** – we might characterise this in many ways, at an individual level in terms of quality of life issues, or at a community level. Measuring social value at the individual level is relatively easy, but it is more challenging to measure collectively (Brooks, 2009; Bridge, Murtah and O'Neill, 2009; Choi and Majumdar, 2014).

□ **Environmental** – social value can involve improvement in terms of waste management, improved green space and generally the creation of healthy environments (Pearce, 2003; Martin and Thomson, 2010; Kroeger and Weber, 2014).

The *Big Issue* demonstrates how social value is created in the economic and societal spheres and, although environmental impact is an important issue, it takes specialist knowledge to calculate if carbon emissions and wastage are to form part of the analysis, and for this reason it will not form part of the forgoing discussion.

■ Big Issue value creation

Economic value

□ It creates employment for a potentially broad range of constituencies.

□ It provides a source of income for homeless people and core staff alike.

□ It reduces governmental intervention through decreased reliance on the public sector in areas such as health benefits and social care.

□ Through greater economic agency, choice becomes more relevant and this encourages and supports healthy markets and economic prosperity more generally.

A monetary value could be ascribed to all of the elements of economic value creation above, making the Big Issue's economic impact easy to quantify.

Social value

Social value creation, on the other hand, is more challenging to measure.

□ It combats social exclusion and provides opportunities for homeless people to engage with the world of commerce.

□ It creates an environment for mutual self-self-help, friendship and development of formal and informal support networks.

□ Homeless people have an opportunity to meet people from a range of socio-economic backgrounds.

□ It improves the confidence of homeless people.

□ It reminds society that homelessness is a real issue that can have dire consequences for those affected.

Measuring increments or the impact of social change on individuals is challenging but possible through the use of benchmarking, questionnaires and interviews; however, how should social value, as it applies to communities, be measured? This is where the theory of *social capital* has application. This theory makes it possible to measure whether a community or society as whole is better off through the value created by a SE. One of the strengths of the theory is that it "shifts the focus of analysis from behaviour of individual agents to the pattern of relations between agents, social units and institutions" (Shuller *et al.*, 2000: 33). It is defined in various ways by scholars and can be split into three types, each with its own theoretical underpinning:

1 The bonds that exist between families and communities in terms of shared values and norms; this is called *bonding* social capital.

2 The linkages between different communities, between unemployed and employed people, for example; this is called *bridging* social capital.

3 Relationships between people from markedly different power or economic structures are referred to as *linking* social capital.

Levels of social capital have been associated with trust, municipality, health, crime and GDP, and a high incidence of social capital is indicative of a healthy society (Bridge *et al.*, 2009). Research has also shown that social capital can characterise good and great companies in both the private and socially entrepreneurial spheres (Collins, 2001; Ridley Duff, 2007). Social capital is also seen as a precursor to community social entrepreneurship, as it acts as a collective force, allowing a community to develop in enterprising ways (Pearce, 2007; Birch,Whittam and Southern, 2009; Danson, 2012). Mull Community Business and McSense are Scottish examples of community social entrepreneurship where a strong community spirit has been the conduit through which community enterprise-based solutions to social problems have been designed and delivered. Through ideals a shared vision can be created: that is social energy (Hirschman, 2013).

Conclusion

During this exploration of social entrepreneurship, two schools of thought have been considered and the strengths and weaknesses of their theoretical bases have been examined. By distinguishing social entrepreneurship from corporate social responsibility and social business and by establishing where it sits within the economy, it is possible to more readily show that it is distinct from other areas of management theory and practice. However, it emerges that determining whether a person, firm or community is socially entrepreneurial is still a challenge.

Based on the analysis and critical evaluation of social entrepreneurship presented, if a venture fulfils the following defining characteristics then it is SE:

Social entrepreneurship test:

- ☐ If it fulfils the characteristics of entrepreneurship as generally conceived by academics and practitioners. This criterion is based on Dees' (2007) view that SEs are just a species of the genus entrepreneur.

- ☐ If the motive is social benefit and social value creation. This is an undisputed aspect of SE.

- ☐ If personal profit is tangential to the social mission or irrelevant to it. This sits comfortably with even the most polarised takes on SE.

- ☐ If it delivers in terms of successful social impact.

In its broadest sense social entrepreneurship embodies the ethos of: "from each according to ability to each according to need", where personal profit is not a force driving the satisfaction of demand. What is clear is that unlike business as practised in the 'for-personal-profit sector' SE offers a different approach to business. This is expressed by Muhammad Yunus (2008:1):

> "We have remained so mesmerised by the success of the free market that we never dared to express any doubt about it. We worked extra hard to transform ourselves, as closely as possible, into the one-dimensional human beings as conceptualised in theory to allow smooth functioning of free market mechanism. Economic theory postulates that you are contributing to the society and the world in the best possible manner if you just concentrate on squeezing out the maximum for yourself. When you get your maximum, everybody else will get their maximum."

Social entrepreneurs like Muhammad Yunus have had substantial impacts on a variety of constituencies. It is clear from the examples considered in this chapter that this model of business can sit successfully alongside traditional conceptualizations of entrepreneurship and business more generally, and that social entrepreneurs really do make a difference!

References

Agafonow, A. (2014).Toward a positive theory of social entrepreneurship: on maximizing versus satisficing value capture. *Journal of Business Ethics,* **125**(4), 709-713.

Austin, J. Stevenson, H. and Wei-Skillern, J. (2006). Social and commercial entrepreneurship: Same, different or both? *Entrepreneurship: Theory and Practice,* **30**(1), 1-22.

Birch, K, and Whittam, G (2009), Market madness or the road to salvation? A critical review of the social enterprise agenda. In: Southern, A (ed.) *Enterprise and Deprivation: Small Business, Social Exclusion and Sustainable Communities.* London: Routledge.

Boschee, J. and McClurg, J. (2003).Towards a Better Understanding of Social Entrepreneurship. SenScot. Available at: http://www.senscot.net/view_art.php?%20viewid=11611. [Accessed 28 February 2015].

Bridge, S., & Murtagh, B. O'Neill, K.(2009). *Understanding the Social Economy and the Third Sector.* Basingstoke: Palgrave.

Brooks, A. C. (2009). *Social Entrepreneurship.* New Jersey: Prentice Hall.

Choi, N., and Majumdar, S. (2014). Social entrepreneurship as an essentially contested concept: Opening a new avenue for systematic future research. *Journal of Business Venturing,* **29**(3), 363-376.

Dacin, P. Dacin, M. and Matear, M. (2010). Social entrepreneurship: Why we don't need a new theory and how we move forward from here. *Academy Of Management Perspectives,* **24**(3), 37-57.

Danson, M.,and Lloyd, G. (2012). Devolution, Institutions, and Organizations: Changing Models of Regional Development Agencies. *Environment and Planning-Part C,* **30**(1), 78.

Deakins, D. and Friel, M. (2012). *Entrepreneurship and Small Firms.* Maidenhead: McGraw-Hill.

Dees, J. G., & Economy, P. (2001). *Social entrepreneurship. Enterprising Nonprofits: A Toolkit for Social Entrepreneurs.* New York: John Wiley & Sons, 1-18.

Dees, J. G., & Anderson, B. B. (2003). Sector-bending: Blurring lines between nonprofit and for-profit. *Society,* **40**(4), 16-27

Dees, J.G. (2007). Taking Social Entrepreneurship Seriously, *Society,* **44**(3), 24-48.

Defourny, J. and Nyssens, M. (2010). Conceptions of social enterprise and social entrepreneurship in Europe and the United States: Convergences and divergences. *Journal of Social Entrepreneurship,* **1**(1), 32-53.

Devinney, T. M. (2009). Is the socially responsible corporation a myth? The good, the bad, and the ugly of corporate social responsibility. *The Academy of Management Perspectives,* **23**(2), 44-56.

5

Gov.uk (2014) https://www.gov.uk/government/news/investing-in-social-enterprise-government-publishes-policy-roadmap

Grönroos, C. (2011). A service perspective on business relationships: The value creation, interaction and marketing interface, *Industrial Marketing Management,* **40**(2), 240-247.

Hirschman, Albert O. (2013). *Getting Ahead Collectively: Grassroots Experiences in Latin America*. Elsevier.

Johnson, G., Scholes, K. and Whittington, R. (2009). *Fundamentals of Strategy*. Harlow: Pearson.

Kirzner, I. M. (1979). *Perception, Opportunity and Profit*. Chicago: University of Chicago.

Knight, F. H. (1921). *Risk, Uncertainty and Profit*. New York: Hart, Schaffner and Marx.

Kroeger, A., and Weber, C. (2014). Developing a conceptual framework for comparing social value creation. *Academy of Management Review,* **39**(4), 513-540.

Kraus, S., Filser, M., O'Dwyer, M., and Shaw, E. (2014). Social entrepreneurship: An exploratory citation analysis. *Review of Managerial Science,* **8**(2), 275-292.

Leadbeater, C. (1997). *The rise of the social entrepreneur* (No. 25). Demos.

Martin, F. and Thompson, M. (2010). *Social Enterprise: Developing Sustainable Business*. London: Palgrave Macmillan.

Meredith, G. G., Nelson, R. E., & Neck, P. A. (1982). *The Practice of Entrepreneurship*, Vol. 30, No. 760. Geneva: International Labour Office.

Nicholls, A. (2010). The legitimacy of social entrepreneurship: Reflexive isomorphism in a pre-paradigmatic field, *Entrepreneurship Theory and Practice,* **34**, 611–633.

One Difference (2015). About Us. Available at: http://onedifference.org/about-us/. [Accessed 28 February 2015].

Pearce, J. (2007). *Social Enterprise in Anytown.* Calouste Gulbenkian Foundation: London.

Porter, M. E., and Kramer, M. R. (2011). Creating shared value. *Harvard Business Review,* **89**(1/2), 62-77.

Reinhardt, F. L., Yao, D. A., & Egawa, M. (2006). *Toyota Motor Corporation: lauching prius*. Harvard Business School

Santos, F. M. (2012). A positive theory of social entrepreneurship. *Journal of Business Ethics,* **111**(3), 335-351.

Sassmannshausen, S. P., and Volkmann, C. (2013).A bibliometric based review on Social Entrepreneurship and its establishment as a field of research (No. 2013-003). Schumpeter Discussion Papers.

Schumpeter, J. (1942). *Creative destruction. Capitalism, socialism and democracy.* New York: Harper.

SEFORIS (2014). The State of Social Entrepreneurship - Key Facts and Figures. Available at:http://www.seforis.eu/upload/reports/1._Key_Facts_and_Figures_of_Social_Entrepreneurship.pdf. [Accessed 20 August 2015].

Skoll Foundation (2015). Institute for OneWorld Health. Available at: http://www.skollfoundation.org/entrepreneur/victoria-hale/. [Accessed 28 February 2015].

Timmons, J. A., & Spinelli, S. (1994). *New Venture Creation: Entrepreneurship for the 21st Century* (Vol. 4). Burr Ridge, IL: Irwin.

Timmons, J.A., and Spinelli, S. (2007). *New Venture Creation: Entrepreneurship for the 21st century.* New York: McGraw-Hill.

Volkmann, C.K., Tokarski, K.O. and Ernst, K. (2012). Background, Characteristics and Context of Social Entrepreneurship.

Young, R. (2006). For what it is worth: Social value and the future of social entrepreneurship. In A. Nicholls (Ed.), *Social Entrepreneurship* (pp. 56–73). Oxford, UK: Oxford University Press

YouTube. (2007). John Bird - Inspiring Entrepreneur. [Online Video]. 26 September. Available from: https://www.youtube.com/watch?v=XTc2Cq6f2BQ. [Accessed: 13 January 2015].

YouTube.(2011). Victoria Hale - Uncommon Hero.[Online Video]. 27 September. Available from: https://www.youtube.com/watch?v=8t2qsX1bWdI. [Accessed: 14 January 2015].

Yunus., M. (2006). Social Business Entrepreneurs Are the Solution. Skoll World Forum on Social Entrepreneurship. Oxford, 29-31 March 2006. Caledonia.

Yunus, M. (2008). Social Business is the Solution. Available at: http://www.mediatheque.lindau-nobel.org/videos/31406/social-business-is-the-solution-2008/laureate-yunus [Accessed: 20th May 2015].

Yunus, M., & Weber, K. (2011). *Building social business: The new kind of capitalism that serves humanity's most pressing needs.* Public Affairs. New York.

Zeyen, A., Beckmann, A., Mueller, S., Dees J. G., Khanin., Krueger, N., Murphy, P.J., Santos, F., Scarlata, M., Walske, J. and Zacharakis., A. (2013). Social entrepreneurship and broader theories: Shedding new light on the 'bigger picture. *Journal of Social Entrepreneurship,* **4**(1), 88-109.

5

6 Corporate Entrepreneurship

Lai Hong Ng

Corporations cannot be static – they must continually adapt and redefine themselves as the development and enhancement of new products, services, processes and technologies are occurring at a phenomenal speed. In the long term, for corporations to remain competitive, corporate entrepreneurship is one of the ways forward. This chapter concentrates on establishing an understanding of corporate entrepreneurship and the approaches corporations can use as pathways to becoming sustainable and successful organizations.

Challenges of corporations

Corporations which once upon a time started as small-sized organizations have moved from being highly entrepreneurial to becoming bureaucratic (Morris *et al.*, 2009). The loss of entrepreneurship poses the danger that corporations will cease to change and innovate. In the long run corporations will face challenges competing with smaller, speedier and more innovative organizations (Naisbitt, 1994; Bratnicka and Bratnicki, 2013). Corporations facing these challenges are known as 'embattled corporations', struggling to survive and thrive in turbulent environments (Morris *et al.*, 2011). These authors highlighted four dimensions through which environmental turbulence has created a need for new management practices:

1 Through customers
2 Through competitors
3 Through technology
4 Through legal, regulatory and ethical standards

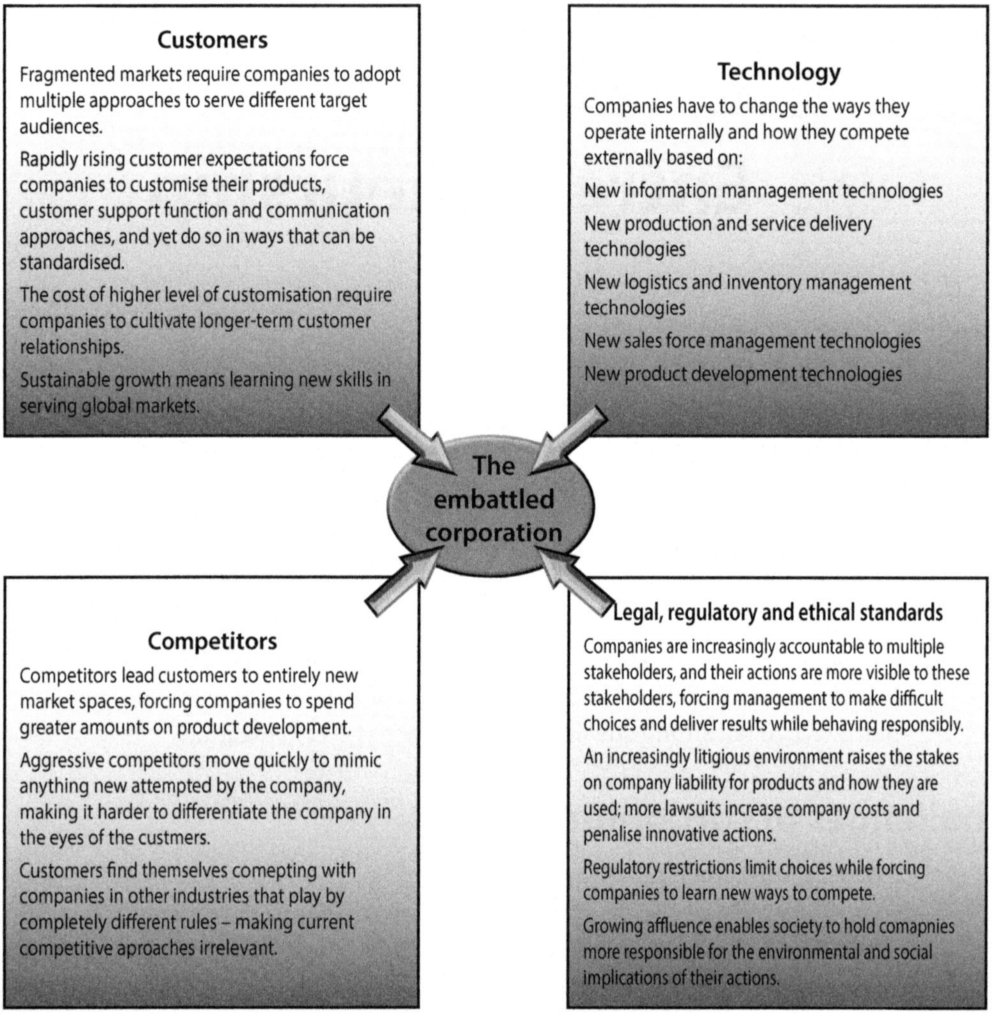

The figure boxes contain the following text:

Customers
Fragmented markets require companies to adopt multiple approaches to serve different target audiences.

Rapidly rising customer expectations force companies to customise their products, customer support function and communication approaches, and yet do so in ways that can be standardised.

The cost of higher level of customisation require companies to cultivate longer-term customer relationships.

Sustainable growth means learning new skills in serving global markets.

Technology
Companies have to change the ways they operate internally and how they compete externally based on:

New information mannagement technologies

New production and service delivery technologies

New logistics and inventory management technologies

New sales force management technologies

New product development technologies

The embattled corporation

Competitors
Competitors lead customers to entirely new market spaces, forcing companies to spend greater amounts on product development.

Aggressive competitors move quickly to mimic anything new attempted by the company, making it harder to differentiate the company in the eyes of the custmers.

Customers find themselves comepting with companies in other industries that play by completely different rules – making current competitive aproaches irrelevant.

Legal, regulatory and ethical standards
Companies are increasingly accountable to multiple stakeholders, and their actions are more visible to these stakeholders, forcing management to make difficult choices and deliver results while behaving responsibly.

An increasingly litigious environment raises the stakes on company liability for products and how they are used; more lawsuits increase company costs and penalise innovative actions.

Regulatory restrictions limit choices while forcing companies to learn new ways to compete.

Growing affluence enables society to hold comapnies more responsible for the environmental and social implications of their actions.

Figure 6.1: Environmental turbulence creating new management practices
Source: Morris *et al.* (2011: p. 6).

Figure 6.1 explains how trends in some of these dimensions force corporations to abandon conventional business practices. Each dimension has vital implications on how things are done in corporations. Many corporations tend to make shorter-term commitments such as rightsizing, outsourcing, leasing and more in order not to miss out on opportunities. For ensuring the long-term sustainability of any corporation, Morris *et al.* (2011) emphasised the need for corporate entrepreneurship – a term used to describe entrepreneurial behaviour inside established, larger organizations. Corporate entrepreneurship is rapidly becoming a weapon of choice for many corporations.

Exercise

Discuss two corporations or brands that face high degrees of environmental turbulence.

What is corporate entrepreneurship?

Corporate entrepreneurship is "the development of new business ideas and opportunities within large and established corporations" (Birkinshaw, 2003: 46). Zahra (1991: p. 259) defined it as "activities that enhance a corporation's ability to innovate, take risk and seize opportunities in its markets" – a call for greater entrepreneurial behaviour that will help in recognising profitable product or market opportunities and in providing new bases for achieving competitive advantage. Corporate entrepreneurship is an attempt to take both the mind and skill sets demonstrated by successful start-up entrepreneurs and instil these characteristics into the cultures and activities of a corporation. This approach can be a powerful solution to corporation staleness, lack of innovation and stagnated growth. Corporations that reveal corporate entrepreneurship are regarded as dynamic, flexible entities prepared to take advantage of new business opportunities when they arise (Hisrich & Kearney, 2012; Kuratko *et al.*, 2014).

Example of corporate entrepreneurship

Nokia's history exhibits corporate entrepreneurship, which has been known as a set of behaviour, processes or activities that renew or reinvent an organization.

1865: Paper Mill

1898: Nokia's rubber business

1912: Nokia's cable businesses

1960: First electronics department

1979: TV and Radio

1991: Nokia equipment is used to make the world's first GSM (Global System for Mobile communication) call.

Source: adapted from Edgar (2013).

Tip: Zahra and Covin (1995) evidenced that corporate entrepreneurship has a positive impact on financial measures of organizational performance. The authors contended that corporate entrepreneurship should not be regarded as a short term solution but as a long-term strategy for achieving higher financial performance. In order to realise the full benefits of corporate entrepreneurship, managers must be willing to sustain their support for entrepreneurial initiatives over a number of years. Without such managerial support, corporate entrepreneurial activities may be discontinued long before they would reasonably be expected to financially benefit the corporation.

How corporate entrepreneurship differs from entrepreneurship?

Independent entrepreneurship and corporate entrepreneurship are differentiated as:

☐ *Independent entrepreneurship* is the process whereby an individual or group of individuals acting independently, create a new organization.

☐ *Corporate entrepreneurship* is the process whereby an individual or a group of individuals, in association with an existing organization, create a new organization or instigate renewal or innovation within that organization. (Sharma and Chrisman, 2007: 92)

Other major differences are illustrated in Table 6.1.

Start-Up Entrepreneurship	Corporate Entrepreneurship
Entrepreneur takes the risk	Company assumes the risks, other than career-related risk
Entrepreneur 'owns' the concept or innovative idea	Company owns the concept, and typically the intellectual rights surrounding the concept
Entrepreneur owns all or much of the business	Entrepreneur may have no equity in the company, or a very small percentage
Potential rewards for the entrepreneur are theoretically unlimited	Clear limits are placed on the financial rewards entrepreneurs can receive
One mis-step can mean failure	More room for errors; company can absorb failure
Vulnerable to outside influence	More insulated from outside influence
Entrepreneur is independent, although successful ones are typically backed by a strong team	Interdependence of the champion with many others; may have to share credit with any number of people
Flexibility in changing course, experimenting, or trying new directions	Rules, procedures and bureaucracy hinder the entrepreneur's ability to manoeuvre
Speed of decision making	Longer approval cycles
Little security	Job security
No safety net	Dependable benefit package
Few people to talk to	Extensive network for bouncing around ideas
Limited scale and scope initially	Potential for sizeable scale and scope fairly quickly
Severe resource limitations	Access to finances, R&D, production facilities for trial runs, an established sales force, brand, databases, and market research resources, distribution channels and customer base

Table 6.1: Corporate and start-up entrepreneurship – major differences

Source: Morris *et al.* (2011: p. 38).

A typology of approaches to corporate entrepreneurship

Wolcott and Lippitz (2007) investigated how corporations succeed in pursuing corporate entrepreneurship and depicted four fundamental models of corporate entrepreneurship as well as identifying two dimensions guiding when each model should be applied (Figure 6.2).

☐ The first dimension is **corporate ownership**: who within the corporation has main ownership for the creation of new businesses? Responsibility either by a focused group (for example, the Producer and the Advocate Models) or diffused across the corporation (for example, the Enabler or Opportunist Models).

☐ The second dimension is **resource authority**: are new business concepts funded in an ad hoc manner (for example, the Advocate and the Opportunist Models) or through dedicated corporate budgets (for example, the Producer or the Enabler Models)?

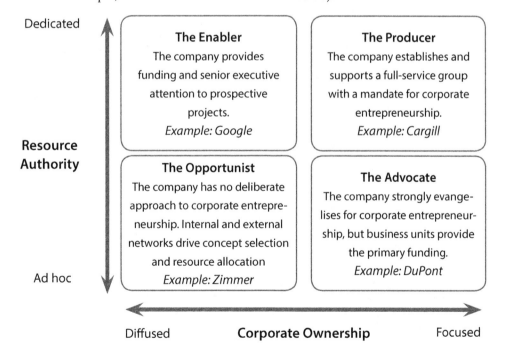

Figure 6.2: The four models of corporate entrepreneurship
Source: Wolcott and Lippitz (2007: pp. 77-78).

The Enabler Model	The Producer Model
Employees willing to develop new concepts if given adequate support. Dedicating resources and processes (but without any formal corporate ownership) enable teams to pursue opportunities on their own insofar as they fit the corporation's strategic frame.	Corporations pursue corporate entrepreneurship by establishing formal corporate ownership with dedicated funds or active influence over business-unit funding. The producer model aims to protect emerging projects from turf battles, encourage cross-unit collaboration, build potentially disruptive businesses and create pathways for executives to pursue careers outside their business units.
The Opportunist Model	**The Advocate Model**
Most corporations begin as opportunists. Without any designated ownership or resources, corporate entrepreneurship is based on efforts and fearless project champions – employees who toil against the odds, creating new businesses often in spite of the corporation.	A corporation assigns corporate ownership for the creation of new businesses while intentionally providing only modest budgets to the core group. Usually advocate corporation facilitates corporate entrepreneurship in conjunction with business units – usually a corporation needed some new thinking because, even though margins and returns had improved but growth had declined.

Example of the **Opportunist Model** (diffused corporate ownership and ad hoc resource authority):

☐ *Zimmer Holdings Inc.*, a medical device company headquartered in Warsaw, Indiana.

☐ No formal department or dedicated resources for corporate entrepreneurship.

☐ When trauma surgeon Dana Mears had an idea for minimally invasive surgery for hip replacements, he presented and explored it informally with Zimmer manager Kevin Gregg.

☐ The two then got the go-ahead from top management, who approved the use of company resources for concept development and experimentation.

☐ The new medical approach required innovations in training, so the company established the Zimmer Institute, and later more than 6,000 surgeons were being trained there in a dozen different types of minimally invasive surgical procedures.

☐ The resulting improvement in patient outcomes (and hence lower total costs) has led to some private insurers paying a premium for certain Zimmer procedures.

☐ Today, that new business has helped Zimmer achieve superior overall growth despite severe industry pricing pressure.

Example of the **Enabler Model** (diffused corporate ownership and dedicated resource authority):

- ☐ At *Google*, employees are allowed to spend 20% of their time to promote their ideas to colleagues, assemble teams, explore concepts and build prototypes.

- ☐ Project groups form based on requirements defined by the teams themselves.

- ☐ If the team believes it has a winner, it appeals to the Google Product Council for funding.

- ☐ This group, which includes the company founders, top executives and engineering team leads, provides broad strategic direction and initial resources.

- ☐ Successful project teams receive assistance from the Google Product Strategy Forum to formulate their business models and set milestones.

- ☐ Importantly, Google applies no preconceived criteria or hurdle rates to the projects.

- ☐ As long as a project appears to have potential and maintains the interest of Google employees, it can continue.

Example of the **Advocate Model** (focused corporate ownership and ad hoc resource authority):

- ☐ *DuPont*, the 200-year-old global conglomerate.

- ☐ In 1999, CEO Chad Holliday realized that the company needed some new thinking because, even though margins and returns had improved during the prior six years, growth had declined.

- ☐ Holliday asked DuPont veteran Robert A. Cooper to head a small internal group that focused on company growth, and the result was the Market Driven Growth initiative.

- ☐ The program provides employees with a wide range of assistance, everything from idea conceptualization through to commercialization.

- ☐ For instance, it includes a four-day business builder session that helps people generate and prioritize different business concepts.

- ☐ After this, a team will typically spend from four to eight weeks developing a detailed business plan, including a 180-day contract with senior management to address major uncertainties of the proposed concept.

- ☐ Then the team and a facilitator from the Market Driven Growth program will present the plan to business-unit leadership for approval.

Example of the **Producer** Model (focused corporate ownership and dedicated resource authority):

☐ *Cargill Inc.*, a global agriculture products and services company has established its Emerging Business Accelerator (EBA).

☐ Prior to the EBA, the company lacked a clearly defined process and budget for pursuing opportunities that fell outside of the scope of existing business units and functions.

☐ The EBA become a global clearinghouse for new concepts and value propositions across Cargill.

☐ The group maintains a website for people to submit ideas, both from inside and outside the company.

☐ When an opportunity appears promising, the EBA develops a high-level plan, performs due diligence, recruits talent and, if approved by the group's board of directors, provides capital and monitors the project's progress.

☐ In the early stages, project teams focus on refining their concept, business model and market offerings.

☐ To do so, they spend time with potential customers to validate the market for their products or services. Projects that achieve validation from real customers graduate into either existing or new business units.

Source: Wolcott and Lippitz (2007: pp. 76-80).

Exercise

Given the different models give further examples of each and how they have had an impact on your life.

Four schools of thought on corporate entrepreneurship

Corporate entrepreneurship can be manifested in different forms and there is a growing literature on this. Birkinshaw (2003) determined four threads of the literature that he calls four basic schools of thought:

☐ Corporate venturing

☐ Intrapreneurship

☐ Bringing the market inside

☐ Entrepreneurial transformation

■ **Corporate venturing**

This school of thought argues the need for corporations to "manage new, entrepreneurial businesses separately from the mainstream activity, or they will not survive long enough to deliver benefit to the sponsoring corporation" (Birkinshaw, 2003: 10). It includes investment by corporations in innovative and high growth smaller organizations in order to gain competitive advantage in a critical area of new trend, segment or technology. This happens in different industries such as pharmaceutical, food and beverage, fast-moving consumer goods and others. Miles and Covin (2002) reported that many corporations pursued venturing for three main reasons:

1 To create an innovative capability as the base for making corporations more entrepreneurial and accepting of change.

2 To expand the scope of operations and competence into areas of strategic significance (Hsu *et al.*, 2014).

3 To generate potential financial gains. The way of achieving successful corporate venturing is strategic fit – searching for investment which has a strong relationship with the core competencies of the venturing corporation (i.e. effective synergy) or acquiring skills, technologies or customers that complement the strategic direction of the venturing corporation (i.e. effective knowledge transfer) (Burns, 2011).

The *advantages* of corporate venturing:

☐ It brings innovation and knowledge into the organization from external sources;

☐ External sources of finance may be more easy to access;

☐ It facilitates the creation of semi-autonomous operating units with their own cultures, incentives and business models;

☐ It is often highly motivating to the staff involved (Burns, 2011: p. 492).

The *disadvantages* of corporate venturing:

☐ It requires investment normally in the form of equity, which can be risky;

☐ It requires the investing company to invest in mechanisms that set up venture management and networks that search out, evaluate and generate deal flows;

☐ The investing company will not be in complete control of the innovation (Burns, 2011: p. 492).

Case study: Pret a Manger

Julian Metcalfe and Sinclair Beecham opened their first Pret a Manger sandwich bar in Victoria Street, central London, in 1986. They made sandwiches in the basement from fresh ingredients bought every morning at Covent Garden market. They built Pret on the simple concept of providing gourmet, fresh and organic fast food in modern, clean surroundings. Pret now sells sandwiches, baguettes, soups, salads, coffees and desserts. It still emphasises its use of fresh, natural ingredients only. Sandwiches are made on the day of purchase in kitchens at the locations. Those not sold on the day they are made are given to charity. The formula has proved successful.

By 2001 Pret has 103 stores in the UK and one in New York, producing a turnover of £100 million and profits of £3.6 million. But Pret does not franchise and finding the funding for expansion was proving challenging. However it came as quite a surprise when McDonald's bought a non-controlling 33 percent interest in the company for an estimated £26 million. The motives were simple enough. McDonald's could provide not only cash but also the support for Pret's global expansion plans and they were happy not to change the Pret formula in any way. McDonald's, who also owned the Aroma coffee bar chain, saw this as a strategic purchase that would advance their long-term strategy of gaining a greater share of the diverse informal eating-out market and spreading their product portfolio into newer, higher-growth market segments.

Source: Burns (2011: p. 472).

Exercise

Choose one of the Virgin brand's business ventures that has been proven successful and analyse why. Also, find an example of corporate venturing that has been proven unsuccessful and analyse why.

■   Intrapreneurship

This school of thought works on the assumption that corporations put in place structures and systems that inhibit initiative so, as intrapreneurs, they have to challenge those systems and to act in entrepreneurial ways (Birkinshaw, 2003). Intrapreneurship was first coined by Pinchot (1985) to describe entrepreneurship in established corporations. An intrapreneur is a "corporate employee who introduces and manages an innovative project within the corporate environment, as if he or she were an independent entrepreneur" (Knight, 1987: p. 285). Pinchot (1985) characterise intrapreneurs as result-orientated, ambitious, competitive, questioning and self-motivated but, unlike entrepreneurs, intrapereneurs are also motivated by corporate reward and recognition. They are comfortable with change, dislike bureaucracy, are adept at politics, have clarity of direction and are able to delegate but are not afraid to roll their sleeves up and do what needs to be done themselves. Stevenson and Jarillo (1990) explained intrapreneurship as a process whereby individuals inside corporations pursue opportunities independent of the resources they currently control. Also, this is known as emergent behaviour – of doing new things and departing from the customary to pursue opportunities – involving innovative activities such as development of new products, services, technologies, administrative techniques, strategies and competitive postures (Antoncic and Hisrich, 2003). They have a good understanding of their corporation and are good at solving problems within the system or bypassing the system – often the intrapreneurial team works outside traditional lines of authority. Refer to Figure 6.3 that illustrates the relationship between intrapreneur and corporation.

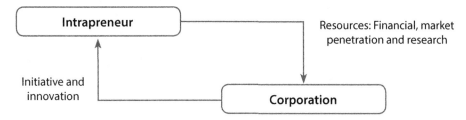

Figure 6.3: Intrapreneur-corporate relationship model
Source: Adapted from Pinchot (1985).

To work effectively intrapreneurs need a certain amount of buffer since they will end up breaking the rules, but likewise they need to be monitored in order to strike a balance (Burns, 2011). They also require a high-level of sponsor to protect them during difficult times whereby the sponsor will help secure resources, provide advice, motivation and contacts (Burns, 2013). This is especially crucial at the early stage of project when things go wrong and visibility of the project is essential – creating a culture that tolerates intrapreneurship. Underpinning this must be a good relationship between the sponsor and the intrapreneur, based on mutual trust and respect.

Examples of intrapreneurs

- 3M: Spencer Silver and Art Fry innovated Post-it Notes.
- Sony Computer Entertainment Inc.: Ken Kutaragi innovated Sony Playstation.
- Kodak: Cheryl Pohlman innovated production of cheaper inkjet cartridges.
- Wal-Mart: Alicial Ledlie innovated in-store health clinics.

Case study: Steve Jobs, the intrapreneur

How to change a company from the inside?

Intrapreneurship is the latest corporate buzzword. But can fusty old companies embrace radical new innovators?

Steve Jobs, the man who turned Apple into a digital cult, once famously described the Macintosh computer team as "a group of people going, in essence, back to the garage, but in a large company".

Corporate America is having another one of its many Steve Jobs moments. As corporate sprawl becomes the norm, some companies are encouraging their workers to break off into entrepreneurial, startup-like teams: giving a section of the office, in effect, to serve as the old California garages that built Hewlett-Packard, Apple and other innovative tech giants. The world has seen too many dominant companies – BlackBerry and Motorola come to mind – who dominate markets and then squander their lead by being too slow in keeping up with new ideas.

Meet the intrapreneurs

That "send in the entrepreneurs" approach to management already has its own corporate buzzword: *intrapreneurship*. Intrapreneurs are supposed to be dynamic employees who create entrepreneurial, profit-making ideas from the inside out. For some employees, who have ideas but yearn for stability, it can be innovation, without the starvation: a start-up feeling with a stable paycheck, a 401k and stock options. Some companies see it as a way to retain employees who might otherwise wander off and take their best ideas with them: Google encourages 20% of employee time to be dedicated to work on anything "cool or innovative".

Yet, as anyone who has worked in a big company knows, innovators are everywhere, and as Jobs himself showed, they usually prefer autonomy and freedom, and have a robust impatience with corporate bureaucracy. As a result, intrapreneurship now has the challenge of proving itself as a real trend and not just corporate wishful thinking.

Source: adapted from Bhanot (2013).

Exercise

Can a traditional manager become an intrapreneur?

■ Bringing the market inside

This approach emphasises the structural changes required to inspire entrepreneurial behaviour (Birkinshaw, 2003). It uses the marketplace metaphor to suggest how corporations should manage resource allocation and people management systems. It argues for greater use of such market techniques as spin-offs (or spin-outs) and corporate venture capital operations (Hamel, 1999; Foster and Kaplan, 2001). For example, Monsanto, Apple, 3M and Xerox use independent venture capital conduits to finance their spin-outs from in-house research (Burns, 2011).

Case study: Xerox Technology spin-outs

When a spin-out is the only answer

If your employees have come up with a promising innovation, a separate venture may be the best home for it

Some companies invest a lot of time and money in innovation in the hope that their staff will come up with profitable ideas. It doesn't necessarily follow, however, that they should develop those ideas themselves. Instead of pursuing innovations in-house, it might sometimes be better to spin them off into new businesses, or even let them leave the company entirely.

For a start, the established structures and processes of an existing business can limit the opportunities for turning an idea into a genuinely new product or service. On top of this, a company may find that attempting to develop new ideas is damaging to the business it already has because it distracts employees or steers it from its core purpose.

Copy the Xerox strategy

Attempting to keep innovation focused on specific business sectors or aligned with corporate strategy does not really work, according to Monica Beltrametti, chief services research officer at Xerox. "You can't restrict research into specific verticals," she said. "If research is successful it will be very broad. It is a matter then of looking for applications."

It is at this point that companies need to decide whether to develop ideas themselves. Xerox patents all its inventions and then assesses whether they fit into one of its core business areas. Those that do not are licensed to other companies. "We licensed a number of patents to Apple and Google," said Beltrametti.

Others are licensed to employees who leave to develop the technology through stand-alone companies. "We encourage it because it means they have a tight relationship with Xerox. They might license some [more] of Xerox's technology, or we could license some of theirs."

Source: adapted from Chynoweth (2014).

Exercise

What do you understand by the term 'bringing the market inside'?

■ Entrepreneurial transformation

This approach assumes that corporations can and should adapt to an ever-changing environment and such adaptation can be achieved by manipulating the corporation's structure, systems and culture, thereby inducing employees to act in a more entrepreneurial way (Birkinshaw, 2003). This line of thinking is shaped by the leadership, strategy, systems, structures and culture in the corporation – coined by Burns (2011) as the entrepreneurial architecture (Figure 6.4). He claimed that the leader's role is crucial in putting the architecture in place especially the structures, culture and strategies. For example, initially Michael Dell's *strategy* was to build good relationships with its global network of suppliers. Today, this has been formalised (*structure*) and most importantly there has built up a *culture* within the organization (Dell, 2014). In the long term Dell has developed competitive advantage based upon the development of distinctive global supply networks. This approach of building entrepreneurial architecture is a systematic exploitation of one of the main capabilities of entrepreneurs. If it is well developed then the architecture is distinctive and difficult to copy.

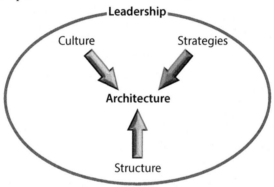

Figure 6.4: Building entrepreneurial architecture
Source: Burns (2011: p. 478).

Exercise

Why is the leader's role vital in encouraging employees to be more entrepreneurial?

Corporate entrepreneurial work environment

As mentioned earlier in this chapter, corporations tend to move from being highly entrepreneurial to becoming large bureaucracies. Corporate entrepreneurship is instrumental for achieving long-term sustainability of a corporation, termed as "corporate entrepreneurship outcomes" by Morris *et al.* (2009). For example, fostering corporate entrepreneurship becomes problematic if leaders do not know what they are trying to achieve. In order to get employees to think and act in entrepreneurial ways, they argue that the starting point is to stipulate desired corporate entrepreneurship outcomes. There are six types of corporate entrepreneurship outcomes and Figure 6.5 describes how the main outcomes fall into six major categories.

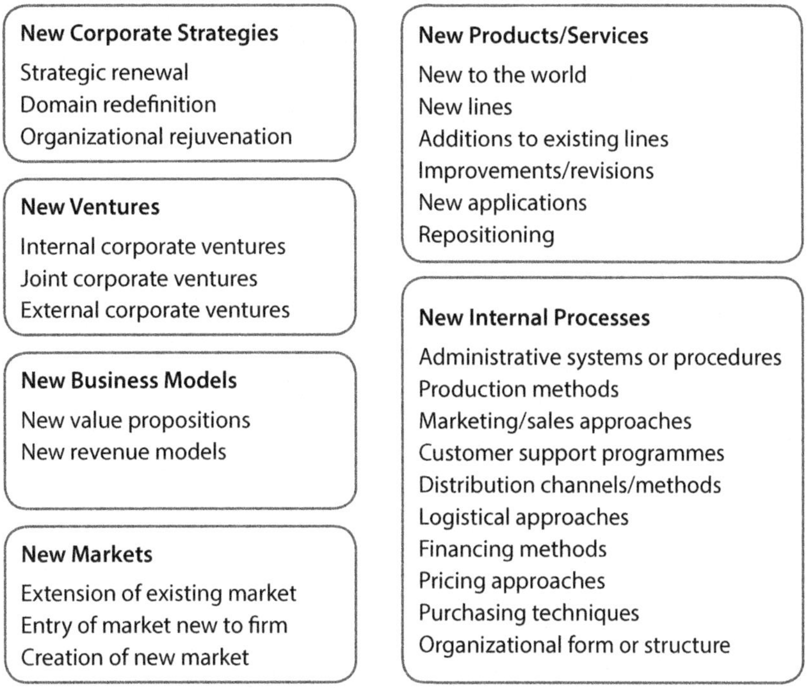

New Corporate Strategies

Strategic renewal
Domain redefinition
Organizational rejuvenation

New Ventures

Internal corporate ventures
Joint corporate ventures
External corporate ventures

New Business Models

New value propositions
New revenue models

New Markets

Extension of existing market
Entry of market new to firm
Creation of new market

New Products/Services

New to the world
New lines
Additions to existing lines
Improvements/revisions
New applications
Repositioning

New Internal Processes

Administrative systems or procedures
Production methods
Marketing/sales approaches
Customer support programmes
Distribution channels/methods
Logistical approaches
Financing methods
Pricing approaches
Purchasing techniques
Organizational form or structure

Figure 6.5: Six types of corporate entrepreneurship outcomes
Source: Morris et al. (2009: p. 430).

The challenge to the corporation is to create a corporate entrepreneurial work environment, i.e. to create work climates that allow employees to recognize and act upon their entrepreneurial potential. Morris *et al.* (2009) also propose a framework that includes four key building blocks vital for designing work environments that support the corporation's entrepreneurial strategy. Figure 6.6 illustrates the variables that combine to promote and support the corporate entrepreneurial work environment: (1) culture, (2) structure, (3) resource controls, and (4) human resource management. For example, values and norms that make up organizational culture are interwoven with the approach to control over resources, which interacts with the organizational structure. Likewise, human resource management practices in areas such as job design, employee recruitment and reward systems affect and are affected by structure, controls and culture. Each variable lends itself to specific managerial actions and they are highly interdependent.

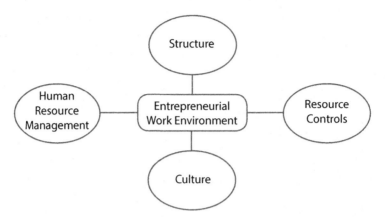

- **Culture:** The organization's basic beliefs and assumptions regarding what the company is about.

- **Structure:** The formal pattern of how people and jobs are grouped, and how the activities of different people or functions are connected.

- **Resource Controls:** The formal and informal mechanisms that help managers ensure that resources are obtained and used efficiently and effectively.

- **Human Resource Management:** The set of tasks associated with acquiring, training, developing, motivating, organizing and maintaining the employees of a company.

Figure 6.6: Variables that combine to create entrepreneurial work environments
Source: Morris *et al.* (2009: p. 432).

Alternatively, Kuratko *et al.* (2014) identified five variables that are significant determinants of an environment conducive to entrepreneurial behaviour: (1) top management support, (2) work discretion/autonomy, (3) rewards/reinforcement, (4) time availability, and (5) organizational boundaries (see Table 2). It is not about which framework to use but a leader's role is crucial in recognising the inherent entrepreneurial potential of employees, determining the corporate entrepreneurship outcome(s) to be achieved and selecting/balancing only relevant variables to create the corporate entrepreneurial work environment (Chen *et al.*, 2014; Bloodgood *et al.*, 2015; Karol, 2015; Tang *et al.*, 2015; Wei and Ling, 2015). Corporate entrepreneurship is the compass that guides these efforts and is quickly becoming an engine of growth and change for many corporations.

Tip: Thornberry (2002) addressed how corporate managers can be trained to act like corporate entrepreneurs via corporate entrepreneurial management development programmes.

Case study: 3M – A culture of innovation

For decades, 3M has been known as an entrepreneurial organization that never stops inventing. Over the years, their innovations have improved daily life of millions of people all over the world. Initially innovation was inspired informally by the founders but through the years some of these rules have been formalised. Above all, a culture of innovation was created and innovation has been the hallmark of 3M's growth, reflecting a culture of shared ideas and technology.

CEO, McKnight, believed in the imperatives of hiring the right people, tolerating mistakes, rewarding through promotion and giving employees freedom to explore in order to foster a culture of innovation. This culture of innovation created a history of success and it perpetuates itself.

Source: adapted from 3M (2012)

Exercise

Select a turbulent industry and research how a corporation within it uses corporate entrepreneurship for achieving one of the corporate entrepreneurship outcomes.

6

Conclusions

Today, corporate entrepreneurial actions are recognized widely as the path to sustainable competitive advantage and success in organizations of all types and sizes (Covin *et al.*, 2000; Hornsby, 2013; Kuratko and Audretsch, 2013; Zahra *et al.*, 2013; Kuratko *et al.*, 2015). Corporate entrepreneurship is not a bandwagon, and it does not produce instant success. It involves time and investment, and there must be continual reinforcement by managers who integrate the corporate entrepreneurial spirit into the mission, goals, strategies, structure, processes and values of the organization (Morris *et al.*, 2011). Flexibility, speed, innovation and entrepreneurial leadership are the cornerstones. A sustainable corporate entrepreneurial orientation will drive organizations to new heights in the long run.

Further reading

Drucker, P. (1985). *Innovation and Entrepreneurship: Practice and Principles*. London: Heinemann.

Hayton, J. C., Hornsby, J. S. and Bloodgood, J. (2013) Part II: The Contribution of HRM to Corporate Entrepreneurship: a review and agenda for future research. *Management* **16**(4): 381-409.

Phan, P., Wright, M., Ucbasaran, D., and Tan, W. (2009). Corporate Entrepreneurship: Current Research and Future Directions. *Journal of Business Venturing* **24**(3): 197-205.

Zahra, S. A. and Randerson, K. (2013). Part I: The Evolution and Contributions of Corporate Entrepreneurship Research. *Management* 16(4): 362-380.

For business and social science students the *Journal of Business Venturing* is a high quality journal dedicated to entrepreneurship. It provides a forum for sharing useful and current theories, narratives and the consequences of entrepreneurship. This multi-disciplinary, multi-functional, and multi-contextual journal aims to extend our understanding of corporate entrepreneurship in its myriad of forms.

The online version of this journal should be available from your University library or otherwise at ScienceDirect.com (http://www.sciencedirect.com/science/journal/08839026).

References

Antoncic, B. and Hisrich, R. D. (2003). Clarifying the Intrapreneurship Concept. *Journal of Small Business and Enterprise Development* **10**(1): 7-24.

Bhanot, V. (2013). How to Change a Company from the Inside? *The Guardian* (15 December). Available: http://www.theguardian.com/business/2013/dec/15/how-to-change-company-from-inside [Accessed 14 July 2015].

Birkinshaw, J. (2003). The paradox of corporate entrepreneurship: Post-Enron principles for encouraging creativity without crossing the line. *Strategy and Business* **30**(1): 46-57.

Bloodgood, J., Hornsby, J., Burkemper, A. and Sarooghi, H. (2015). A system dynamics perspective of corporate entrepreneurship. *Small Business Economics* 45(2): 383-402.

Bratnicka, K. and Bratnicki, M. (2013). Linking two dimensions of organizational creativity to firm performance: The mediating role of corporate entrepreneurship and the moderating role of environment. *Advances in Business-Related Scientific Research Journal* **4**(2): 153-163.

Burns, P. (2011). *Entrepreneurship and Small Business* (3rd ed.). UK: Palgrave Macmillan.

Burns, P. (2013). *Corporate Entrepreneurship: Innovation and Strategy in Large Organizations* (3rd ed.). UK: Palgrave Macmillan.

Chen, Y., Tang, G., Jin, J., Xie, Q. and Li, J. (2014). CEOs' Transformational leadership and product innovation performance: The roles of corporate entrepreneurship and technology orientation. *Journal of Product Innovation Management* **31**(1): 2-17.

Chynoweth, C. (2014). When a spin-off is the only answer. *The Sunday Times* (23 March). Available: http://www.thesundaytimes.co.uk/sto/public/Appointments/article1390360.ece [Accessed 14 July 2015].

Dell (2014). About Dell: Press Release – Dell Takes Position as World's Fastest Growing, Integrated Technology Company. Available: https://www.dell.com/learn/us/en/uscorp1/secure/2014-11-04-dell-fastest-growing-integrated-technology-company [Accessed 8 August 2015].

Edgar, J. (2013) Microsoft Buys Nokia: 150-year History of Finnish Company with Humble Beginnings. *The Independent* (3 September). Available: http://www.independent.co.uk/news/business/analysis-and-features/microsoft-buys-nokia-150year-history-of-finnish-company-with-humble-beginnings-8795907.html [Accessed 5 August 2015].

Foster, R.N. and Kaplan, S. (2001). *Creative Destruction: Why Companies that are Built to Last Underperform the Market – and How to Successfully Transform Them.* New York: Currency Doubleday.

Hamel, G. (1999). Bringing Silicon Valley inside. *Harvard Business Review* **77**(5): 70-84.

Hisrich, R. D. and Kearney, C. (2012). *Corporate Entrepreneurship: How to Create a Thriving Entrepreneurial Spirit throughout your Company.* US: McGraw-Hill.

Hornsby, J. (2013). The Role of corporate entrepreneurship in the current organizational and economic landscape. *International Entrepreneurship and Management Journal* 9(3): 295-305.

Hsu, C. C., Tan, K. C., Jayaram, J. and Laosirihongthong, T. (2014). Corporate entrepreneurship, operations core competency and innovation in emerging economies. *International Journal of Production Research* **52**(18): 5467-5483.

Karol, R. A. (2015). Leadership in the context of corporate entrepreneurship. *Journal of Leadership Studies* **8**(4): 30-34.

Knight, R.M. (1987). Corporate innovation and entrepreneurship: A Canadian study. *Journal of Product Innovation Management.* **4**(4): 284-297.

Kuratko, D. F. and Audretsch, D. B. (2013). Clarifying the domains of corporate entrepreneurship. *International Entrepreneurship and Management Journal* **9**(3): 323-335.

Kuratko, D. F., Hornsby, J. S. and Covin, J. G. (2014). Diagnosing a firm's internal environment for corporate entrepreneurship. *Business Horizons* **57**(1): 37-47.

Kuratko, D. F., Hornsby, J. S. and Hayton, J. (2015). Corporate entrepreneurship: The innovative challenge for a new global economic reality. *Small Business Economics* **45**(2): 245-253.

Miles, M. P. and Covin, J. G. (2002). Exploring the practice of corporate venturing: some common forms and their organizational implications. *Entrepreneurship*

6

Theory and Practice **26**(3): 21-40.

Morris, M. H., Kuratko, D. F. and Covin, J. G. (2011). *Corporate Entrepreneurship and Innovation* (3rd ed.). USA: Cengage Learning.

Morris, M. H., van Vuuren, J., Cornwall, J. R. and Scheepers, R. (2009). Properties of balance: A pendulum effect in corporate entrepreneurship. *Business Horizons* **52** (5): 429-440.

Naisbitt, J. (1994). *Global Paradox: The Bigger the World Economy, the more Powerful its Smaller Players*. London: BCA.

Pinchot, G. (1985). *Intrapreneuring: Why You Don't Have to Leave the Corporation to Become an Entrepreneur*. New York: Harper and Row.

Sharma, P. and Chrisman, S. J. J. (2007). Toward a reconciliation of the definitional issues in the field of corporate entrepreneurship. In Cuervo, A., Ribeiro, D. and Roig, S. (eds.) *Entrepreneurship: Concepts, Theory and Perspective* Heidelberg: Springer.

Stevenson, H.H. and Jarillo, J.C. (1990). A paradigm of entrepreneurship: entrepreneurial management. *Strategic Management Journal* **11**: 17–27.

Thornberry, N. E. (2002). Corporate Entrepreneurship: Teaching Managers to be Entrepreneurs. *Journal of Management Development* **22**(4): 329-344.

Tang, G., Wei, L. Q., Snape, E. and Ng, Y. C. (2015). How effective human resource management promotes corporate entrepreneurship: evidence from China. *International Journal of Human Resource Management* **26**(12): 1586-1601.

Wei, L. Q. and Ling, Y. (2015). CEO characteristics and corporate entrepreneurship in transition economies: Evidence from China. *Journal of Business Research* **68**(6): 1157-1165.

Wolcott, R.C. and Lippitz, M. J. (2007). The four models of corporate entrepreneurship. *MIT Sloan Management Review* **49**(1): 75-82.

Zahra, S. A. (1991). Predictors and financial outcomes of corporate entrepreneurship: An exploratory study. *Journal of Business Venturing* **6**(4): 259-285.

Zahra, S. A. and Covin, J. (1995). Contextual Influences on the Corporate Entrepreneurship- Performance Relationship: A Longitudinal Analysis. *Journal of Business Venturing* **10**(1): 43-58.

Zahra, S. A., Randerson, K. and Fayolle, A. (2013). Corporate Entrepreneurship: Where are we? Where can we go from here? *Management* **16**(4): 357-432.

3M (2012). *3M Brochure: A Culture of Innovation*. Available: http://solutions.3m. com/3MContentRetrievalAPI/BlobServlet?lmd=1349327166000&locale =en_WW&assetType=MMM_Image&assetId=1319209959040&blobAttribute=Imag eFile [Accessed 10 August 2015].

7 **Family Business**

John Sanders

National statistics across countries suggest that 60% to 70% of all small firms (less than 50 employees) are family-owned. However, family firms can be difficult to define and categorize, as they participate in a myriad of activities and take many forms. Despite this diversity, common patterns and characteristics of working occur amongst family-owned firms. To appreciate family businesses requires an understanding of these unique characteristics and how they develop. The unique characteristics possessed by family businesses include the influence of family relationships, company culture and succession planning. Investigating the scope of family business research conducted is also worthwhile, as there are many gaps in our understanding of how family companies operate.

Exercise

Think of a family business you know well from television or the newspapers. What do you think distinguishes this family business from non-family businesses?

Family businesses

The small and medium-sized business sector in most countries includes a predominance of family businesses. Family businesses account for nearly two-thirds or 66 per cent of the small and medium sized enterprise firms within the United Kingdom (UK) private sector according to the Institute for Family Business (Institute For Family Business, n.d.). This 66 per cent represents more than 3 million family businesses in the UK, which between them provide 9.4 million jobs and create 25 per cent of UK's gross domestic product (Institute For Family Business, n.d.). In developing countries like Latin America, Southeast Asia and Africa, the proportion of businesses that are family concerns is believed to be even higher.

Exercise

Visit the Institute for Family Business website (www.ifb.org.uk). Use the content of the website to identify the main challenges confronting family-owned businesses.

There are a great variety of different types of family firms, as they can range from small lifestyle businesses to large multinational corporations. In between these two extremes there are innumerable different types of family businesses. A characteristic of family businesses is that they can endure for many years, as family members across multiple generations commit to their survival. The UK's oldest family-based business is a Dorest-based butchers shop, R J Balson and Son. Over twenty-five generations of family members have owned and operated this family business since its establishment in 1535!

However, the number of family firms surviving through to the third generation and beyond is small. According to Leach and Bogod (1999) only 24 per cent of family businesses survive to the second generation, while just 14 per cent survive to the generation beyond that. Similarly Smyrnios and Walker (2003) discovered that about 55 and 28 per cent of family businesses in Australia survive to the second and third generations respectively. Data from France shows that the number of family firms surviving to the second generation or beyond never exceeded 35 per cent (Lescure, 1999).

Tip: Family-owned businesses account for approximately two-thirds of all small businesses across developed and developing countries.

Despite the low survival rates beyond the third generation, some family firms go on to become major global companies. The German-based company Bosch is a good example. Robert Bosch established his family company in a small workshop and employed just two people in 1886. Today the company has grown into a multinational company employing approximately 300,000 employees around the world. The Bosch group is one of the world's largest suppliers of automotive components. It also manufactures industrial machinery, hand tools and domestic appliances. The company has sales of over €50 billion and production facilities all over the world. Robert Bosch's values and principles continue to influence the company even today. The Bosch Family still owns 8% of the company.

Another family firm that grew into a global enterprise is Banco Santander. Emilio Botin inherited a minor regional Spanish bank from his father in 1986. Established in 1857 the bank had been owned and managed by two previous generations of the Botin family. Emilio built the small regional bank into Spain's largest banking group, with branches in Chile, Mexico, UK and other European countries. Other examples of family firms growing into multinational companies include Samsung, Porsche, Levi-Strauss, Mars, Wal-Mart Stores and Michelin.

Defining the family business

There are many definitions of the family firm. The definition of family business is important, as researchers like to compare and contrast the performance characteristics and activities of family and non-family businesses. Foundational work carried out by Shanker and Astrachan (1996) developed a criteria for classifying family businesses based on broad, middle, and narrow definitions. The authors' definitions helped to demonstrate the influence family firms had on the US economy, which promoted the importance of family businesses, as being critical entities with unique organizational characteristics. Despite the work of Shanker and Astrachan there is a general consensus amongst researchers that it is impossible to compose a universal definition of family businesses due to the distinctive business laws and regulations that operate in various countries around the world. Nevertheless, it is important that any study investigating family businesses clearly states what they understand by the term. As you can appreciate, differing classifications of family businesses can lead to diverse findings depending on how the sample was selected and defined.

7

Despite the absence of a universal definition, family business research has identified three commonly used dimensions that set family businesses apart from other businesses. These three dimensions help us to better understand how we might generally define a family business. The dimensions are ownership (one or several family members hold a major stake in the company), management (family members hold top management positions), or board-membership (family members hold major control over the company via their board membership). It is important to emphasize that family can include immediate family, extended family (cousins, uncles, aunts), and family by marriage. Subsequent generations of these various elements of the family can be involved in the business as well. If business ownership is shared between and amongst these different parts of a family, then researchers tend to refer to them as a family firm.

> **Tip**: Ownership, management and board-membership are three common dimensions used to understand how a family business is defined.

Global significance

As indicated above, most family firms are small (fewer than 50 employees) and generally wish to maintain a certain level of income that allows them to enjoy a particular lifestyle. In many cases these small, local family firms are handed from one generation to the next, like funeral directors, fishing boats, bakeries, butchers, builders, electricians etc. In contrast, there are many examples of family firms which have moved beyond being a simple lifestyle business and grown into large, powerful multinational corporations that have demonstrated entrepreneurial flair and innovation, like Bosch, Banco Santander (as previously mentioned), Mars, ArcelorMittal, Hyundai Motor, BMW Group, Fiat S.p.A., Samsung Electronics, Tata, Toyota, Volkswagen and Walmart etc.

The Center for Family Business at the University of St. Gallen, Switzerland, complies a Global Family Business Index that contains the largest 500 family firms in the world by revenue (http://familybusinessindex.com). The family businesses contained in the index account for a combined $US6.5 trillion in annual sales. European-based family firms dominated the index with nearly 50 per cent of the index companies based in this region. Behind Europe was North America, which accounted for 24 per cent. The index demonstrates that large family firms generate massive value and constitute a significant economic force in the world.

Characteristics of family firms

Interest in family businesses is based on their unique merits and disadvantages compared to non-family businesses. Certainly when they are compared to a non-family business this uniqueness comes to the fore during their development. For instance, when a business venture is first established reliance on family is common, but this has both benefits and drawbacks. Business advice from experienced family members and low or zero interest rate funding from family members can have a significant benefit for new ventures. On the contrary, family members may attempt to interfere with the running of the business, particularly if they have provided the funding. A number of unique issues can also arise for family businesses, compared to non-family businesses, once they are established and begin growing. The most significant of these issues include the relationships between family members, company culture and succession planning. These issues can be the making or breaking of a family firm. In the next section the negative and positive impact of these three issues will be discussed.

■ Family relationships

According to Kennedy (2000, p.1) "[b]eing part of a family is a universal human experience, at once suffocating, infuriating, comforting and supportive." This statement effectively expresses the benefits and drawbacks of family run businesses. Leach (2007) adds that the complex relationships involved in a family business need to be managed carefully for the benefit of both the family and the firm. Some of these complex relationships can cause conflict, so they need to be carefully managed and monitored.

Exercise

Identify how family relationships might benefit or harm the operations of a business.

Discussed below is how family relationships can affect the management of a family business. First, the hiring and promotion of family members within a family business is often based on blood ties rather than on superior management skills. This phenomenon is called nepotism and can have both negative and positive effects on relationships within family businesses. The danger of placing blood ties before experience and competence is that the link between performance and compensation is lost. However, the biggest danger is that an incompetent family member is promoted to a position from which he or she cannot be dismissed! The promotion of incompetent family members creates mistrust and dissatisfaction amongst non-family employees (Whyte, 1996). The risk of this phenomena is that family firms lose skilled non-family employees who seek career advancement elsewhere, or if they stay, their motivation to perform optimally for the family firm will be reduced due to perceived inequalities. On the other hand, nepotism can have a positive influence on family business performance, as it can enhance communications due to the maintenance of familiar and trusting family relationships (Jaskiewicz *et al.*, 2013). Sometimes to resolve inequalities or conflict family members will deliberately divide the family resources or establish a breakaway firm. An example of the deliberate establishment of a breakaway firm to avoid conflict is the German sportswear companies Puma and Adidas.

7

Case study: Puma and Adidas

Adi and Rudolf Dassler began manufacturing sports shoes together in their mother's washroom in the 1920s. However, during World War II, the brothers' diverging political beliefs caused considerable tension and disagreement between them. As a result of this rift the brothers founded separate businesses on either side of a river in the Bavarian town of Herzogenaurach in southern Germany. When the brothers set up their separate companies in 1948 the town was also split, with residents loyal to one or other of the only major employers. Puma is now largely owned by PPR, the French luxury goods maker. Adidas Group is much more widely owned company, with no individual shareholder having more than 5%.

In general, the success of this solution depends on its timing and the perceived fairness of the split between family members.

Second, if multiple family members are employed in a family firm, the selection of who is, and who is not promoted, within the business can cause problems; for example, female family members may be overlooked in favour of male family members based on traditional sexual stereotyping. As a result, female family members can lose faith in the fairness and equity of the promotion procedures utilized within the family firm and seek job opportunities elsewhere (Dhaliwal, 1998).

Third, contradictions that exist between family demands and the needs of the business can cause relationship conflict. Owners of family businesses often find it difficult to perform the dual roles of being a parent during nonbusiness hours and a manager to family members in business hours. Unfortunately, these conflicting roles for business owners often mean disagreement and conflict between family members. Greenhaus and Beutell (1985) suggest that relationship conflicts arise in family businesses because of the time-pressure difficulties of coping with these dual roles. The decision-making time required for a single role can make it difficult to perform other roles effectively, which can lead to discord and arguments. The authors also suggest that the behaviour required for one role maybe at odds with that required for the other roles. For example, an autocratic approach to decision-making used by the owner within the family would be entirely inappropriate to employ amongst experienced, non-family professional employees working within the family business.

Relationship conflict can also arise because of too much involvement by family members in the day-to-day operations of the firm. Too much involvement increases the probability that one or more family or non-family members will disagree over the firm's goals or activities. It has been suggested by Greenhaus and Beutell (1985) that limiting the decision-making within a family firm to a few select individuals is a key way of reducing conflict.

> **Tip:** Common causes of family business conflict include nepotism, unclear family and nonfamily roles, succession issues, and family ownership and control.

A further common reason for relationship conflict is the delayed succession of the oldest son to replace his father. This can cause bad feelings between father and son, which can affect firm performance. Similarly relationship conflict can occur if the father or founder remains active within the business for some time after the son or daughter has officially taken charge. In addition, Morris *et al.* (1997) states that relationship conflict can often arise when the founding entrepreneur retires or leaves. Founders often know the business best, and the way it should operate, so if they leave it is likely that ambiguity and confusion could occur amongst the remaining family members and professionals employed by the firm, as they try to impose their different views on how it should operate.

Another source of relationship conflict can occur if both a husband and wife are involved in the family firm. Studies suggest that if a husband's involvement is greater than his wife in a business, then there is less tension; but if a husband thinks he is making fewer decisions than his wife then tension increases (Collins, 2012).

Finally, a common source of relationship conflict is from the amount of ownership and control individuals have in a family firm. Family owners / managers are often reluctant to hand too much power to outsiders due to a fear of losing control of the business (Chua *et al.*, 2003). For many family firms, ownership and control may change over time as shareholders and non-family members are hired. Changes in ownership and control can give rise to differences of opinion over a firm's investment options, and its purpose and developmental opportunities, for example. Family ownership may shift from absolute control to a minority holding via the introduction of private or public shareholders. Typically the life cycle of these developments starts with the entrepreneurial owner-manager, who is then succeeded by a new generation after training and experience is obtained. If the family firm continues to grow this usually coincides with changes in its direction, product offerings and the participation of new partners and shareholders. Overall, if these changes are managed successfully the family firm's ownership generally transfers to professional management. Despite diminishing family ownership, it is common that the family name and key individuals are retained because of their importance to shareholders and customers.

7

Exercise

Imagine that you are the owner/manager of a family business, what steps would you take to lessen the potential for family conflict?

■ Company culture

A common justification given for the success of family firms is the existence of a common set of values and principles that guide company performance and behaviour. This common set of values and operating principles often provides family firms with a distinctive company culture, which endows them with certain competitive advantages. Some of these competitive advantages include the existence of a distinctive "sense of future," because there is an expectation that the family firm will be passed on to the next generation. This sense of future means owners generally take a judicious and long-term view of the company and its survival. As a result family firms tend to avoid making drastic or risky changes to the way the firm operates (Kachaner *et al.*, 2012).

Family firms in particular are better prepared to view economic downturns as a temporary phenomenon, as they remain focused on their long-term goals due to this sense of future. Kachaner *et al.* (2012) also state that family firms tend to encourage all employees, whether they are non-family or family members, to view the company's money as family money as well. As a result, family firms tend to have leaner cost structures, which enable them to better survive recessions (Kachaner *et al.*, 2012).

Often the founder's entrepreneurial flair and passion also inspires and motivates other family members and subsequent generations. Certainly past successes and the experience of previous generations can provide family members with a base of knowledge, skills and business contacts that can be invaluable for successfully operating the family business.

Another cultural advantage possessed by family firms is their reputation. When a family firm's reputation improves, so do employee expectations of how they should perform their jobs. The family business literature reports many examples of family businesses that have been successful due to a shared culture and cooperation, long-term vision and established reputation. Paisner (1999) states that a company culture is built by involving family members from an early age in what the business is all about. This involvement starts when children listen to their parents and grandparents discussing business at their dinner table. This early and constant contact means family members develop deep and detailed knowledge of the business, its products, contacts and customers. This accumulated knowledge along with emotional ties to the firm can provide a family business with a significant competitive advantage. It can also provide a clear focus on value and success. Family values can also be extended to non-family members as well. For example, Robert Bosch established such a strong set of values and guiding principles on the importance of innovation, training and development, and social responsibility within the Bosch Company that non-family members have wholeheartedly adopted them.

Despite the benefits and advantages a family company culture can provide, it can also be detrimental too, as discussed previously under family relationships. Family culture can strengthen a business, but it can also be an acrimonious dynamic, and its importance to succession planning is discussed next.

Tip: A distinctive company culture based on strong family values and beliefs is often cited as positively enhancing family business performance.

■ Succession planning

Succession planning is a method for identifying and developing potential candidates to fill important leadership positions within a company. The purpose of succession planning is to increase the availability of experienced and skilled employees that can fill key organizational roles as they become vacant. Succession planning not only affects family firms, but it is also a critical issue for privately owned businesses. Commonly succession is regarded as coming about due to the retirement of the owner or founder of the business. However, there are other reasons for succession occurring such as ill health, death or the early exit of the founder to pursue other interests.

Harvey (2004) reports a number of approaches used by family firms to ensure the transition of ownership between generations. First, the appointment of a single heir, 'the crown prince'. Second, is an approach that creates a 'sibling partnership', where roles are allocated according to the capacities of the family. Third, the 'cousin consortium', where different levels of family involvement happen, some members are active at senior levels, while others are at junior levels and working their way up the company. Other family members may also be inactive shareholders.

The next approach is the 'stop-gap manager', who looks after the management of the company until the next generation is ready. A further approach is the appointment of professional management to run the business, while the family retains ownership and control. This situation arises when no one in the family wants to run the business, or no one is capable enough, so professionals are hired while the family retains ownership. A final approach is a management buyout. This approach involves selling the business to interested professional / non-family members working within the company.

> **Tip**: Succession planning is a method for identifying and developing potential candidates to fill important positions within a company.

Succession planning can be difficult for a number of reasons. First, the next generation of family members can have very different ambitions and attitudes towards the business. Potential heirs in particular may wish to establish themselves in different careers and industries. Studies have discovered that first-generation immigrants typically start ventures in retailing and catering, but subsequent generations often have very different aspirations. As a consequence finding a sibling willing to succeed the founder can be a significant problem. Often immigrant children are not prepared to spend the long hours necessary to run such a business. Indeed it is not unusual for the new generation of family members to have no desire to be involved in the business.

Second, it may not always be the best course of action for the firm to be passed on to the next generation, as the founder originally intended, especially when the heir is less able, unqualified or ill-equipped to run the firm. Certainly professional or non-family staff members can become very dissatisfied and frustrated if they possess the much needed knowledge or skills the firm requires, but are overlooked or ignored in favour of a less competent family member.

Case study: Luxottica

An example of a family business experiencing succession problems is Luxottica, an Italian luxury eyewear company. It is the world's biggest eyewear company. The 79-year-old founder and chairman of the company, Leonardo Del Vecchio, continues to take an active role in the company's management despite officially retiring on several occasions. His refusal to relinquish control and his continuing to micro-manage firm operations has seen the departure of several professional /non-family chief executive officers hired to replace him. The Italian business press has widely criticized the corporate governance of the firm for allowing Mr. Del Vecchio to continue to wield power. The exit of several non-family chief executive officers has been blamed on several other Del Vecchio family members as well; they also desire to have greater family influence on how the company is run. Nicoletta Zampilla, Mr. Del Vecchio's, wife is thought to have increased her influence since departure of the CEOs in particular, which has annoyed many of the firm's non-family executives.

Luxottica is also an example of a family business where the owner, Mr. Del Vecchio, does not want to relinquish control, because he believes that his successors are not good enough to do the job. Mr. Del Vecchio has also taken exception to the desire of his successors to change the vision and direction of the organization.

Third, there are many company examples of sibling rivalry causing problems during the succession process. At the time of writing, Rupert Murdoch the founder, chairman and CEO of global media company News Corporation, the world's second-largest media conglomerate, is planning to 'step down' in the near future. The heirs to his empire are his two sons, who already hold senior positions in his media empire: James, his youngest son holds the CEO title of 21st Century Fox, while the eldest son Lachlan holds the title of co-executive chairman of both News Corporation and 21st Century Fox.

Rumours and media reports suggest that a bitter power struggle is occurring between the two brothers over who will take control of their father's media empire when he retires or dies. Former senior employees of the media empire state that, despite moves establishing James as CEO of 21st Century Fox, Lachlan has reportedly been trying to undermine his authority within the company. Lachlan has informed 21st Century Fox executives that he, rather than

James, is the ultimate decision-maker within the company. Rupert Murdoch has realized that if he doesn't put in place the right succession plan before he leaves, the sons' intense rivalry will cause problems for the company and its survival. Interestingly it appears Rupert Murdoch is not prepared to promote his own daughters: Elisabeth, Lachlan and James's sister from their father's second marriage, as she has not been considered for a senior position; nor has their half-sister, Prudence. The youngest daughters from Rupert Murdoch's third marriage, Grace and Chloe are both too young and outside the voting structure of the family trust that controls the company. The Murdoch family controls almost 40% of the global media group.

Fourth, a high proportion of owners ignore the need for a successor altogether. According to Fleming (2000), some family firms ignore the succession issue because it may unearth underlying family problems and issues that would cause pain and conflict. Fleming goes on to argue that succession issues are also unpleasant to contemplate for the founder / owner, because it forces him or her to face their mortality and losing control of the business. A noteworthy study conducted by Nicholson (2003) discovered that over half of its 150 UK company respondents did not have a succession plan, for either a family member or someone from outside the business, to take over the running of the company. Small firms with less than 50 employees or owner-managed firms without a clear management team are considered to be the most vulnerable to succession failure. Statistics suggest that some 54,000 small firms in the UK were at risk of succession failure.

A particular succession issue arising for daughters is that they can receive contradictory messages from their parents; on the one hand they wish for them to take over the business, while on the other hand they desire grandchildren (Cole, 1997). These conflicting demands are bound to cause tension between the founder and daughter. A further major problem is when the successor does not take full responsibility for making decisions while the founder is still alive, even though he or she has officially exited from the firm. Further issues occur when no natural internal successor exists, so the founder has to continue until an alternative manager can be found or an heir comes of age. When this situation occurs high levels of communication and cooperation are required, so a shared vision can be established for the future of the organization.

Heller (1998) offers some useful practical advice for handling succession within family firms. He states that the use of an experienced mentor to guide the successor is important. He also argues that the successor needs to keep close to the firm's customer base, so he or she understands how the company's products serve their needs. Successful succession in a family business requires the successor to obtain relevant training and experience as well.

Succession planning guides are widely available from government agencies in most developed countries, as they generally have a remit to assist small family firms. For example, the Scottish Government provides access to free business support services via an agency called the 'Business Gateway'. The Business Gateway service operates from offices that resemble retail outlets, and are readily accessible across the whole of Scotland. Research shows that businesses that have used the services provided by the Business Gateway in Scotland have a significantly better chance of surviving more than three years, which is longer than the national average.

Within the UK the Institute for Family Business (http://www.ifb.org.uk) supports and promotes the family-owned business sector through training events, networking, publications and research etc. Available on the Institute's website are a number of publications and guides outlining the succession planning process. These guides typically identify the following issues as being critical:

☐ The time and effort required to produce a succession plan cannot be underestimated;

☐ Owners should plan for succession proactively and early;

☐ Owners should create a written succession plan that includes the involvement of appropriate family and business colleagues;

☐ Owners should make use of external assistance and support offered by government agencies such as Scotland's Business Gateway and establish a training process for the next generation.

The involvement of outside investors makes succession planning particularly important, as they wish to see their investment protected. Investors also want a clear understanding of where the company will go if something happens to the current owner. Like most investors around the world they crave stability and certainty, so the personal qualities of the successor, the way he or she has been chosen, trained and the involvement of the outgoing leader are all very important considerations for them.

Exercise

Search through news media websites like the BBC (www.bbc.co.uk) to discover examples of family businesses experiencing succession issues.

Family business research

Despite the obvious economic importance of family firms (as discussed above) relatively little academic research has been conducted in this area. In stark contrast there has been much written in the popular press (magazines, books and newspapers) about the management and operation of family businesses. For example, the popular press has highlighted family business case studies, profiles of key family members and stories about how founders established their companies etc.

The scarcity of family business research means there are many opportunities for academic researchers to investigate unexplored aspects of their operations and behaviour. Certainly in recent years a burgeoning number of studies using the family firm as a unit of analysis has emerged. Like the popular press, succession is the most widely academically researched area for family businesses. It is a critical area of investigation, because a lack of succession planning is considered to be a primary reason for family business failure (Tatoglu *et al.*, 2008). This area of investigation also includes studies looking at leadership, conflict between generations, succession, the relationship between succession and various dimensions of organizational behaviour. Another popular area of research interest focuses on corporate governance. This line of research describes the rights and responsibilities amongst the various stakeholders within family businesses. Generally this concentrates on how family involvement affects the management of power and control within family businesses. A seminal article in this area of study was prepared by Jensen and Meckling (1976) and describes the best form of government structure for family businesses to utilize. The authors argue that family owners have stronger incentives than minority stakeholders to monitor the performance of managers.

Studies linking organizational theory to family business activity are another major area of investigation. These have utilized a variety of theories to investigate family businesses and their links between various disciplines such as individual and group behaviour, organizational structure and managerial practices. Comparative studies between family and non-family businesses are popular within this area. Another major dimension within family business research is culture. Culture affects succession, governance and other management issues that are unique to family businesses. Some key articles in this area have compared the impact of culture on family and non-family firm performance.

Tip: Some common areas of family business research include performance comparisons between family and non-family business, succession, and family conflict and management governance.

In contrast to these popular areas of investigation, a poorly studied topic has been gender and ethnicity within family businesses. For instance, the involvement of females within a family firm is often hidden or undervalued. Research conducted by Hamilton (2006) counters this notion, as she provides evidence of apparently male owner dominated firms, as perceived by outsiders, actually being controlled by the husbands' wives. Hamilton (2006) demonstrates that firms often deliberately reinforce sexual stereotypes, so they can obtain greater acceptance within their industry and community about who should be in charge. Anecdotal evidence also indicates that many husbands may appear to own a family firm, and hold the title of general manager, but wives who have active roles in the business often have a significant influence on the firm's direction and how it operates.

A consequence of this burgeoning literature has been the emergence of three peer-reviewed journals dedicated specifically to the field of family businesses research. These dedicated journals included the *Family Business Review*, *Journal of Family Business Strategy* and the *Journal of Family Business Management*. According to Smyrnios, Poutziouris and Goel, the field is making great progress and is gradually gaining acceptance amongst academics as a mainstream research topic. Certainly the level of sophistication of family business research has improved; for example, contemporary studies are addressing more complex research questions, these questions are being underpinned by established theory, and the methods of analysis applied are now consistent with other management disciplines, as advanced statistical methods, like structural equation modeling and multivariate analysis, are being commonly employed (Smyrnios *et al.*, 2013). Those interested in family businesses should examine the 'Who to read' list at the end of the chapter to discover additional topics covered in the area of family business research. Investigating family businesses offers a rich area of research possibilities for those interested in the entrepreneurship and small business disciplines.

Conclusions

Family businesses play an important role in the economies of most nations around the world. It has been estimated that family businesses generally constitute between 60 to 70% of all small firms across nations. Some even suggest that this figure is even higher in developing nations. Although many struggle to survive, e.g. it is rare for family-owned businesses to reach a third-generation of ownership and beyond, some do obtain significant growth, influence and power. Some family businesses have grown to become multinational corporations and make a significant economic contribution like BMW, Ford, Samsung, Tata, and Toyota to name a few. If the number of small businesses and multinational corporations that are family-owned were amalgamated, their economic worth to the world and nation states would be considerable.

The significance of family businesses is well understood, but assessing their true dimensions and nature is difficult, because defining and classifying them is still problematic. Many researchers have attempted to define family businesses, but no universal way of undertaking this task exists. A lack of consensus means that researchers use a variety of definitions. Therefore, anyone evaluating studies investigating family businesses needs to carefully scrutinize how they were defined and selected by the researchers involved. While no consensus exists on a single definition for family businesses, researchers generally agree that certain unique dimensions exist that mark them out as being different from non-family businesses, i.e. ownership, management and board-membership.

The key characteristics that distinguish family businesses from non-family businesses concern the influence of family relationships, company culture and succession planning. The influence of family relationships has both positive and negative dimensions for family businesses. A positive dimension is the enhancement of communications and high levels of trust because of close family ties. However, a negative aspect of family relationships can be nepotism. Nepotism can occur through the promotion of family members over non-family members who have greater experience and qualifications for the position they are given. This can give rise to dissatisfaction in the workforce and the loss of very able members of staff.

Another important characteristic of family businesses is their company culture. The culture of the family firm often leads to the development of superior teamwork, a common vision and greater resilience than nonfamily businesses. The culture of the family firm is created by the collective involvement of family members and their common goals and vision. A common vision is important to all firms, but has more impact within the family firm because of family relationships and ties.

The last key characteristic is succession. Succession for family firms is critical for ensuring a family firm's long-term success. Early planning is important and it is vital that all shareholders are involved. Formal training is also a critical ingredient for executing the plan, particularly if the heir is inexperienced. While succession can arise through death or retirement, there may be other reasons, such as ill health or the founding entrepreneur wishing to move on to new opportunities. Succession can lead to considerable relationship conflict. It is sometimes the case that the founder will allow a family member to take control regardless of their suitability or competence. This can create dissatisfaction amongst both competing family and non-family members.

Finally, family business research is an underdeveloped area of academic research. This is surprising given their economic significance. However, since the 2000s there has been a marked increase in the volume of family business research being undertaken. Favourite areas of academic research mirror the unique characteristics identified in this chapter, i.e. the influence of family relationships, company culture and succession planning. An important gap within the academic literature is the limited number of studies examining gender and ethnicity issues.

Who to read

Some of the notable authors in family business research include Pramodita Sharma, W. Gibb Dyer and Joseph H. Astrachan. Pramodita Sharma, alongside various colleagues such as James J. Chrisman and Jess H. Chua, has produced widely-cited family business research exploring issues such as succession and strategic management in family businesses. She has also produced a widely-cited family business research review. Another well-cited author conducting family business research is W. Gibb Dyer. Professor Dyer is a recognized authority on family business and entrepreneurship. Finally, Joseph H. Astrachan is a prolific family business researcher. He has written about various aspects of family businesses such as their economic contribution, succession planning, human resource practices etc.

References

Chua, J. H., Chrisman, J. J. & Sharma, P. (2003). Succession and nonsuccession concerns of family firms and agency relationship with non-family managers. *Family Business Review*, **16**(2), 89–107.

Cole, P. M. (1997). Women in Family Business. *Family Business Review*, 10(4), 353–371.

Collins, L. (2012). The family business. In L. Collins, L. Grisoni, C. Seaman, S. Graham, D. Otten, R. Fakoussa & J. Tucker (Eds.) *The Modern Family Business: Relationships, Succession and Transition*, (pp. 3-44), Basingstoke: Palgrave Macmillan.

Dhaliwal, S. (1998). Silent contributors: Asian female entrepreneurs and women in business. *Women's Studies International Forum*, **21**, 463–474.

Fleming, Q.J. (2000). *Keep the Family Baggage out of the Family Business*, New York: Simon & Schuster.

Greenhaus, J. H. and Beutell, N. J. (1985). Sources of conflict between work and family roles. *The Academy of Management Review*, **10**(1), 76–88.

Hamilton, E.E. (2006). Whose story is it anyway? Narrative accounts of the role of women in founding and establishing family businesses, *International Small Business Journal*, **24**(3), 253-271.

Harvey, D. (2004). *Keeping it in the Family*, London: ACCA.

Heller, R. (1998). *Goldfinger: How entrepreneurs grow rich by starting small*. London: Harper-Collins Business.

Institute For Family Business. (n.d.). *Media*. Retrieved from http://www.ifb.org.uk/media/44219/theukfamilybusinesssectorreportnov2011_final.pdf

Jaskiewicz, P., Uhlenbruck, Klaus, Balkin, D.B. & Reay, T. (2013). Is nepotism good or bad? Types of nepotism and implications for knowledge management. *Family Business Review,* **26**(2), 121-139.

Jensen, M., & Meckling, W. (1976). Theory of the firm: managerial behavior. Agency costs and ownership structure. *Journal of Financial Economics*, **3**(4), 305–360.

Kachaner, N., Stalk, G. & Bloch, A. (2012). What you can learn from family-run companies, *Harvard Business Review*, **90**(11), 102-106.

Kennedy, C. (2000). *The Merchant Princes*, London: Hutchinson.

Leach, P. (2007). *Family Businesses*, London: Profile Books.

Leach, P. & Bogod, T. (1999). *The BDO Stoy Hayward Guide to the Family Business*, (3rd. ed.), London: Kogan Page.

Lescure, M. (1999). Small and medium industrial enterprises in France 1900-1975. In K. Odaka amd M. Sawai (Eds.), *Small Firms, Large Concerns*, (pp. 140–167), Oxford: Oxford University Press.

Morris, M. H., Williams, R. W., Allen, J. A. & Avila, R. A. (1997). Correlates of success in family business transitions. *Journal of Business Venturing*, 12(5), 385–401.

Nicholson, N. (2003). *Leadership in Family Business*, London: London Business School.

Paisner, M.B. (1999). *Sustaining the family business*, New York: Basic Books.

Shanker, M. C., & Astrachan, J. H. (1996). Myths and realities: family businesses' contribution to the US economy: a framework for assessing family business statistics. *Family Business Review*, 9(2), 107–123.

Smyrnios, K.X, Poutziouris, P.Z. & Goel, S. (2013). Introduction: Trends and developments in family business research. In K. Smyrnios, P.Z. Poutziouris and S. Goel (Eds.), *Handbook of Research on Family Business*, (pp. 1-13), Cheltenham: Edward Elgar Publishing Limited.

Smyrnios, K.X. & Walker, R.H. (2003). *The Boyd Partners Australian Family and Private Business Survey*, Melbourne: RMIT University.

Tatoglu, E., Kula, V., & Glaister, K. W. (2008). Succession planning in family-owned businesses: Evidence from Turkey. *International Small Business Journal*, **26**(2), 155–180.

Whyte, M. K. (1996). The Chinese family and economic development: Obstacle or engine? *Economic Development and Cultural Change*, **44**, 1–30.

7

8 Entrepreneurial Leadership

UmmeSalma Mujtaba

The study of leadership has certainly come a long way since Thomas Carlyle wrote about heroes and hero worship in 1841 (Bryman, 2011). From the organizational perspective, the most significant role of a leader is to influence and provide direction to their followers and provide them with the much needed support for its success (Wood, 2009). Conversely, an ineffective leader does the adverse and can, in fact, detract from organizational goal accomplishment. Leadership has been defined from various viewpoints and each definition allows exploring the concept from a wider and diverse angle. Furthermore, over time, scholars have proposed many different styles of leadership, interestingly; yet, there is no particular style of leadership that can be considered universal. This chapter concentrates on leadership styles and theories and begins by defining leadership. It also incorporates entrepreneurial leadership (EL) as EL exists at the intersection of entrepreneurship and leadership; we take a look at the leading scholar Gupta's definition of EL (Gupta *et al.* 2004).

Leadership – a definition

According to Stogdill (1948), there are nearly as many definitions given to leadership as there have been researchers who have written about the concept. Conger (1992: p. 18) defines leadership as "individuals who establish direction for a working group of individuals who gain commitment from this group of members to this direction and who then motivate these members to achieve the direction's outcomes". Essentially Conger's definition involves the following:

1 The individuality of leaders.

2 Their focus in providing direction.

3 The presence of a group; that is, leadership operates in groups.

4 The involvement of the followers via commitment (the degree of commitment can differ).

5   Leadership is about influencing through motivation.

6   Leadership includes the achievement of goals, which leaders and follows share.

As such, to ensure that one understands leadership, it needs to be said that leaders are not better than followers, nor are they above followers. On the contrary, leaders and followers are intertwined in a way that requires them to be understood in their relationship with each other and as a collective body of two or more people (Burns, 1978; Hollander, 1992; Dubrin, 2007).

The key writers on the subject 'leadership' among many have been Stogdill, Bass, Burns, Hersey and Blanchard and the more recent ones, Schyns and Northouse.

Leadership styles

A leadership style is the manner and approach of providing direction for a team, implementing plans and motivating people to complete a task. There are several different leadership styles, each with advantages and disadvantages.

Lewin (1939) led a group of researchers to identify different styles of leadership. In the study, groups of school children were allocated into three different groups with three diverse types of leaders: authoritarian, democratic and a laissez-faire. The children's behaviour was recorded in response to the different styles of leadership in an arts and crafts project. This early study has been very influential and established three major leadership styles.

■ Autocratic leadership style

In an autocratic leadership style, staff and team members have little opportunity to provide their input suggestions, and leaders have complete power over their staff. In terms of disadvantages, most staff members resent being dealt with in this way, therefore it is deemed that autocratic leadership is often best used in situations of crisis. Autocratic leadership is often used synonymously with a directive style of leadership; Tepper (2000) uses 'abusive supervision' and Einarsen, Aasland and Skogstad (2007) have used 'tyrannical leadership' to describe the 'autocratic'.

Generally, the autocratic leadership style is not considered to be the most suitable way to get the best response from a team, but it has distinct advantages in situations where there is great urgency and pressure to achieve, such as the armed forces. Autocratic leaders tend to be the sole decision makers for their group (Van Vugta et al., 2004).

An autocratic leader: Howell Raines, of the New York Times

The New York Times had a lot of autocratic leaders like Howell Raines and Abraham Rosenthal. Howell Raines, executive editor, is an example of a very efficient autocratic leader, as the newspaper industry is highly demanding, with a lot of associated pressures and requiring quick decision-making. The newspaper industry requires different forms of autocratic leadership styles to meet the deadlines, day after day. Nevertheless, Raines was dismissed after almost two years in the job, because his leadership style caused distress amongst the journalists and quality declined.

Source: Adapted from Kellerman (2004).

Appropriate conditions when an autocratic leadership style is best suited:

☐ When decisions need to be made quickly and do not necessarily require the team's input.

☐ You are working to a tight deadline.

☐ The team is well motivated and used to working for an authoritarian leader.

Benefits of autocratic leadership

☐ Quick decision making

☐ Streamlined work process

☐ Absolute control

☐ Close supervision

☐ Maintains order and discipline

8

Exercise

In small groups, discuss the disadvantages of autocratic leadership.

■ Democratic leadership style

The term 'democratic leadership' has been replaced by 'participative leadership' (Yukl, 2000). Participative leadership is the degree to which a leader shares the influence on decision making with his followers in a workgroup (Somech, 2003). Democratic leaders make the final decisions, but they include team members in the decision-making process. They encourage creativity, and people are often highly engaged in projects and decisions. This is not always an effective style to use, though, when you need to make a quick decision.

Democratic leadership cultivates a sense of responsibility in team members who feel that they have an entrusted concern in the success of the operation. It also allows a leader to draw upon the knowledge and capabilities of the team in order to achieve the best and to develop the skills of individuals in the team. Hoch (2013) notes that participative leadership will foster shared leadership development in teams. Democratic leadership style was the commonest style of leadership used by principals of senior secondary schools in Nigeria (Adeyemi, 2010). The study found a significant relationship between principals' democratic leadership style and students' academic performance suggesting that the more democratic a principal is in his or her leadership style the better the academic performance of students in the schools.

Drawbacks of democratic leadership

☐ A time-consuming approach

☐ Not be the most cost effective way of organizing a service.

☐ Team members need to be carefully selected

Exercise: Local city council and leadership

Your local city council has reported an increase in youth crime. Chris is the Senior Community Police Officer involved who has taken on the initiative to reduce the amount of youth crime occurring. The first step on the action plan is to call a meeting to deliberate upon the situation. The agenda is to discuss the current preventative action and subsequently produce an effective plan to better the service.

The meeting invitation has been sent to the youth action groups, the Probation Service, local business owners and social services. After reviewing his preparation notes for the meeting, Chris has decided to take on a democratic approach to the meeting rather than using another style.

1 Do you think Chris has made the right choice; if so, why?

2 What are the main drawbacks of using this style and how could this affect the project as a whole?

■ Laissez-faire leadership style

First described by Lewin, Lippitt and White in 1938, the laissez faire leadership style is sometimes described as a 'hands off' leadership style because the leader provides little or no direction to their followers. This style allows complete freedom to the group to make decisions without the leader's participation. Thus, subordinates are free to do what they like. Piccolo *et al.,* (2012) note that laissez-faire is the avoidance or absence of leadership, indicating leaders who avoid making decisions hesitate in taking action, and are absent when needed.

In this style the leaders normally do not want to impose their interference in decision making processes. Subordinates are free to work in their own way and they are also responsible for their decisions. This style varies from the autocratic and participative style of leadership, in that the leader exercises very little control over the subordinates and allows them to establish their own roles and responsibilities.

Appropriate conditions when laissez-faire leadership style is best suited:

☐ When a group of followers are highly motivated.

☐ When a group of followers are experienced.

☐ When a group of followers are well trained.

☐ When a leader can trust the groups to complete tasks without control.

Exercise

Suggest different situations where a laissez-faire leadership style is not suitable.

Benefits of laissez-faire leadership style

☐ Instills high sense of responsibility in team

☐ Boosts the commitment of team members

☐ Bring out the best in members, encouraging greater innovation and out-of-the-box initiatives.

Following from the three styles discussed above, the 'situational leadership style' offers a new dimension.

■ Situational leadership style

The fundamental underpinning of the situational leadership theory is that there is no single 'best' style of leadership. This addresses the common criticism of leadership styles that 'one-size-fits-all', which ignores possible variety, or gender, race and other aspects of cultural diversity (Western, 2008). Effective leadership varies, not only with the person or group that is being influenced, but it also depends on the task, job or function that needs to be accomplished. Theories related to situational leadership are addressed later (p. 142 ff.).

Exercise

Discuss the factors that determine the right leadership style. The aim of the exercise is that participants engage in a discussion on 'right' leadership. This would help them understand that 'right' leadership centers on various parameters.

Hint: Ibara (2010, pp. 74-76) outlines a number of factors that help define which type of leadership style is most in effect and/or when to draw on a different or a combination of leadership styles.

- Size of the organization.
- Degree of communication.
- Members' personalities.
- Goal congruency.
- Level of decision making.

Theories of leadership

A *leadership theory* is an explanation of some aspect of leadership; theories have practical value because they are used to better understand, predict, and control successful leadership. Over time, a number of theories of leadership have been proposed.

■ Great Man and trait theory

The Great Man theory evolved around the mid-19th century. This approach is essentially the 'great person' theory of leadership, and takes a tactic which tries to identify the noteworthy features of recognized leaders. Early approaches to the study of leadership (mostly undertaken before and shortly after the Second World War) dwelt on the personal qualities and characteristics of successful leaders in an attempt to isolate the 'magic ingredients of a leader'. The theory focused on identifying the innate qualities and characteristics possessed by great social, political, and military leaders.

Examples of 'Great Man' leaders.

- ☐ Catherine the Great.
- ☐ Mohandas Gandhi.
- ☐ Indira Gandhi.
- ☐ Abraham Lincoln.
- ☐ Joan of Arc
- ☐ Napoleon Bonaparte.

■ Trait theory

Bearing similarity to 'Great Man' theories, the trait theory posits that traits of leadership are intrinsic, implying that leaders are born and not made. The traits theory researchers looked for evidence of mysterious qualities and believed they were frequently passed between generations (Klingborg *et al.*, 2006). Their focus was to identify specific personal qualities that qualify an individual for leadership. This involved observing leaders and analyzing personality traits that made them successful. Not surprisingly, the number of traits identified was roughly equal to the number of studies undertaken (Bolden *et al.*, 2003; Winston & Patterson, 2006).

After several years of such research, it became apparent that no consistent traits could be identified. Although some traits were found in a considerable number of studies, the results were generally inconclusive. Some leaders might have possessed certain traits but the absence of them did not necessarily mean that the person was not a leader. Table 8.1 highlights the different traits applied by Stogdill (1974).

Traits	Skills
- Adaptable to situations	- Clever (intelligent)
- Alert to social environment	- Conceptually skilled
- Ambitious and achievement-orientated	- Creative
- Assertive	- Diplomatic and tactful
- Cooperative	- Fluent in speaking
- Decisive	- Knowledgeable about group task
- Dependable	- Organized – good administrative ability
- Dominant (desire to influence others)	- Persuasive
- Energetic (high activity level)	- Socially skilled
- Persistent	
- Self-confident	
- Tolerant of stress	
- Willing to assume responsibility	

Table 8.1: Traits and skills, by Stogdill
Source: Stogdill, (1974, p. 81).

■ Leadership instrument

Recent research has extensively demonstrated that traits matter, as do 'deep' determinants going back to genes (Arvey *et al.*, 2006; Arvey *et al.*, 2007). In many organizations, it is common practice to use standard personality measures such as the Minnesota Multiphasic Personality Inventory or the Myers-Briggs Type Indicator®. These measures are said to provide valuable information to the individual and the organization about the individual's unique attributes for leadership and where the individual could best serve the organization.

The Leadership Trait Questionnaire (LTQ) is provided as an example of a measure that can be used to assess your personal leadership characteristics. The LTQ quantifies the perceptions of the individual leader and selected observers, such as subordinates or peers. It measures an individual's traits and points the individual to the areas in which that individual may have special strengths or weaknesses. By taking the LTQ, you can gain an understanding of how trait measures are used for leadership assessment. You can also assess your own leadership traits.

The leadership trait questionnaire (LTQ)

Instructions: The purpose of this questionnaire is to measure personal characteristics of leadership. The questionnaire should be completed by the leader and five people who are familiar with the leader. Make five copies of this questionnaire.

This questionnaire should be completed by you and five people you know (e.g., room-mates, coworkers, relatives, friends).

Using the following scale, have each individual indicate the degree to which they agree or disagree with each of the 14 statements below. Do not forget to complete one for yourself.

_____ (*leader's name*) **is**

Key: 1= Strongly 2= Disagree 3= Neutral 4= Agree 5= Strongly agree

1. Articulate: Communicates effectively with others	1 2 3 4 5
2. Perceptive: Is discerning and insightful	1 2 3 4 5
3. Self-confident: Believes in himself/herself and his/her ability	1 2 3 4 5
4. Self-assured: Is secure with self, free of doubts	1 2 3 4 5
5. Persistent: Stays fixed on the goals, despite interference	1 2 3 4 5
6. Determined: Takes a firm stand, acts with certainty	1 2 3 4 5
7. Trustworthy: Is authentic and inspires confidence	1 2 3 4 5
8. Dependable: Is consistent and reliable	1 2 3 4 5
9. Friendly: Shows kindness and warmth	1 2 3 4 5
10. Outgoing: Talks freely, gets along well with others	1 2 3 4 5
11. Conscientious: Is thorough, organized, and controlled	1 2 3 4 5
12. Diligent: Is persistent, hard working	1 2 3 4 5
13. Sensitive: Shows tolerance, is tactful, and sympathetic	1 2 3 4 5
14. Empathic: Understands others, identifies with others	1 2 3 4 5

Scoring

1 Enter the responses for Raters 1, 2, 3, 4, and 5 in the appropriate columns as shown below. The example has hypothetical ratings to help show how the questionnaire can be used.

2 For each item, compute the average of the five raters and write that in the *Average* column.

3 Place your own scores in the *Self-rating* column.

Example 2.1: Leadership traits questionnaire ratings

	Rater 1	Rater 2	Rater 3	Rater 4	Rater 5	Average	Self-rating
1. Articulate	4	4	3	2	4	3.4	4
2. Perceptive	2	5	3	4	4	3.6	5
3. Self-confident	4	4	5	5	4	4.4	4
4. Self-assured	5	5	5	5	5	5	5
5. Persistent	4	4	3	3	3	3.4	3
6. Determined	4	4	4	4	4	4	4
7. Trustworthy	5	5	5	5	5	5	5
8. Dependable	4	5	4	5	4	4.4	4
9. Friendly	5	5	5	5	5	5	5
10. Outgoing	5	4	5	4	5	4.6	4
11. Conscientious	2	3	2	3	3	2.6	4
12. Diligent	3	3	3	3	3	3	4
13. Sensitive	4	4	5	5	5	4.6	3
14. Empathic	5	5	4	5	4	4.6	3

Trait studies attempted to find the 'great man' who had the natural characteristics necessary to be a good leader: the focus was on selection. Critiques of the leader trait paradigm (Jenkins, 1947; Stogdill, 1948) prompted scholars to look beyond leader traits and consider how leaders' behaviours predicted effectiveness. One flaw with the earlier line of thought was in ignoring the situational and environmental factors that play a role in a leader's level of effectiveness (Horner, 1997). By the late 1940s, leadership studies began to look at what leaders do, rather than at their personalities.

Behavioural theory

From the perspective of leadership theories, there is a shift in focus to: "leaders can be made, rather than are born". Researchers studying the behavioural approach determined that leadership is composed of two kinds of behaviours:

☐ **Task behaviours**: The task leader is a leader who is concerned with accomplishing a task by organizing others, planning strategy, and dividing labour. Task behaviours facilitate goal accomplishments.

☐ **Relationship behaviours**: The relationship leader is a leader who is concerned with reducing tension, patching up disagreements, settling arguments, and maintaining morale. Both of these functions are important leadership roles. Thus, in general, leaders must be concerned with both the social-emotional and task functions.

The central purpose of the behavioural approach is to explain how leaders combine these two kinds of behaviours to influence followers in their efforts to reach a goal. To investigate this many studies were conducted. Leading studies under the heading have been:

☐ The Ohio State studies.

☐ The Michigan studies

☐ Blake and Mouton's (1964) Managerial G rid.

The Ohio State studies

Studies were conducted at Ohio State University in the late 1940s, based on the findings of Stogdill's (1948) work. A series of studies at the University indicated that two clusters of behaviours had an important role in successful leadership. Those dimensions are 'initiating structure' and 'consideration':

Initiating structure refers to the extent to which a leader is likely to define and structure their own role as well as the roles of subordinates in the search for goal attainment. It includes behaviour that attempts to organize work, work relationships and goals. The leader characterized as high in initiating structure specifies the task to be performed by each member of his group, sets down deadlines, gives directions and puts pressure on them for its fulfillment.

Consideration refers to the extent to which a leader is likely to have job relationships which are characterized by mutual trust, respect for subordinates' ideas and regard for their feelings. S/he shows concern for her/ his followers' comfort, well-being, status and satisfaction.

Initiating structure behaviours were essentially task behaviours and consideration behaviours were relationship behaviours. The Ohio State University studies viewed these two behaviours as distinct and independent. The Ohio State Studies suggested that the 'high-high' leadership style (high in initiating structure as well as in consideration) generally results in positive outcomes but there are exceptions which indicate that situational factors should be integrated into the theory.

		Low	High
Consideration	**High**	**Low structure, high consideration.** Less emphasis is placed on structuring employee tasks while the leader concentrates on satisfying employee needs and wants	**High structure, high consideration.** The leader provides a lot of guidance about how tasks can be completed while being highly considerate of employee needs and wants
	Low	**Low structure, low consideration.** The leader fails to provide necessary structure and demonstrates little consideration of employee needs and wants	**High structure, low consideration.** Primary emphasis is placed on structuring employee tasks while the leader demonstrates little consideration of employee needs and wants

Low   High

Initiating structure

Initiating structure - (organizing work, organizing and defining relationships or roles, establishing well-defined patterns of organization, channels of communication, and ways of completing jobs).

Consideration - (building friendship, mutual trust, respect and camaraderie).

Figure 8.1: Ohio State Leadership Styles
Source: Northouse (2007, p.70-71).

The Michigan studies

The focus of the Michigan studies was to determine the principles and methods of leadership that led to productivity and job satisfaction. Two types of leadership behaviours were identified:

☐ **Employee orientation** – stress on the human-relations aspect, employees are viewed as human beings with personal needs.

☐ **Production orientation** – stress on the technical and production aspects of the job, employees viewed as the means of completing tasks.

Leaders with an employee orientation showed genuine concern for interpersonal relations. Those with a production orientation focused on the task or technical aspects of the job.

To locate behavioral characteristics of leaders that appeared related to performance effectiveness.

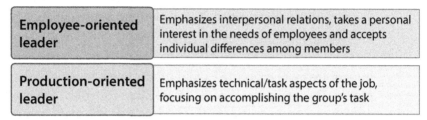

Employee-oriented leader	Emphasizes interpersonal relations, takes a personal interest in the needs of employees and accepts individual differences among members
Production-oriented leader	Emphasizes technical/task aspects of the job, focusing on accomplishing the group's task

Figure 8.2: University of Michigan Studies
Source: Adapted from Ian and Cooper (2015, p. 107).

The treatment of task orientation and people orientation as two independent dimensions was a major step in leadership studies. Building on the work of the researchers at these Universities, Robert Blake and Jane Mouton in the 1960s proposed a graphic portrayal of leadership styles through a Managerial Grid (sometimes called the Leadership Grid).

Blake and Mouton's (1964) Managerial Grid

The Managerial Grid focuses on task (production) and employee (people) orientations of managers, as well as combinations of concerns between the two extremes: a grid with concern for production on the horizontal axis and concern for people on the vertical axis, and plots five basic leadership styles (Figure 8.3).

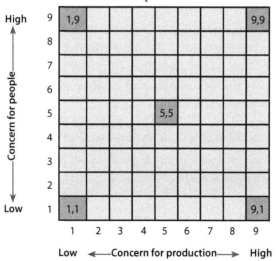

Figure 8.3: Blake and Mouton's (1964) Managerial Grid
Source: Robbins, Odendaal and Roodt (2011, p. 244).

The five resulting leadership styles are as follows:

☐ **Impoverished management** (1, 1): Managers with this approach are low on both dimensions and exercise minimum effort to get the work done from subordinates. The leader has low concern for employee satisfaction and work deadlines and as a result disharmony and disorganization prevail within the organization. The leaders are termed ineffective wherein their action is merely aimed at preserving job and seniority.

☐ **Task management** (9, 1): Also called dictatorial or perish style. Here leaders are more concerned about production and have less concern for people. The employees' needs are not taken care of and they are simply a means to an end. The leader believes that efficiency can result only through proper organization of work systems and through elimination of people wherever possible. Such a style can definitely increase the output of organization in the short run but, due to the strict policies and procedures, high labour turnover is inevitable.

☐ **Middle-of-the-road** (5, 5): This is basically a compromising style wherein the leader tries to maintain a balance between goals of the company and the needs of people. The leader does not push the boundaries of achievement resulting in average performance for organization. Here neither employee nor production needs are fully met.

☐ **Country club** (1, 9): This is a collegial style characterized by low task and high people orientation where the leader gives thoughtful attention to the needs of people thus providing them with a friendly and comfortable environment. The leader feels that such a treatment with employees will lead to self- production and lead to questionable results.

☐ **Team management** (9, 9): Characterized by high people and task focus, and has been termed as the most effective style according to Blake and Mouton. The leader feels that empowerment, commitment, trust, and respect are the key elements in creating a team atmosphere which will automatically result in high employee satisfaction and production.

Exercise: Applying the Blake Mouton Managerial Grid

Discuss a few leadership positions in your degree/job and place the leaders on the grid according to where you believe they fit.

■ Situational or Contingency Theory

Situational or Contingency Theory is a class of behavioral theory that claims that there is no best way to organize a corporation, to lead a company, or to make decisions. Instead, the optimal course of action is contingent (dependent) upon the internal and external situation. A contingent leader effectively applies their own style of leadership to the right situation.

The Hersey-Blanchard (1969) situational leadership model suggests that successful leaders adjust their styles as follows:

1 **Telling** (high task/low relationship): the leader defines roles and routines and tells followers what, how, when, and where to do (directive behavior)

2 **Selling** (high task/high relationship): the leader provides both directive and supportive behaviour

3 **Participating** (low task/high relationship): shared decision making with followers, focuses on facilitation and communication

4 **Delegating** (low task/low relationship): little direction and support.

Tip

- Telling – Leaders tell their people what to do and how to do it.

- Selling – Leaders provide information and direction, but there's more communication with followers. Leaders 'sell' their message to get people on board.

- Participating – Leaders focus more on the relationship and less on direction. The leader works with the team, and shares decision-making responsibilities.

- Delegating – Leaders pass most of the responsibility onto the followers or group. The leaders still monitor progress, but they're less involved in decisions

---

Leaders and Followers: The models discussed so far have deliberated on the leader as someone who stands out from the rest in 'leading' the people. The discussion now moves to recognition of the prominence of the leader's' relationship with his/her followers and an interdependency of roles.

Transactional leadership

Transactional leadership styles are more concerned with maintaining the normal flow of operations. Transactional leadership can be described as 'keeping the ship afloat'. Transactional leaders use disciplinary power and an array of incentives to motivate employees to perform at their best. The term 'transactional' refers to the fact that this type of leader essentially motivates subordinates by exchanging rewards for performance. Bass *et al.* (2003) emphasized that transactional leadership can build a base level of trust in the leader as he/she clarifies expectations and rewards and reliably executes what has been agreed. However there are recent studies, such as Moriano *et al.*, (2014), who discuss the negative influence of transactional leadership on employees' intrapreneurial behaviour.

A transactional leader generally does not look ahead in strategically guiding an organization to a position of market leadership; instead, these managers are solely concerned with making sure everything flows smoothly today.

Transformational leadership

The second form of leadership is transformational leadership, which serves to change the status quo by appealing to followers' values and their sense of higher purpose. A transformational leader goes beyond managing day-to-day operations and crafts strategies for taking his company, department or work team to the next level of performance and success. Transformational leadership is associated with enhanced effectiveness of employees and their leader (Spreitzer 2007; Nemanich and Keller 2007). Transformational leadership styles focus on team-building, motivation and collaboration with employees at different levels of an organization to accomplish change for the better. Transformational leaders set goals and incentives to push their subordinates to higher performance levels, while providing opportunities for personal and professional growth for each employee. Braun *et al.* (2013) note that transformational leadership was positively related to followers' job satisfaction at individual as well as team levels of analysis and to objective team performance. Noruzy *et al.*, (2013) also link the positive influence of transformational leadership to organizational innovation and organizational performance of manufacturing firms.

Even though transformational leadership is important for successfully guiding employees, at the same time it can draw too much attention to a leader's vision and lead to the potentially valuable perspectives of their followers being ignored (Poel *et al.*, 2010).

Exercise

In groups discuss: among all the positives, Ashford *et al.* (2003)'s study notes that the visionary and charismatic characteristics of transformational leaders may leave little room for employees to have their own ideas, reflect upon and criticize their ways of working.

Case study: Transformational leader – Nelson Mandela

South Africa was ruled by a white minority government for much of the past 200 years. Although blacks made up over 75% of the populace, whites owned most of the property, ran most of the businesses, and controlled virtually all of the country's resources.

Moreover, blacks did not have the right to vote and often worked under horrible conditions for little or no wages. Seeing the frustration of his people, Nelson Mandela spent 50 years working to overturn white-minority rule. He started by organizing the African National Congress, a nonviolent organization that protested white rule through work stoppages, strikes, and riots. Several whites were killed in the early riots, and in 1960 the police killed or injured over 250 blacks in Sharpeville. Unrest over the Sharpeville incident caused 95% of the black workforce to go on strike for two weeks, and the country declared a state of emergency. Mandela then orchestrated acts of sabotage to further pressure the South African government to change. The organization targeted installations and took special care to ensure no lives were lost in the bombing campaign. Mandela was arrested in 1962 and spent the next 27 years in prison. While in prison he continued to promote civil unrest and majority rule, and his cause eventually gained international recognition. He was offered but turned down a conditional release from prison in 1985. After enormous international and internal pressure, South African President F. W. de Klerk 'unbanned' the ANC and unconditionally released Nelson Mandela from prison. Nonetheless, South Africa remained in turmoil, and in 1992 four million workers went on strike to protest white rule. Because of this pressure, Mandela forced de Klerk to sign a document outlining multiparty elections. Mandela won the 1994 national election and was the first truly democratically elected leader of the country.

Source: Higher than Hope: The Authorized Biography of Nelson Mandela (1990).

Different researchers lay down that both transactional and transformational leadership styles are related to leader effectiveness, with the best leaders demonstrating both transactional and transformational behaviors (Avolio, 1999; Bass, 1985; Judge and Piccolo, 2004).

Exercise

Is a football coach striving for his team to win the league, a transactional or a transformational leader?

8

What is entrepreneurial leadership?

Entrepreneurial leadership literature came into existence when researchers have tried to combine two concepts (entrepreneurship and leadership) into one concept. Let's consider the definition of entrepreneurship: it is the pursuit of opportunity beyond the resources one currently controls (Stevenson and Gumpert, 1985). Kuratko (2002) notes that it is none other than the passion and drive of entrepreneurs that moves the world of business forward as they challenge the unknown and continuously create the future.

Case study: Entrepreneurial leader - John Peters

John Peters, now the CEO of broadband service provider Sigma Networks, embodies himself as a 'serial entrepreneur'. He says, "I just thrive on the uncertainty, the challenge and the creativity of starting a company. I like the blank piece of paper." His way of working around start-ups is to spend about 4 years with each initiative. Peters, surely fits in to the definition of an entrepreneur as he yearns for new beginnings and thrives on risk.

Source: KNOWLEDGE@WHARTON. (2011)

Interestingly, studies today show these characteristics must not only be limited to entrepreneurs, i.e. entrepreneurs aren't the only ones who should be able to clinch the opportunity of that 'blank piece of paper'. Management professor at Fordham, Vipin Gupta, and Ian C. MacMillan, director of Wharton's Sol C. Snider Entrepreneurial Center, use a term coined by MacMillan – 'entrepreneurial leader' – to summarize the style, they believe today's managers must nurture. Let us understand who is an entrepreneurial leader.

Since entrepreneurial leadership (EL) exists at the intersection of entrepreneurship and leadership, it would be important here to look at some definitions of EL. Here we take a look at the leading scholar Gupta's definition of EL. Entrepreneurial leadership has been defined as a form of leadership behaviour distinctive from other types of leadership behaviours that are required for highly turbulent, challenging and competitive environments (Gupta *et al.* 2004).

This is a leader who can operate in a world that is highly volatile and in which competitive action unstoppably and speedily erodes whatever advantage the firm develops and aims to enjoy. In other words, in this turbulent environment and competitiveness across industries, firms do not have the luxury of relaxing, once a competitive advantage is established. The role of an entrepreneurial leader in such an environment is that, instead of attempting to develop in-depth strategies based on precise forecasts (that may be ineffective in the face of increasing uncertainty) which lead to sustainable advantage (that may be short-lived in the face of increasing rivalry), the entrepreneurial leader forges an organizational unit that is persistently repositioning itself to capture opportunities.

Many theorists study the common qualities between entrepreneurs and leaders (Gupta, MacMillan and Surie, 2004; Fernald *et al.*, 2005; Renko *et al.*, 2015). Fernald *et al.* (2005) adapt this approach, investigating the separate literatures of entrepreneurship and leadership, from which they derive a set of similar characteristics common to both leaders and entrepreneurs: vision, problem-solving, decision-making, risk-taking and strategic initiatives.

Parallels between the two disciplines are evident, leading some scholars to also look at the behavioural similarities in both entrepreneurs and leaders and identify most of the entrepreneurs' behaviours as leadership behaviours. Some have even defined entrepreneurship as a type of leadership, arguing that entrepreneurship is merely leadership in a special context. From our previous knowledge of types of leadership, let us look at entrepreneurial leadership and transformational leadership, and discuss the similarity.

Transformational leaders demonstrate some features and behaviours that also characterize entrepreneurial leaders. Recall that: transformational leaders go beyond managing day-to-day operations and craft strategies for taking their organization, department or work team to the next level of performance and success; this sounds part of an EL's way of working.

Exercise

Take an example of a local transformational leader (a union president or head of the department) and discuss the similarities between transformational and entrepreneurial leaders.

■ Entrepreneurs and leaders: how do they view themselves?

Looking at this from the actors' perspectives, the actors being the entrepreneurs and the leaders themselves, most successful entrepreneurs view themselves as leaders because they had the vision that empowered them to deliver valuable output economy. A successful start-up required of them the skills to steer through many risks, some of which were calculated and others just series of potential hazards. Equally, most leaders of large establishments would regard themselves as entrepreneurial too, irrespective of whether they founded the company or not. The most successful of today's CEOs include a few founders, but primarily they are comprised of those, like Jack Welch and Michael Eisner, who restructured and recreated existing companies, returning higher profits, shareholder value and rewriting history.

It is clear that one can draw differences between entrepreneurs and leaders. An entrepreneur is by far more than just a leader who performs in any reputable organization, s/he starts a firm from scratch, faces different challenges and crises (Gupta *et al.* 2004) and in addition leads in an extraordinary complex situation (Cogliser and Brigham, 2004). Discussing the personalities of both entrepreneurs and leaders Matare (2008) notes that entrepreneurs are more complex in personality attributes and skills because they need to play different roles simultaneously.

This surely implies that entrepreneurial leadership is an interesting discipline and leaders who are put into situations where their actions and behaviour are required to be entrepreneurial need to go an extra mile. Therefore, entrepreneurial leaders need to develop more specific competencies to be able to successfully create a new venture and lead it to success and development.

Following from the discussion above, it can be summarized that:

Not all leaders are entrepreneurs, but entrepreneurs are leaders in their own right.

8

■ Entrepreneurial leadership skills

As discussed above, entrepreneurial leaders have the capacity to explore their environments, ascertain prospects that could be exploited whilst also motivating others to keenly participate in this development towards value creation.

There are two main approaches that scholars have discussed in entrepreneurial leadership competencies. Here, these are defined as the specific abilities to perform leadership roles and tasks in entrepreneurial endeavours (Lans and Mulder 2009).

The 'work-oriented approach'

This style considers entrepreneurial leadership competencies as the essential and indispensable attributes of entrepreneurial leaders. The understanding is that EL must possess these attributes to successfully play the challenging roles and tasks of the leader in different stages of their business growth and development. In order to understand these attributes we can learn from a few definitions proposed for entrepreneurial leadership.

The discussion of these definitions is out of the scope of the chapter; however, these indicate that three specific personal competencies for entrepreneurial leader are identified: proactiveness, innovativeness and risk taking (Chen 2007; Kuratko 2007). These are discussed below in detail.

The 'socio-cultural and situated approach'

It is reasoned that entrepreneurial competencies and in particular entrepreneurial leadership can be learned and developed (Baron and Ensly 2006; Kempster and Cope 2010). The socio-cultural and situated approach explains entrepreneurial leadership development as a social process of continuous and gradual learning and 'becoming' that is located in particular contexts and communities, and where entrepreneurs and leaders are continually learning and developing their capabilities through a range of situational influences.

In the following paragraphs each of the personal competencies discussed in 'the work-oriented approach' of entrepreneurial leaders is explained.

Proactiveness

We have discussed earlier that entrepreneurial leadership is a proactive response to environmental opportunities. Proactiveness is being active to create and lead the future rather than waiting to be influenced by it. In a study conducted by Crant (1996) that examined the relationship between proactive personality and entrepreneurial intentions, proactive personality was positively associated with entrepreneurial intentions. People with a proactive personality may be more inclined to mobilizing the resources and gaining the commitment required for value creation that the entrepreneurial leader faces. More proactive people also have a greater desire to become entrepreneurial leaders in order to help create value for their firm.

It is this typical personality characteristic of entrepreneurial leaders that enables them to manage their own business (Fuller and Marler 2009) and to anticipate future problems, recognize opportunities and identify the needs for change and improvement (Kuratko *et al.* 2007). This is because a proactive personality, which is the tendency to show initiative and take action in one's environment in order to effect meaningful change, not only impacts on business success and growth, it also positively affects their creativity, perseverance to achieve the vision, and desire and intention to initiate entrepreneurial activities (Zampetakis 2008). The proactive trait in leaders is all about challenging the status quo rather than passively adapting to present conditions.

Risk taking

This very important aspect of entrepreneurship is probably the most misunderstood of all. Many assume it is just 'risk–taker'. However, that is not the case: rather it is about *calculated* risk taking. Sensible and premeditated risk taking is one of the common characteristics of entrepreneurial leaders, particularly, in the early stages of the entrepreneurship process (Robinson *et al.* 2006). After careful evaluation, the 'worth-taking' risks are determined, especially if their variables can be examined and then worked out and if the majority of these uncertainties are determined to be good for the business.

One must keep in mind, though, that risk taking is the willingness of entrepreneurial leaders to absorb uncertainty and take the burden of responsibility for the future. Furthermore, entrepreneurial leaders are characterized as having a greater propensity to take risks than managers would and they need to take various risks in different stages of their venture creation and development (Mueller and Thomas, 2000).

Innovativeness

The observation of an entrepreneur as an innovator is based on the model which puts the entrepreneur as a person involved in the identification of prospects and employs the innovation tool for developing successfully new business. Therefore, innovativeness has been defined as the tendency and ability of entrepreneurial leaders to think creatively and develop novel and useful ideas in entrepreneurial opportunity recognition, resource utilization and problem solving (Mattare, 2008). Innovativeness is the attribute that differentiates entrepreneurs from those who want just to be self-employed (Kuratko 2005). At a macro level, countries with the largest economies can be associated with great commitment to innovation and research. Entrepreneurial leadership and innovation is discussed at length in the section below.

Case study: Entrepreneurial leadership and innovation

According to a study conducted by IBM's Global Business Services (2006), innovation is vital to growth and sustainability in the current era of rapid change and globalization. Innovation has become essential to the success of individuals as well as of new and existing organizations. Drucker (1985, p 36) states that innovation is the knowledge base of entrepreneurship, in the light of the same statement, let us look at Drucker's definition of an entrepreneur: "someone who creates something new or different, transmuting or changing values, shifting resources from low to high productivity".

Exercise

Discuss in class where is the overlap between innovation and entrepreneurship?

An entrepreneurial leader is an individual, with the readiness and the competence to transform inventions into innovations. While invention refers to generating novel ideas, innovation makes these ideas alive, and entrepreneurial leaders take risks in the process of making the ideas alive, all of which determine business success. The fundamental goal of entrepreneurial leaders is to create an atmosphere of innovation while helping the constituents themselves become more entrepreneurial.

Conclusion

Leadership is an intriguing topic, and leaders are seen in many different roles. Researchers have studied it at length rendering three major styles: autocratic, democratic and laissez-faire. The situational leadership style offers a new dimension, supporting that there is no single 'best' style of leadership. An approach that might answer the question "What type of leadership actions and behaviours are appropriate?" with the phrase "It depends on the circumstances".

Different leadership theories, such as trait studies, attempted to find the 'great man', followed by the behavioural school of thought that was a big leap from trait theory, in that it assumes that leadership capability can be learned, rather than being inherent. Leading studies under the behavioural school have been the Ohio State studies, The Michigan studies and the managerial grid by Blake and Mouton.

James MacGregor Burns (1978) believed that leadership could take one of two forms: transactional leadership, which occurs when leaders and followers are in some type of exchange relationship in order to get needs met; and transformational leadership, which serves to change the status quo by appealing to followers' values and their sense of higher purpose.

A newer form of leadership, the entrepreneurial leadership, exists at the intersection of entrepreneurship and leadership. Those traits of entrepreneurial leaders include being risk averse, proactive and innovative. The entrepreneurial dimension of leaders focuses through innovativeness the search for creative and meaningful solutions to operational problems and needs. Risk-taking involves the willingness to commit resources to opportunities. Proactiveness is concerned with execution, and assisting to make actions materialize through appropriate means, which typically includes the efforts of others. The exercise of effective entrepreneurial leadership is thereby fulfilled within an array of exciting activities and new creative developments.

Further reading

Burns, J. M. (1978), *Leadership*, New York: Harper and Row.

Bryman, A. (Ed.). (2011). *The SAGE Handbook of Leadership*. Sage Publications.

References

Adeyemi, T. O. (2010). Principals' leadership styles and teachers' job performance in senior secondary schools in Ondo State, Nigeria. *International Journal of Educational Administration and Policy Studies*, **2**(6), 83-91.

Arvey, R.D., Rotundo, M., Johnson, W., Zhang, Z., & McGue, M. (2006). The determinants of leadership role occupancy: Genetic and personality factors. *The Leadership Quarterly*, **17**(1), 1–20.

Arvey, R.D., Zhang, Z., Avolio, B.J., & Krueger, R. F. (2007). Developmental and genetic determinants of leadership role occupancy among women. *Journal of Applied Psychology*, **92**(3), 693–706

Ashford, S.J., Blatt, R., and van de Wall, D. (2003), Reflections on the looking glass: a review of research on feedback-seeking behavior in organization, *Journal of Management*, **29**, 773–799

Avolio, B.J., (1999). *Full Leadership Development: Building the Vital Forces in Organizations*. Thousand Oaks, CA: Sage.

Baron, R.A., and M.D. Ensley. (2006). Opportunity recognition as the detection of meaningful patterns: Evidence from the comparison of novice and experienced entrepreneurs. *Management Science* 52, no. 9: 1331–44.

Bass, B.M., Avolio, B. J., Jung, D. I., & Berson, Y. (2003). Predicting unit performance by assessing transformational and transactional leadership. *Journal of Applied Psychology*, **88**, 207 – 218.

Bass, B.M., (1985). *Leadership and Performance Beyond Expectation*. New York: Free Press.

8

Blake R.R., Mouton J.S. (1964). *The Managerial Grid*. Houston, TX: Gulf.

Bolden, R., Gosling, J., Marturano, A., & Dennison, P. (2003). *A review of leadership theory and competency frameworks*. Report for Chase Consulting and the Management Standards Centre. University of Exeter: Center for Leadership Studies.

Braun, S., Peus, C., Weisweiler, S., & Frey, D. (2013). Transformational leadership, job satisfaction, and team performance: A multilevel mediation model of trust. *The Leadership Quarterly*, **24**(1), 270-283.

Bryman, A. (Ed.) (2011). *The SAGE Handbook of Leadership*. London: Sage Publications

Burns, J. M. (1978), *Leadership*, New York: Harper and Row.

Chen, M.-H. (2007). Entrepreneurial leadership and new ventures: Creativity in entrepreneurial teams. *Creativity and Innovation Management* **16**,(3), 239–49.

Cogliser, C. C., & Brigham, K. H. (2004). The intersection of leadership and entrepreneurship: Mutual lessons to be learned. *The Leadership Quarterly*,**15**(6), 771-799.

Conger, J. A. (1992), *Learning to Lead*. San Francisco: Jossey-Bass.

Crant, J. M. (1996). The proactive personality scale as a predictor of entrepreneurial intentions. *Journal of Small Business Management*, **34**, 42-49.

De Poel, F. M., Stoker, J. I., & Van der Zee, K. I. (2012). Climate control? The relationship between leadership, climate for change, and work outcomes. *International Journal of Human Resource Management*, **23**(4), 694-713.

Drucker, P.F. (1985). *Innovation & Entrepreneurship*. New York, NY: HarperCollins.

Dubrin, A. J. (2007). *Leadership: Research findings, practice and skills* (5th ed.). Boston: Houghton Mifflin Company.

Einarsen, S., Aasland, M.S. and Skogstad, A. (2007). Destructive leadership behaviour: a definition and conceptual model, *Leadership Quarterly*, **18**, 207–216.

Fernald, L., Solomon, G. and Tarabishy, A. (2005), A New paradigm: Entrepreneurial Leadership, *Southern Business Review*, Spring

Fuller, J.B. and Marler, L.E. (2009). Change driven by nature: A meta-analytic review of the proactive personality literature. *Journal of Vocational Behaviour*, **75**: 329–45.

Gupta, V., MacMillan, I.C. & Surie, G. (2004). Entrepreneurial leadership: Developing and measuring a cross-cultural construct. *Journal of Business Venturing* **19**, 241–60.

Hoch, J. E. (2013). Shared leadership and innovation: The role of vertical leadership and employee integrity. *Journal of Business and Psychology*, **28**(2), 159-174.

Hollander, E. P. (1992). Leadership, followership, self, and others. *The Leadership Quarterly*, **3**(1), 43-54.

Horner, M. (1997). Leadership theory: past, present and future. *Team Performance Management: An International Journal*, **3**(4), 270-287.

Ibara, E. C. (2010). *Perspectives in Educational Administration*. Port Harcourt, Nigeria: Rodi Printing and Publishing.

IBM Global Business Services. (2006). *Expanding the innovation horizon: The global CEO study 2006. Somers*, NY: IBM Corporation.

Jenkins W.O. (1947). A review of leadership studies with particular reference to military problems. *Psychological Bulletin*, **44**, 54–79.

Judge, T.A. and Piccolo, R.F. (2004). Transformational and transactional leadership: a meta-analytic review of their relative validity. *Journal of Applied Psychology* **89**, 755–768.

Kellerman, B. (2004). *Bad Leadership: What it is, How it Happens, Why it Matters.* Harvard Business Press.

Kempster, S.J., and J. Cope. (2010). Learning to lead in the entrepreneurial context. *Journal of Entrepreneurial behaviour and Research* **16**(6), 5–34.

Klingborg, D. J., Moore, D. A., & Varea-Hammond, S. (2006). What is leadership? *Journal of Veterinary Medical Education*,**33**, 280–283.

KNOWLEDGE@WHARTON. (2011). What Makes a Good Entrepreneurial Leader? Ask Middle Managers. http://knowledge.wharton.upenn.edu/article/what-makes-a-good-entrepreneurial-leader-ask-middle-managers/ [Accessed July 2015].

Kuratko, D. F. (2002). *"Entrepreneurship," International Encyclopedia of Business and Management*, 2nd ed.(London: Routledge Publishers), 168–176.

Kuratko, D.F. (2005). The emergence of entrepreneurship education: development, trends, and challenges. *Entrepreneurship Theory and Practice* **29**(5), 577–97.

Kuratko, D.F. (2007). Entrepreneurial leadership in the 21st century. *Journal of Leadership and Organizational Studies* **13**(4),1–11.

Kuratko, D.F., Hornsby, J.S. and Goldsby, M.G. (2007). The relationship of stakeholder salience, organizational posture, and entrepreneurial intensity to corporate entrepreneurship. *Journal of Leadership and Organizational Studies* **13**(4), 56–72.

Lans, T., & Mulder, M. (2009). Competence, empirical insights from a small-business perspective. In *Proceedings of the ECER VETNET Conference.*

Lewin, K., Lippitt, R., & White, R. K. (1939). Patterns of aggressive behavior in experimentally created "social climates". *The Journal of Social Psychology*,**10**(2), 269-299.

Maritz, D. (2011). Leadership and Trust. In Robbins, S.P., Odendaal, A., Roodt, G. (Eds.). *Organisational Behaviour: Global and Southern African Perspectives,* (pp. 241-265). South Africa: Pearson.

Mattare, M. (2008). Teaching entrepreneurship: The case for an entrepreneurial leadership course. *USASBE proceedings*, 78-93.

8

Moriano, J. A., Molero, F., Topa, G., & Mangin, J. P. L. (2014). The influence of transformational leadership and organizational identification on intrapreneurship. *International Entrepreneurship and Management Journal,***10**(1), 103-119.

Mueller, S.L. and Thomas, A.S. (2000). Culture and entrepreneurial potential: A nine country study of locus of control and innovativeness. *Journal of Business Venturing* **16**, 51–75.

Nemanich, L.A., and Keller, R.T. (2007), Transformational leadership in an acquisition: A field study of Employees, *The Leadership Quarterly*, **18**, 49 – 68.

Northouse, P. G. (2007). *Leadership: Theory and Practice.* 4th ed. Thousand Oaks, CA: Sage Publications.

Noruzy, A., Dalfard, V. M., Azhdari, B., Nazari-Shirkouhi, S., & Rezazadeh, A. (2013). Relations between transformational leadership, organizational learning, knowledge management, organizational innovation, and organizational performance: an empirical investigation of manufacturing firms. The *International Journal of Advanced Manufacturing Technology*, **64**(5-8), 1073-1085.

Piccolo, R. F., Bono, J. E., Heinitz, K., Rowold, J., Duehr, E., & Judge, T. A. (2012). The relative impact of complementary leader behaviors: Which matter most? *The Leadership Quarterly*, **23**(3), 567-581.

Renko, M., El Tarabishy, A., Carsrud, A. L., & Brännback, M. (2015). Understanding and measuring entrepreneurial leadership style. *Journal of Small Business Management*, **53**(1), 54-74.

Robbins, S.P., Odendaal, A., Roodt, G. (Eds.). *Organisational Behaviour: Global and Southern African Perspectives,.* South Africa: Pearson.

Robinson, D.A., Goleby, M. and Hosgood, N. (2006). *Entrepreneurship as a values and leadership paradigm.* http://epublications.bond.edu.au/ business pubs/10 (accessed July 12, 2013).

Rothmann, I and Cooper, C (2015). *Work and Organizational Psychology.* New York: Routledge.

Somech, A. (2003). Relationships of participative leadership with relational demography variables: a multi-level perspective. *Journal of Organizational Behavior*, **24**(8) 1003-1018.

Spreitzer, G.M. (2007), Giving peace a chance: organizational leadership, empowerment, and peace, *Journal of Organizational Behavior*, **28**, 1077– 1095.

Stevenson, H. and Gumpert, D. (1985), The heart of entrepreneurship, *Harvard Business Review*, March-April

Stogdill RM. (1948). Personal factors associated with leadership: A survey of the literature. *Journal of Psychology*, **25**, 35–71

Stogdill, R. M. (1974). *Handbook of Leadership*. New York: Free Press.

Tepper, B. J. (2000). Consequences of abusive supervision. *Academy of Management Journal*, **43**(2), 178-190.

Van Vugta, M., Jepsona, S. F., Harta, C. M., & De Cremer, D. (2004). Autocratic leadership in social dilemmas: A threat to group stability. *Journal of Experimental Social Psychology*, **40**(1), 1–13

Western, S. (2008). *Leadership: A Critical Text*. London: Sage.

Winston, B. E., & Patterson, K. (2006). An integrative definition of leadership. *International Journal of Leadership Studies,***1**, 6–66

Wood, J. (2009), *Communication in Our Lives*. (5th Ed). Boston, USA: Learning

Yukl, G. (2000). *Leadership in Organizations*, 4th edn. Englewood Cliffs, NJ: Prentice Hall

Zampetakis, L.A. (2008). The role of creativity and proactivity on perceived entrepreneurial desirability. *Thinking Skills and Creativity* **3**, 154–62.

8

9 International Entrepreneurship and Growth

Yen Tran and Spiros Batas

Globalization allows not only the international expansion of multi-national companies (MNCs) but also the growing success of early internationalizing firms, who go global and succeed in multiple foreign markets at birth or early in their operation as part of their early growth strategy. This chapter focuses on these early internationalising firms and will help you understand how these firms excel with their performance in competitive global markets. You should then be able to:

☐ Understand the globalization influences, the emergence of early internationalized firms;

☐ Understand and explain the theoretical foundation of international entrepreneurship;

☐ Identify different motivations for international entrepreneurs;

☐ Examine the characteristics and traits of an international entrepreneur;

☐ Build international entrepreneurial capabilities for starting and growing an international venture.

Globalization and the internationalization of start-up firms

In today's world of a truly globalized economy, consumers are familiar with buying products and services which are made in not just one country but in multiple countries. A daily product such as a smart phone has its components coming from different OEMs (Original Equipment Manufacturers) in Taiwan and Korea, memory chips from Europe, is designed in America and assembled in China. The product is truly made globally.

■ Globalization influences

Globalization – the continuous integration of the countries in the world towards a liberalised and unified global market – impacts on all national economies. The increasingly free market is opening up opportunities for firms and individuals to interact and do business, even virtually, regardless of geographical locations. The movement of many previously controlled economies in the former Soviet blocs towards more free and market-oriented systems, the development of the Pacific Rim, the emergence of new markets in Asia, Latin America and Middle East have brought about countless opportunities for firms to start new businesses or to expand their business globally.

Decreased trade barriers and facilitating institutions have been observed to initiate many international business set-ups and expansions. Since after World War II, the growth of international trade and investment has been faster than the growth of domestic economies, including those of the United States and China (Hisrich, 2013). The development of trading blocs, such as NAFTA (North American Free Trade Agreement) and the European Union, with tax exemption policies, have lowered the barriers for firms to import and export their products to other countries within these customs unions.

Facilitated by advances in information and communication technology in particular, the boom of the internet, international transport, advances in process technology and integration of world financial markets, the impact of increased levels of globalization on entrepreneurship has been witnessed more than ever before. Increases in efficiency due to advancement in information, production and communication technologies have reduced costs and raised efficiency thus making it possible for firms to internationalised rapidly (Knight and Cavusgil, 2005).

Firms once focused solely on domestic markets have been recognising constraints in business development locally and the new opportunities to do business globally. We have observed many big companies, from small nations such as the Nordic countries, prove their success globally; to name just a few: H&M (a global clothing fashion company from Sweden), IKEA (a global furniture company from Sweden), LEGO (a world-leading toy company from Denmark). These companies have quickly expanded their business abroad due to the limited sizes of their home markets and the prospect of entering growing markets elsewhere. The entrance of new international competitors who are penetrating local markets has changed the competitive nature of local industries, putting pressure on domestic firms to adapt and look beyond their local territories. High labour costs, high R&D costs in the domestic markets further urge domestic firms to outsource their business in other countries (Vestring *et al.*, 2005)

■ Internationalization of start-up firms

The globalization trend of international markets has stimulated the international business expansion of multinational companies (MNCs) in the last few decades. However, this globalization of markets and new technologies allows not only the international expansion of large established firms such as IKEA, Zara, H&M and Lego, but also the growing success of firms who internationalized and succeed in multiple foreign markets at birth (international start-ups) or early in their operation, despite limited resources.

Cochlear – an Australian company producing implants for the profound deaf is an example of a 'born-global' firm. The company has relied on their strong relationship with hospital and research centres located all around the world right from inception to maintain a strong technological base for their product innovation. Its technological partners and network of institutions are located in Australia, Switzerland, Germany and the United States. (Rennie, 1993).

> **Tip**: Early internationalising firms succeed in multiple foreign markets early in their operation despite limited resources. Consider if resource constraint would be an opportunity for firms to be innovative and an option for growth strategy.

Logitech – a world famous mouse device company – was founded by one Swiss and two Italians, who had a strategic vision from the start to build a global new venture. The company has two headquarters, in the US and Switzerland, and later on has expanded to Taiwan and Ireland. Its customer base has been globally built, e.g. a Japanese company was the first customer to sign a commercial contract with Logitech (Alahuta, 1990).

Easyjet – a well-known international low cost airline– was founded by a Greek entrepreneur. Stelios Haji-Ioannou, who lives in the UK, travelled to the US and realised the potential of replicating the low cost airline business model by American based Southwest Airlines in the UK market. Stelios has been successfully adapting the business model in the international context, focusing on multiple markets as its initial strategy. These companies are excellent examples of early internationalized firms or born-global firms.

9

Case study: Skype– global from the start

Skype provides free internet phone and messaging services and is a born-global start up. Users need to install software with internet phone technology to communicate with others. There are millions of users logged in on Skype and the program and service has made such a strong impression that the term "Skype me" has replaced "call me" in some circles. Niklas Zennstrom and Janus Friis, the same two entrepreneurs who invented

KaZaA (one of the most popular internet file-sharing software programmes in the world) also developed Skype. Initially founded in Sweden as Tele2, Skype is now headquartered in Luxembourg and has offices in Europe, the United States, and Asia. Skype has received significant funding from some of the largest venture-capital firms in the world. Skype is a typical born global start-up with characteristics of being innovative, seeking for global resources to make them succeed.

Source: http://www.skype.com.

Case study: Seaflex – seeking new international markets

Seaflex was founded in Sweden with ten employees in 1999. The product of the company is an environmentally friendly elastic mooring system that secures pontoons and buoys or floating docks without damaging the sensitive ecosystem on the seabed. Due to the limited domestic market, Seaflex mainly relies on foreign sales which account for 98% of turnover. Over eight years, Seaflex has increased its sales by around 30% each year and doubled its staff. The company in recent years has expanded its traditional markets in Europe and the United States into new and emerging markets in the Middle East and Asia. CEO Lars Brandt made it clear: "During those first years, I tried to find international customers because Sweden is so small and I think if you have a product that everyone else can use, it is a missed opportunity to sell it only on the domestic market ... the whole world is our market!"

Source: http://www.seaflex.net, Adapted from Eurofound, 2012

Knight and Cavusgil (2005) confirmed the emergence of a uniquely characterised breed of international firms whose origins and initial orientations are international and from infancy seek to gain competitiveness through establishing significant foreign sales. McKinsey in 1993 spotlighted the emergence of small and medium enterprises who successfully competed almost from their inception against large and established players in the competitive global market (Rennie, 1993). The study of young Austrian firms also showed that these firms began exporting only two years after their foundation and 76% of their total sales came from export activities. (Rennie, 1993). About 20% of new enterprises in Europe are born-global firms and they comprise up to half of young firms in Romania, Belgium and Denmark. (Eurofound, 2012). This reflects partly the limited market size of some European countries and also the regional integration trend leading to international firm foundation (Eurofound, 2012). Another study by Madson and Servais (1997) on 328 export-oriented enterprises from Sweden, Norway, Finland and Denmark revealed that most export enterprises began their international activities right after their establishment, with offshore business accounting for 20% in the first year, and after just two years reaching more than 50%. These are firms taking advantages of international resources early in their business cycle to produce and sell their products in multiple countries to attain competitive advantage. Therefore, early internationalising firms or born-global firms could be considered to be more common in countries with smaller domestic markets.

> **Tip**: If you are from a small country with limited domestic market size and you would like to set up a new business, it is advisable to have an international mindset right from the start. This is one of the success factors of Scotland in international markets "It is exactly this kind of international mindset that we want to embed even more in our culture and in our attitudes" (Lena Wilson, CEO of Scottish Enterprise).

Due to the nature of their young age, born-globals tend to be mainly micro or small enterprises. Entrepreneurs and staff in such firms tend to be highly skilled and educated, particularly with technological and language knowledge which commands higher than average wages (Tran, 2014). Furthermore, due to their relationships with other firms via partnership (e.g. through supply chains, R&D collaboration) and their business models (e.g. outsourcing), there is a clear evidence that born-globals help to create more jobs in other companies. (Eurofound, 2012)

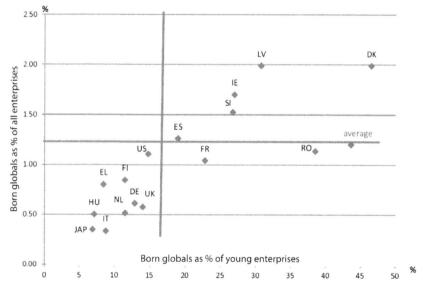

Figure 9.1: Born globals as a proportion of young and all enterprises, in selected EU member states, US and Japan, 2008.
Source: Eurofound. 2012. *Born Global: The Potential of Job Creation in New International Businesses,* Publications Office, the European Union, Luxembourg.

Takeaways

■ The globalization contextual factors for internationalization of firms

■ Advances in international communication, information technology

■ Pace of technological change in production and transportation

■ Advances in international transport

■ Integration of world's financial markets

■ Market-oriented and globalization polices

■ Limited home market

■ International nature of industry

■ Homogeneity of international market

■ International competition

The theoretical foundations of international entrepreneurship

International entrepreneurship refers to the "the process of an entrepreneur conducting business activities across national boundaries" (Hisrich, 2013). The concept was first defined by McDougal (1989, p.389) as "the development of international new ventures or start-ups, that from inception, engage in international business, thus viewing their operating domain as international from the initial stages of the firm's operation". The authors later on introduced this broader concept to include established firms: "international entrepreneurship is a combination of innovative, proactive, and risk-seeking behaviour that crosses national borders and is intended to create value in organizations" (McDougall and Oviatt, 2000:903).

In this chapter, we focus on early internationalising firms who either start up globally (born global firms/BGFs) or internationalised shortly after their inception (international new ventures/INVs). Scholars use different terms to describe the early internationalising firms as 'born globals' (first coined by McKinsey company (Rennie, 1993), then by Knight and Cavusgil, (1996); Madsen and Servais, (1997), as 'global start-ups' (e.g. McDougall *et al.*, 1994), as 'international new ventures' (Oviatt and McDougall, 1994) and as 'instant exporters' (e.g. Coviello and McAuley, 1999). Most of the literatures, however, focus more on born global firms and international new ventures which emphasises the important role of timing on internationalization (Jones and Coviello, 2005).

Many scholars have provided an explanation of the characteristics of such companies. Some have criticized and questioned if born globals are truly global, and have suggested that a more appropriate name would be the 'born international' (Hashai, 2011). Hashai described these companies as firms that continuously expand their operations geographically. Moreover, he stated that born globals prefer to focus on a single expansion path, at a certain time period, but might change their expansion path over time. The definition of born global firms includes companies with 25% of foreign sales out of their total turnover, and those that internationalised within 3 years of their inception (Knight and Cavusgil, 2004; Kuivalainen *et al.*, 2007; Gabrielson *et al.*, 2008). Gabrielsson *et al.* gave their own definition of born global firms. According to them "born globals have products with global market potential". These products, in addition with the entrepreneurial capability, help the early and rapid internationalization. It is crucial for these firms to target international markets from their inception. Finally, born globals should not be a spin-off of a large company; and entrepreneurs should be prepared to take risks similar to those of a small start-up firm.

Oviatt and McDougall (1994) found that a number of companies internationalised rapidly and share common characteristics with born globals, the so-called 'international new ventures (INV)'. They introduced and defined an INV as "a business organization that from inception, seeks to derive significant competitive advantage from the use of resources and the sale outputs in multiple countries" (Oviatt and McDougall, 1994: p. 49)

Entrepreneurs who can identify and act on international market opportunities and be able to manage effectively different resources from multiple countries can drive their INVs to success. There are four types of INVs:

- ☐ Export/import start-ups
- ☐ Multinational trader
- ☐ Geographically focused start-ups
- ☐ Global start-ups

Export and import start-ups and multinational traders are characterised as new international market makers by Oviatt and McDougall (1994). In particular:

- ☐ The export and import start-ups concentrate on limited countries for trading where the entrepreneur is knowledgeable;
- ☐ The multinational traders operate in a number of countries and continually scan for new opportunities where "their networks are established or where they can quickly be set up";
- ☐ Geographically focused start-ups possess their advantages by offering their services as "the specialised needs" of a particular geographic region via the use of foreign resources.

Unlike multinational traders, the geographically focused start-ups focus on geographic regions where the needs are specialised. They also differ from the export/import start-up in activities of inbound and outbound logistics. These enterprises are able to coordinate various value chain activities, for example developments in technology, human resources and production. This type of firm may sustain their advantage by working closely with an "exclusive network of alliances" in the area in which they operate.

The last type of INV is the global start-up, which is the most radical manifestation of the INVs. This type develops its competitive advantage from various organizational activities where their locations are globally dispersed. Global start-ups proactively capture and identify opportunities regarding the acquisition of resources from multiple geographic locations, especially resources that offer great value (Oviatt and McDougall, 1994).

Global start-ups "appear to have the most sustainable competitive advantages due to a combination of historically unique, causally ambiguous, and socially complex inimitability with close network alliances in multiple countries", Oviatt and McDougall (1994: p. 60). Undoubtedly, the importance of networks is highlighted in the four types of INVs. Networks not only can sustain the competitive advantage of the INVs but also assist them in their process of internationalization. Moreover, many have highlighted the importance of technology and the internet in accelerating internationalization of these global start-up firms (e.g. Oviatt and McDougall, 1994; Singh and Kundu, 2002; Petersen and Welch, 2003; Yamin and Sinkovics, 2006; Reuber and Fischer, 2011; Fischer and Reuber, 2011).

Theoretically, international entrepreneurship is one of the key research areas of international business and entrepreneurship and strategic management (see Wright and Ricks, 1994; Zahra et al, 1999; Hitt and Ireland, 2000; Keupp and Gassmann, 2009; Rialp *et al.*, 2005; Coombs *et al.*, 2009; Jones *et al.*, 2011). Research in the IE field has surged dramatically in recent decades (Young *et al.*, 2003). Building on the foundation of international business theories– which originated from Adam Smith's work *The Wealth of Nations* with the focus on the national level, and later since the 1950s on the firm level ,with theories of multinational corporations (Mtigwe, 2006), the field of international entrepreneurship has emerged since 1994 as a new and promising research area. Scholars have mainly borrowed from international business theories the resource-based view, and an institutional and network perspective to explain the emergence and growth of international entrepreneurship (Young et al, 2003). However, international entrepreneurship theories lack a solid theoretical foundation and can be regarded as still independent from international business. That means there is a need to employ broader approaches from entrepreneurship and other fields to appropriately emphasise the international characters of international entrepreneurship. McDougall *et al.* (1994) argued that internationalization theories would not offer any explanation to the INV phenomenon because those presume and support internationalization as a gradual process. They also added that entrepreneurs of INVs have capabilities such as knowledge and networks that assist them to identify opportunities that are not seen by others. Ford and Leonidou (1991) and Ramaswamy *et al.* (1996) identified a problem in the theoretical frameworks used in the international business field. First of all, those frameworks lacked sophisticated variables, which could explain the idiosyncrasies and complexity of the observed phenomena. Many scholars understood the dynamic and important role of small entrepreneurial firms in national economies (Prefontaine and Bourgault, 2002; Mtigwe, 2006). According to Mtigwe (2006) international entrepreneurship theory along with network theory are the best representatives of the recent development in international business theory. The international entrepreneurship theory cannot, however, be sufficiently explained by only one approach or context. Many scholars (e.g. Zahra and George, 2002; Oviatt and McDougall, 2005) identified a key issue in international entrepreneurship theory: the main focus of the research is on small businesses and born global companies. Zahra and George (2002) also proposed that future research should not only research small firms because theories might be excluded. The international entrepreneurship theory helped international business theory to move forward because it helped to focus on the entrepreneur level rather than the firm level. Finally, the international entrepreneurship theory has helped scholars to understand how international business takes place.

> **Tip**: If you are interested in doing research in international entrepreneurship, start with the work by leading scholars such as Zahra, Oviatt, McDougal, Coviello, Knight and search in *Journal of International Business Studies* for some classic studies.

9

We will now refer to those firms who are born-globally or internationalised soon after their birth as 'early internationalising firms'.

Takeaways

- International Entrepreneurship is the emergent research area at the intersections of International Business, Entrepreneurship and Strategy
- International Entrepreneurship studies "the process of an entrepreneur conducting business activities across national boundaries"
- International Entrepreneurship concerns early internationalized firms, being born global firms, and international new ventures and entrepreneurial-established firms
- International Entrepreneurship is considered as an international growth strategy

Motivations for international entrepreneurship

Why do firms internationalize so early in their business cycle? What are the motivations for firms to start globally? There are various reactive and proactive reasons motivating start-up firms either to set up at the outset taking into account the global market and network or to internationalize their activities soon after foundation. Globalization influences, as discussed previously, are the pull or reactive factors which urge firms to adapt, and hence to go global. Other proactive factors, which we discuss below, are those which firms choose when selecting to set up globally. These are also challenges start-up firms are facing, overcoming and turning into new business opportunities.

Case study: Overcoming the constraint of local market

Zoobug is a UK based company founded by Julie Diem Le, a former employee of the NHS and member of the Royal College of Ophthalmologists, which provides children's high quality sunglasses. "Zoobug is a specialist brand of kid's eyewear, designed in London and created by an ophthalmologist to help children see well and look great". The uniqueness of the product is the combination of fashionable style and ophthalmically correct range of sunglasses with 100% UV protection as adult sunglasses in stylish frames designed by Italian designer. Zoobug proved its success instantly in the domestic UK market. However, after two summers of poor weather in the UK, the company felt the need to expand its market internationally: "I had to look overseas for new business because there was not any sun in Britain". By 2009, the sales increased substantially especially with the addition of optical frames and the company was selling in 20 countries, with France as the biggest market. Some of the production is now outsourced to Italy to take advantage of high quality of craftsmanship and to Asian countries for lower priced ranges. Zoobug has proved its success, with international expansion shortly after formation due to the constraints and disadvantages in home market.

Adapted from Burns, 2009. Additional source: http://www.zoobug.com/

Start-up firms, especially in small economies in Nordic countries, usually face the problem of local market constraint. That can be the limited size of the market, for example Seaflex AB where Sweden does not provide enough demand for their innovative products. Another example is the case of Zoobug, of which the founder Diem Le had to look overseas for new business simply because "there is not enough sun in Britain to sell sunglasses" (see the Case study above). By going global, small firms can also achieve economies of scale through selling the same types of products across multiple markets. This is particularly relevant when the products target niche markets or a specific market segment, such as the sea environmental industrial products by Seaflex AB, or the flight control systems for unmanned aerial vehicle application and general aviation by UAV Navigation (http://www.uavnavigation.com/). Besides, there is a tendency of international consumers nowadays to demand more special-ized and customized products rather than standard ones; therefore, small firms have found niche markets an important source of new business opportunities. With their small size being more flexible to accommodate new international market demand compared with large established firms, small firms are far more motivated to grow internationally.

In many industries, as the product life cycles are shortened firms expand their markets internationally quicker to maximise the values offered by their products before they reach their matured and declined stages. ASOS – an internationally successful online fashion retailer based in the UK– offers the same styles of products in different international markets simultaneously to maximize the relevant fashion trend rather than sequentially selling in domes-tic markets then abroad. Early internationalized firms take their advantages of small size to be more adaptable and cost effective to meet the quick changes of international consumers' preferences. The limited size of local markets also means that domestic competition is fiercer, forcing firms to go global from the start.

Most of the small early internationalising firms have shortages of resources, including financial, human and other physical tangible assets, such as machin-ery, equipment, properties (Knight, *et al.*, 2004). Tapping into global networks helps start-ups secure diverse resources for their setting up, survival and growth. With these networks and being flexible, they have the possibility to take on larger competitors, chase global opportunities and create new products and services (Isenberg, 2008). Limited funds forced Heartware International Corporation – an international start up from USA – to rely on a strategic alliance with the University of Maastricht for R&D and for production of its electro-physiology equipment (McDougal, *et al.*, 1994). Having international financial providers also means it is easier for firms to gain access to international markets. A start-up firm with financial support from a French investor would naturally enter the French home market much earlier. Logitech – a global firm offering a computer mouse and other devices – also had a foreign investor at the founding stage. In order to grow early in their operation, in November 2007, Facebook – a global social network company who internationalized just barely four years after foundation – attracted $60 million from a large international investor Li Ka-shing (HongKong billionaire) and, in May 2009, $200 million investment from Digital Sky Technologies (an internet investment group active especially in Eastern Europe and Russia). As a result, Facebook reached 400 million users in February 2010 and doubled in size by September 2011.

> **Tip**: Forming strategic alliances with international partners helps a firm not only to access international markets but also international finance providers including equity funders.

Case study: Accessing international start-up funding

Profitero was established in late 2010 in south County Dublin. The company was truly international from the first stages. The founders (one Ukrainian and two Belarussian entrepreneurs) had prior international experience working for large firms. All three entrepreneurs gained international business experience at top-tier technology companies, like IBM, Microsoft and Google, before setting up their own business. The company offers prototype solutions to trawl retail websites and get real-time pricing information so that retailers can create competitive pricing. During the inception phase, the company raised €750,000 in venture capital from Delta Partners, which manages the Bank of Ireland Start-up and Emerging Sectors Equity Fund, Enterprise Ireland, the Irish government agency for the development and growth of Irish enterprises in world markets, and Seedcamp, an angel investor. After two years, the company had 15 full-time employees in Dublin and in the development centre in Belarus. It monitored 27.5 million products across 2,500 European retail websites, and planned to grow this to 100 million products by the end of 2012.

Source: www.profitero.com adapted from Eurofound, 2012

The lack of traditional tangible resources of early internationalized firms can act as one of the key success factors of these firms. Knight *et al.* (2004) discovered that, due to the lack of resources, these firms are forced to leverage other intangible resources which are more related to their strategies, marketing orientations, skills, know-how, previous experiences and founders' networks. This in turn helps firms to be more innovative, proactive and usually ahead of their competitors in international strategic growth.

Takeaways

- Motivations for early internationalization as growth strategy
- Overcome local market constraints: limited size of domestic markets
- Pursue unique international niche market: specialised products
- Shorten product life cycles
- Need to access to foreign resources: financial, human and technological capital
- Exploit proprietary technology internationally
- Avoid domestic inertia within firm
- Seek for lower costs: labour cost, R&D cost, tax
- Advantages of small firms in quicker response time, higher flexibility, adaptability
- Competitiveness of domestic markets

Characteristics of international entrepreneurs

International entrepreneurs are the founders of earlier internationalizing firms. They share many characteristics similar to any other entrepreneurs such as being visionary, risk taking, resilient, independent, ambitious and determined (Burn, 2007). However, due to the different context of international and cross-cultural settings, international entrepreneurs bear the following additional traits (Knight, 2004; Karra, 2008; McDougal *et al.*, 1994). They have global vision and strong commitment to engage and expand markets internationally from the beginning. They desire to be international market leaders with the products targeted at international rather than domestic consumers. Their origins and fundamental orientation are strongly international. The vision of Facebook's founder Mark Zuckerberg right from the start was global: "Give people the power to share and make the world more open and connected", and the commitment to date stays the same (Facebook, 2015). International entrepreneurs view international markets as opportunities rather than obstacles. They are known to have higher tolerances for ambiguity, which is far more unpredictable in international markets. This complex ambiguity is due to differences among countries in stages of economic development, types of economic system, political-legal environment, cultural environment, technological development, local foreign competition and government policies (Hisrich, 2013). International founders value their learning-while-doing and knowledge they achieve through international strategic moves. All of these help them to address challenges dealing with the complexities of international markets.

> **Tip**: If you have a cross-cultural background, for example you have been living or studying in different countries, you already possess an important factor helping you in setting up and running a successful international business

9

To stay committed and be able to make bold international strategic decisions, international entrepreneurs rely on their international experience from their cross-cultural background or from what they achieved from previous employment with MNCs. As described earlier, both Logitech and Profitero (see the Case study on page 173) were founded by migrant entrepreneurs from different countries who had gained international business experience at top-tier technology companies before setting up their own enterprises. Founders at NEXIA STT, an auditing and accounting management company from Vietnam, are former employees of the Big Four in auditing and accounting service industry, namely KPMG and Ernst and Young. In the current success of their own company, they clearly value their prior experiences and knowledge obtained from working in MNCs and their local knowledge; the company offers the same services as their previous employers but with good local and regional adaptation (Tran, 2014).

Having such a prior experience in a cross-cultural context, these international entrepreneurs are more alert to new business opportunities. They are more reactive to the business potential of combining profitable resources across countries. Ismail Karov, founder of a leather goods company in Russia, is a Turkish Bulgarian who quickly identified the business opportunities to produce designed leather products to be sold in Russia and Eastern Europe after the collapse of the Soviet Union. He used his experience of working with Turkish leather production companies and the shortages of supply to Russian markets for high quality leather goods to set up a successful leather goods business. "[I saw] many stylish women on the street of Moscow carrying their belongings in plastic bags. Not that they wanted to do that, but because they had no option. There were no purses or bags available at that time… I saw the opportunity in the market and I acted on it" (Karra *et al.*, 2008, p:446). Xiaojing Chu is the founder of her own company in the UK providing consumer retail goods made in the UK to Chinese customers who have preferences for foreign made products but cannot travel to the UK to buy them. These business opportunities are more evident for such international entrepreneurs with multiple cultural backgrounds and prior business experiences. They are more alert to the possibilities of combining resources from different national markets because of the competencies that they have developed from their earlier activities (McDougal *et al.*, 1994). It can be argued that the entrepreneurs with these competencies are better able to combine a particular set of resources across national borders with a high level of integrity and form a new born-global or new international venture.

Takeaways

- Characteristics of international entrepreneurs
- Global vision and commitment
- International market orientation
- International experiences
- Alert to the possibilities of combining resources form different national markets
- Cross-cultural background and network
- Innovative mindset, entrepreneurial orientation
- Emphasis on learning and knowledge development
- Flexibility to adapt to changing conditions abroad
- Emphasise differentiation and/or focus strategies (e.g. super product quality)

Building international entrepreneurial capability for growth

Besides those characteristics of international entrepreneurs, studies have shown many successful ways to build international entrepreneurial capabilities for start-up founders. These are skills and competencies that enable entrepreneurs to create new international ventures (Karra *et al.*, 2008; Isenberg, 2008; McDougal, 1994). In particular, "entrepreneurial capability is the ability to identify new opportunities and to build the resource base to exploit them" (Karra *et al*, 2008, p 446)

■ Articulating a global purpose

It is essential for entrepreneurs who want to grow in the international markets to develop a clear rationale for being global right from as early as possible in their operation. Research has suggested that the organizational routines and capacities that firms use for domestic markets can make firms become path dependent, constraining their capacity to expand later on internationally (Dosi, Teece and Winter, 1990; Teece *et al.*, 1990; Ghosal, 1987; McDougal *et al.*, 1994). Many domestic firms who wish to go global after being well established in their domestic market find inertia (from old routines, employee resistance, etc.) a big problem because it creates obstacles in adapting to differences in the new international markets. Therefore, it is important for firms to develop routines for managing multi-cultural workforces, for coordinating resources coming from different countries, for serving customers from different geographical markets (McDougal *et al*, 1994). The online education programmes of Edinburgh Business School set a clear mission from the start to target international students. A founder of an American based international new venture stated "We hire either people who are foreign immigrants, who have done work in their own cultures and have come here to work, or Americans who have lived in different foreign cultures and have learned how to have sympathy for it" (McDougal *et al.*, 1994).

■ International market opportunity identification

International entrepreneurs can use different methods to identify business opportunities which can turn into new ventures. Studies on opportunity identification suggest active search, passive search and creativity with imagination as three ways to start identifying opportunities (Karra *et al.*, 2008; DeTienne and Chandler, 2004; Dess *et al.*, 1997). Active search can be undertaken with superior search skills and the capacity to scan the environment for gaps in the markets. Passive search refers to prior experience or knowledge of the founders, and these are evident in many cases of international entrepreneurs as discussed previ-

9

ously. Creativity and imagination are done through the cognitive processes that help entrepreneurs to envision new trends, new resource combinations from different strategic partner networks, different locations and different markets. A successful international entrepreneur demonstrates the ability to connect the dots across different international contexts to find their 'sweet spot' for the right opportunity. Steve Jobs is an example of an entrepreneur having the vision of new products, such as the iPad, without conducting the market research to find out what customers want. In style-based industries such as art, industrial design, fashion or music, creativity and imagination are the key elements in the business opportunity recognition process of entrepreneurs. (Tran, 2010)

■ Institutional bridging

For many international entrepreneurs, being international from their background gives them the ability to sense the market gap and seize new business opportunities. This ability is defined by Karra *et al.* (2008) as 'institutional bridging'. The concept refers to the ability to span the institutional distance between national contexts, and the ability to translate business concepts and opportunities to adapt into different national contexts. Many international entrepreneurs have been successful by applying a known business idea in a new context or by showing how a set of business competencies in one country has the potential for value creation or can be adapted in a new novel way in another country (Karra *et al.*, 2008). This capability can be developed with the strong preference of international entrepreneurs for cross-cultural collaboration and their competencies in combining resources for different national markets (McDougal, 1994). Asian Dane use Danish design but are produced by a network of handcrafted workshops in Vietnam.

■ Strategic alliance building and supply chain network creation

The process of setting up a global start-up requires sufficient resources usually in a relatively short period of time as cash flow can lead to the failure of the firm. Therefore, it is unlikely that global start-ups will make substantial investment from the beginning on their own. They instead choose to go for strategic alliances (Isenberg, 2008) or hybrid structures to control their vital assets (Vesper 1990; Oviatt and McDougal, 1994). That means they search for other partners and rely on them for funding, equity sharing, R&D, market expertise, etc. This collaboration strengthens their position in the market but also create threats of opportunism with hybrid partners. Some entrepreneurs have to enter into such deals from positions of weakness, hence the alliance can potentially lead to failure (Isenberg, 2008). The case of Heartware mentioned previously shows that the firm had to rely on a strategic alliance with the University of Maastrict for R&D and for production of their equipment. Isenberg (2008) pointed out that start-ups can have problems communicating with global partners due to the geographic and psychic distances with their alliances.

Case study: Supply chain at the heart of the business

Winery Exchange, a California-based venture manages a 22-country network of wineries and breweries and was co-founded by Peter Byck in 1999. Winery Exchange's business model relies on a close network with retail chains, for example Kroger, Tesco and Costco, to develop premium private label products. The company has an excellent supplier network which produces and packages the wines at the lowest cost. The success of the firms is due to its links with relatively small suppliers and with large retailers, in combination with its product development expertise. In 2006, Winery Exchange sold 2 million cases of 330 different brands of wine, beer, and spirits to retailers on four continents.

Adapted from Isenberg (2008)

Entrepreneurs must often choose suppliers on the other side of the world and monitor them without having managers nearby. Besides these ongoing issues, the best manufacturing locations may change as labour and fuel costs rise and as quality problems show up, as they did in China where a study by the American Chamber of Commerce in Shanghai revealed that currency and shipping costs were rising by 5% and wages up to 30% annually. Labour costs for blue-collar workers rose by 12% in Guangdong and 14% in Shanghai from 2002 to 2009 (Economist, 2012). Start-ups find it daunting to manage complex supply networks, but they gain competitive advantage by doing so. Sometimes the global supply chain is the business opportunity for the firm (Isenberg, 2008).

Seeking for institutional support for the international growth

Due to the young age and being in early start up process, most small and medium enterprises (SMEs) need to rely on the government or other institutional organizations for the initial support of their growth. Such organizations set out to provide support including market research, guidance, experience, contacts and funding to such firms in the transition from domestic markets to international markets.

Case study: ROVOP – growth with institutional funding

Founded in 2011, ROVOP is a Scottish-based firm supplying subsea remotely operated vehicle services – ROV – for the energy sector in deep water drill support, sea construction, survey and pipe/cable laying support. The company commits to the highest quality of equipment, service and expertise. With a global mindset, the company is targeting at international markets as part of its growth strategy and has had instant success with 50% revenue growth rate of £15.3 million in 2014. ROVOP has proactively searched for various institutional funds to support its ambitious international expansion, such as Royal Bank of Scotland and Scottish Loan Fund. Scottish Enterprise and Scottish Development International had provided £60,000 to allow the firm to explore business opportunities overseas. Recently in April 2015, the company received £10m of funding from Business Growth Fund to continue growing in international markets. ROVOP's CEO Steven Gray (2014 UK Earnst and Young Entrepreneur winner) made it clear that the various funding was an endorsement of ROVOP's growth plans and that adding the focus on international markets was a vital step for the company. He said: "The ability to operate the most modern and capable ROVs is vital to fulfil contracts available to us in the global subsea market". Maureen McChlery, ROVOP's account manager at Scottish Enterprise, said: "ROVOP is a great example how we can work with an ambitious Scottish company to accelerate its growth plans and help it secure access to growth finance."

Source: Energy Voice, 09/08/2012, 23/04/2015 **http://www.rovop.com/**

Tip: Most countries and regions have business development agencies which provide dedicated support for internationalising start-ups and SMEs, e.g. Scottish Enterprise (http://www.scottish-enterprise.com/services) provides free direct support for start-ups and firms doing business outside Scotland and promotes the international growth of firms with financial support. Scottish Development International (http://www.sdi.co.uk) helps local enterprises make the most of international trade and global markets.

Takeaways
- Building international entrepreneurial capability for growth
- Articulating a global purpose.
- International market opportunity identification: connect the dots
- Institutional bridging: preference and capacity for cross-cultural collaboration
- Strategic alliances building
- Supply chain creation
- Taking the advantage of institutional support

(Adapted from Karra *et al.*, 2008; Isenberg, 2008)

Conclusion

International entrepreneurship is a growth path for young domestic firms who wish to grow globally in their early years of operation or later after becoming established in their domestic markets. International entrepreneurship concerns early internationalizing firms who internationalized their operation right at birth or after a few years serving local markets, with high export shares or business activities in several foreign countries. They come from different sectors of the economy with a high level of innovative products or services, advanced technology or exclusive design. These firms try to get gain access to international networks such as strategic business partnership and international investors for their resource exploitation and supply chain management as part of their growth strategy. However, being at a young age with less experience, early in the set-up process, pursuing new ideas with new and unique products to the international markets, these SMEs can face potential threats for their growth and survival. Firms can lack the required high levels of technical and managerial expertise, the experience with procedures and markets, and be without a high level of commitment and engagement. As shown previously, some firms are struggling with limited resources and hesitance from external investors to finance their untested business ideas. Many institutions such as Scottish Enterprise or Scottish Development International in Scotland have provided substantial support to such firms in funding and business consultancy. However, such early internationalizing firms or SMEs are vulnerable to economic developments and thus calls for more government help in all countries to support their growth potential.

9

References

Alahuhta, M. 1990. *Global growth strategies for high technology challenges.* ACTA Polytechnica Scandinavia. Electrical Engineering Series No 66. Helsinki: Doctoral Thesis.

Batas, S. 2015. *The internationalisation process of high technology INVs: The role of social capital and network relationships.* University of Edinburgh: Doctoral Thesis.

Burn, P. (2007). *Entrepreneurship and Small Business: Start-up. Growth and Maturity.* Palgrave Macmillan.

Coombs, J.E., Sadrieh, F., Annavarjula, M. (2009). Two decades of international entrepreneurship research: what have we learned - where do we go from here?. *International Journal of Entrepreneurship,* **13**: 23-64.

Coviello, N. and McAuley, A. (1999). Internationalisation and the smaller firm: A review of contemporary empirical research. *Management International Review,* **39**(3): 223-256.

Dess, G., Lumpkin, G. and Covin, J. (1997). Entrepreneurial strategy making and firm performance: test of contingency and configurational models, *Strategic Management Journal,* **18**(9): 677-695.

DeTienne, R. and Chandler, G. (2004). Opportunity identification and its role in the classroom: a pedagogical approach and empirical test, *Academy of Management Learning and Education,* **3**(3): 242-257.

Dosi, G., Teece, D. and Winter, S,. (1990) Frontiers of businesses : Towards a theory of coherence of big business, *Journal of Industrial Economics,* **51**: 238-254.

Eurofound. (2012). *Born global: The Potential of Job Creation in New International Businesses,* Publications Office, the European Union, Luxembourg.

Facebook (2015). Investor Relations. Facebook company website. http://investor. fb.com/faq.cfm

Fischer, E. & Reuber, A. R. (2011). International entrepreneurship in internet-enabled markets. *Journal of Business Venturing,* **26**(6): 660-679.

Gabrielsson, M., Kirpalani, V.H.M., Dimistratos, P., Solberg, A., & Zucchella, A. (2008), Born-global: Propositions to help advance the theory, *International Business Review,* **17** (4): 385-401.

Ghosal, S., (1987). Global Strategy: An organizing framework. *Strategic Management Journal,* **8**: 425-440.

Hashai, N,. (2011). Sequencing the expansion of geographic scope and foreign operations by born global firms. *Journal of International Business Studies,* **42** (8): 995-1015.

Hisrich, R. (2013*). International Entrepreneurship: Starting, Developing and Managing a Global Venture.* Sage Publication Inc.

Hitt, M.A. & Ireland. R.D. (2000). The intersection of entrepreneurship and strategic management research. In D.L. Sexton and H. Landstrom, (eds.), *The Blackwell Handbook of Entrepreneurship,* Oxford: Blackwell Publishers Ltd.: pp. 45-63.

Isenberg, D. (2008). The Global Entrepreneur. *Harvard Business Review.* December

Jones, M. V., Coviello, N., & Tang, Y. K. 2011. International Entrepreneurship research (1989-2009): A domain ontology and thematic analysis. *Journal of Business Venturing,* **26** (6): 632-659.

Jones, M. and Coviello, N. (2005). Internationalisation: Conceptualising an Entrepreneurial Process of Behaviour in Time. *Journal of International Business Studies.* **36**(3): 84-303.

Karra, N., Phillips, N. and Tracey, P. (2008). Building the born global firm. Developing entrepreneurial capabilities for international new venture success. *Long Range Planning,* **41** (2008): 440 -459.

Keupp, M. M. and Gassmann, O. (2009). The past and the future of international entrepreneurship: A review and suggestions for developing the field. *Journal of Management,* **35**(3): 600-633.

Knight, G. & Cavusgil, S.T. (1995). The born global firm: Challenge to traditional internationalization theory. In *Proceedings of the Third Symposium of the Consortium for International Marketing Research*, Tage Madsen, ed. Odense, Denmark: Odense University.

Knight, G. & Cavusgil, S.T. (1996). The born global firm: A challenge to traditional internationalization theory. In S.T. Cavusgil and T. Madsen (eds.) *Advances in International Marketing*, **8**: 11-26. Greenwich, CT: JAI Press.

Knight, G. & Cavusgil, S.T. (2005). A Taxonomy of Born-Global Firms. *Management International Review*, **45**(3): 15-35.

Knight, G. & Cavusgil, S.T. (2004). Innovation, organizational capabilities, and the born-global firm. *Journal of International Business Studies*, **35**(2): 124–141.

Knight, G., Madsen, T. K., & Servais, P. 2004. An inquiry into born-global firms in Europe and the USA. *International Marketing Review*, **21**(6): 645-665.

Kuivalainen, O., Sundqvist, S. and Servais, P. (2007). Firms' degree of bornglobalness, international entrepreneurial orientation and export performance. *Journal of World Business*, B(3): 253-267.

McDougall, P. P., Shane, S., & Oviatt, B. M. (1994). Explaining the formation of international new ventures - the limits of theories from international-business research. *Journal of Business Venturing*, **9**(6): 469-487.

Madsen, T. K., & Servais, P. (1997). The internationalization of born globals: An evolutionary process? *International Business Review*, **6**(6): 561-583.

Mtigwe, B. (2006). Theoretical milestones in international business: The journey to international entrepreneurship theory. *Journal of International Entrepreneurship*, **4**: 5-25.

Oviatt, B. M. and McDougall, P. P. (1994). Toward a theory of international new ventures. *Journal of International Business Studies*, **25** (1), 45-64.

Oviatt, B. M. and McDougall, P. P. (2005). Defining international entrepreneurship and modeling the speed of internationalization. *Entrepreneurship Theory and Practice*, **29**(5): 537-554.

Petersen, B. and L.S. Welch (2003): International business development and the internet – post-hype, *Management International Review*, **43**, Special Issue 1: 7-29.

Prefontaine, L. and Bourgault, M. (2002). Strategic analysis and export behaviour of SMEs: a comparison between the United States and Canada. *International Small Business Journal*, **20**(2): 123-138.

Rennie, M. (1993). Born global. *McKinsey Quarterly* (4): 45–52.

9

Reuber, A. R. and Fischer , E. (2011). International entrepreneurship in internet-enabled markets. *Journal of Business Venturing*, **26**(6): 660-679.

Rialp, A., Rialp, J. and Knight, G.A. (2005a): The phenomenon of early internationalizing firms: What do we know after a decade (1993-2003) of scientific inquiry?, *International Business Review*, **14**(2): 147-166.

Singh, N. & Kundu, S. (2002). Explaining the growth of e-commerce corporations: An extension and application of the eclectic paradigm. *Journal of International Business Studies*, **33**(4): 679-697.

Teece, D., Pisano, G. and Shuen, A,. (1990). *Firm Capabilities, Resources, and the Concept of Strategy*. Center for Research in Management. University of California, Berkeley. CCC Working Paper 90-8.

The Economist (2012). The end of cheap China. What do soaring Chinese wages mean for global manufacturing, March 10.

Tran, Y. (2008) *Fashion in the Danish Experience Economy: Challenges for growth*. Samfundsliteratur and Imagine.

Tran (2014). Founding of sustainable new ventures by MNC employees in emerging markets: An exploration study of professional service ventures in Vietnam. *Working paper*

Vestring, T., Rouse, T., Reinert, U. and Varma, S. (2005). *Making the Move to Low-Cost Countries*. Bain & Company

Wright, R.W. and Ricks, D. A. (1994). Trends in international business research: Twenty-five years later. *Journal of International Business Studies*, **25**: 687-701.

Yamin, M. and Sinkovics, R. (2006). Online internationalisation, psychic distance reduction and the virtuality trap. *International Business Review*, **15**(4): 339-360.

Young, S., Dimitratos, P. and Dana, LP. (2003). International entrepreneurship research: What scope for international business theories? *Journal of International Entrepreneurship*, **1**(1): 31-42.

Zahra, S. and George, G. (2002), Absorptive capacity: A review, reconceptualization, and extension. *The Academy of Management Review*. **27**(2): 185-203

Zahra, S., Ireland, R., & Hitt, M. (2000). International expansion by new venture firms: International diversity, mode of market entry, technological learning, and performance. *Academy of Management Journal*, **43**(5): 925-950.

10 Exit: Failure and Success

Jaydeep Pancholi and Norin Arshed

It may seem odd to learn about business exit and failure in a book about entre-preneurship and starting and growing successful businesss. However, it has been reported by the U.S. Small Business Administration that approximately 10% of all firms in the United States fail each year (Knott and Posen, 2005). In the UK, the rate is thought to be similar with 20% of businesses failing in their first year while a further 30% fail within the first three years (BIS, 2013). It is crucial to understand what is meant by business exit and failure to ensure that entrepreneurs and governments can learn from, and respond to failure. This chapter explores the meaning and importance of business failure followed by why firms fail and the effect this can have on the entrepreneur. It also discusses how to avoid such failures and provides an insight into some famous failures.

Understanding the meaning of failure

Understanding failure can be a challenging concept; terms such as 'failure', 'business death', 'closure' and 'exit' can be used to describe how an entrepreneur leaves a business, frequently overlapping in definition. The definition of busi-ness failure can be summarised as "a business that has fallen short of its goals or become insolvent, thus requiring involuntary termination or discontinuation of the business" (Politis and Gabrielsson, 2009, p. 365). In other words, business failure is the "cessation of involvement in a venture because it has not met a minimum threshold for economic viability as stipulated by the entrepreneur" (Ucbasaran *et al.*, 2013, p188). Other terms used can be defined as:

- ☐ **Business closure:** A situation in which a business entity discontinues in its existing form (Stokes and Blackburn, 2002). The inability of the busi-ness to survive and thus a discontinuance of the business (Hall, 1995).

- ☐ **Owner's exit:** The act of departing from a business ownership by the business owner (Stokes and Blackburn, 2001).

☐ **Exit:** No longer trading in a specific market or producing a particular product.

Famous failures

Polaroid – The camera that gave instant pictures was not only an admired form of photo-graphy but also a cultural phenomenon. A leader in photographic technology, Polaroid created a name for itself in the 1980s. However, through the weight of competition, technological advancements and change in consumer trends Polaroid went bankrupt in 2005.

Phones 4 U – Once a well-known independent retailer of mobile phones in the UK, Phones 4 U had gained a successful business strategy in offering special deals. However, in 2014 the company had become dependent upon contract deals with EE and Vodaphone, two major networks within the UK mobile phone industry. Failing in negotiations, contracts were not renewed, which led to business failure and store closures.

In 2014 there was 5.2 million businesses recorded in the UK, with 346,000 business births and 238,000 business deaths that year (Rhodes, 2014). New firms are the most vulnerable (Headd, 2003). Despite the most conservative estimates suggesting these rates are inflated (Levie *et al.*, 2011), the common consensus is that business failure is a common phenomenon and prevalent mostly amongst early stage ventures.

Given such statistics, the term 'failure' can hold a negative connotation, discouraging many from starting a business (Stokes and Blackburn, 2002). Business failure can be due to many reasons where entrepreneurs have not been able to sustain financial benefit through offering a product or service. When examining why a business fails, several factors can arise, questioning the lack of experience, strength of competition and changes in consumer trends. However, once a business has reached its peak in trading operations, managerial decisions will have to be taken on how an entrepreneur wishes to exit. Two options remain for an entrepreneur to exit their business: *voluntary* or *involuntary*.

Voluntary exit can be initiated by an entrepreneur knowing that their business is on the decline in the life cycle. As a result, an entrepreneur can put their business into liquidation; bringing the business activities of the company to an end (DeTienne *et al.*, 2014). However, it must be noted that there can be further reasoning for an owner liquidating their business, such as retirement or lack of interest, therefore this form of business exit could also end with a surplus rather a loss. For example, The Falck Group, now a successful Italian energy firm, had liquidated its initial steel business in the 1990s. The company had been in the family for five generations and they were able to raise investment for a new venture into renewable energy (Detienne and Chirico, 2013), once again becoming successful in their new venture. However, for many entrepreneurs with a failing business, liquidation is an inevitable process before funds dissolve.

Instead of liquidation, as another form of voluntary business exit an entrepreneur can sell the business. If a business is profitable or has scope to achieve another business's objectives, such as capturing the same target market, an entrepreneur can attract the interest of their competitors or specific interest groups. This form of business exit would be more attractive for an entrepreneur who wants to end their business venture and leave with a surplus.

Case study: WhatsApp

The sale of WhatsApp, a mobile messaging application, to Facebook provides a good example of a profitable business exit. Facebook purchased WhatsApp for $19 billion in 2014 (Bhattacharya, 2014). With 450 million active users at the end of 2014, WhatsApp undertook a positive exit strategy enticing Facebook with a customer community which they had developed. Being purchased by a larger company proves to be a profitable exit strategy for mobile app developers with the rise of consumer usage.

For the majority of cases, business failure is led by an involuntary exit where an entrepreneur is forced to leave their business venture (Stokes and Blackburn, 2001). A case could arise through insolvency, where an entrepreneur has lost control of their financial balance sheets resulting in an increase of debt with insufficient income to cope with financial repayments. In this case an entrepreneur can declare bankruptcy – a legal clearance allowing an entrepreneur to be free of debt by directly handing over their bank accounts. This form of exit would also impede the entrepreneur's viability to future financial borrowing power, where lenders would question the track record of the individual. Any assets in the business owner's name would also be taken to pay towards the debt. However, the European Commission has reviewed the difficulties for failed entrepreneurs to gain finances, allowing a 'second chance' legal framework to encourage entrepreneurs to continue entrepreneurial activity in the hope of generating future income for the European Union (European Commission, 2011: p. 19).

10

Case study: Blockbuster

An example of bankruptcy can be demonstrated by movie rental store Blockbuster. Not being able to withstand online competition through the rise of the digital era the company had to declare bankruptcy (Hill and Gareth, 2013). In direct competition with a growing online rental company Netflix, Blockbuster was forced to close their 5000 stores in US and later in the UK.

In some cases of insolvency, a business can go into administration; handing over the company to a third party (an administrator) in an attempt to revive financial stability and set a plan of recovery.

Case study: HMV

Administration has been the case for high street music store HMV. With 73% of music and films downloaded online and a further projection of increasing to 90% by the end 2015, HMV have been attempting to maintain consumer interest (McDonald and Ailsa, 2014). HMV had to appoint management consultancy firm Deloitte after music suppliers refused to provide £300 million in additional financing to pay their bank debts. Deloitte had tried to find a buyer for the company and save some of the larger stores closing down. However, many of the company's assets were used to pay their debts. Nevertheless, today the company is still surviving, with the help of Hilco UK (a firm specialising in reconstructing failing firms).

Having looked into key terms used in both voluntary and involuntary forms of business exit, it is equally important to review the term 'failure'. Scholars of business exit have demonstrated that many companies have become successful in their business venture after failing several times, where not only experience was gained but also expertise (Müller and Stegmaier, 2015; Wolfe and Shepherd, 2015; Yamakawa *et al.*, 2015). Examples of famous failures (before success) include the likes of Richard Branson who failed in several businesses before establishing the Virgin brand – an entrepreneur's learning experience from failure may positively change their behavioural actions alongside their learning through success.

Exercise

Research and provide one example of a company for each of the following business exits: liquidation, exit and bankruptcy that has affected the student population. Justify your answer.

Why is business closure important?

There are five main categories of why entrepreneurs closed or changed their business in the UK (Figure 10.1). It is evident that the two main reasons may not be related to financial performance but due to a change in the owner's objectives or in finding a buyer for their business (Justo *et al.*, 2015; Levie *et al.*, 2011). Showing the different reasons why entrepreneurs close their business is important as it allows us to analyse the social and economic impacts of business closure.

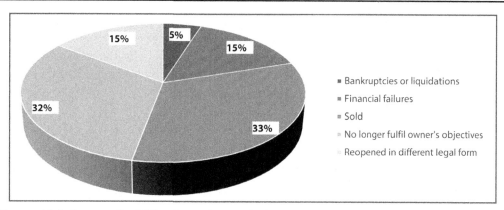

Figure 10.1: Reasons for UK business closures in 2011
Source: (Levie *et al.*, 2011: p.198).

■ Social

As reviewed earlier, a business failing to maintain a financial objective could force an entrepreneur to close down the venture. However, as an outcome the learning experience gained for an entrepreneur can be justified as a strong return on investment (Toft-Kehler *et al.*, 2014). It is because of this failing experience that the entrepreneur can create another start-up with prior experience leading to success (Hsu *et al.*, 2015). However, conceptualising failure as a positive outcome for an entrepreneur can be viewed differently for other members. There have been studies that have reviewed the 'aftermath' and 'costs of business failure' (Ucbasaran *et al.*, 2013: 174) identifying the financial, psychological and social costs (Byrne and Shepherd, 2013; Jenkins *et al.*, 2014; Lofstrom *et al.*, 2014). A business closure affects not only the entrepreneur but is also likely to affect their family and friends. A level of distress would need to be taken into account, where lifestyle, family commitment and pride could mean significant costs for the business not succeeding (Singh *et al.*, 2014). This can be the case where an entrepreneur is providing financial support for their family; in particular entrepreneurs often rely on personal sources of finance from family and friends (Roper and Scott, 2009).

Not all business closures are linked to a negative outcome. As seen from the reasons of business closures (Figure 10.1), a majority are 'successful closures' (Levie *et al.*, 2011). An entrepreneur's change in personal objectives could alter, such as retirement or change of interests, resulting in closing business operations. Many times if a business has been successful, they can be offered a 'buy out' deal, where if the offer is attractive, they would sell the business to another owner. This can be a quick exit strategy if the entrepreneur wishes to gain their return on investment at a faster rate. This was the case of American

10

toy manufacturer Sprig Toys being bought by Wham-O's (known for toys such as the Frisbee and the Hula Hoop) who decided to sell due to the need for capital (Sarason *et al.*, 2014). As a result, successful closures can provide an entrepreneur with personal endorsements, ending their venture to either keep or reinvest their money into another business.

■ Economic

From an economic perspective, a key area which enforces the importance of business closure is dominated by finances. An entrepreneur could have raised their finances to start up their business through personal savings. Along with this initial financial investment, the entrepreneur is also subjected to the 'opportunity cost' of their time; these are the potential earnings they could have made if they were in full time employment for an established company as an employee (Burke and van Stel, 2014). Through failure, these finances – money and other earnings foregone – would be lost whereby an entrepreneur is left with the same or most likely less than what they started with. To raise the capital to start their business venture, family, potential business partners, shareholders or financial lenders are often used. This creates a wider issue as the closure of a business would directly affect the stakeholders who have invested into the business. If the business was closed with an inability to pay back the investment, a level of debt exists which may cause concern for many.

In a few cases there is an element of intentional business failure by money lenders where fraudsters set up fake business to siphon money (Olaison and Sørensen, 2014). Furthermore, large scale business closures may raise national interest and concerns at the cost of unemployment. For example, at the peak of the financial downturn British high street chains Woolworths and Borders Books were both forced to cease trading resulting in thousands becoming unemployed (Lai *et al.*, 2015). Such large redundancies usually have a direct effect on the individuals involved by causing financial restraint. In turn the national economy is impacted with the loss of jobs, rise of unemployment, potentially increasing social welfare transfers to aid those affected. Both on an individual and national level, unemployment would thus change the lifestyle and national prosperity.

Small to medium size enterprise (SMEs) are particularly vulnerable to economic recession. Within the UK 99% of British firms fall into this category therefore making SMEs a strong area of concern for the government to ensure resilience in all economic climates (Lai *et al.*, 2015). This highlights the importance of understanding business closure because of factors that are of economic relevance and stability. Furthermore, although business failures are not productive or inductive of economic growth, failure can improve:

☐ **Market efficiencies**, e.g. through cheaper transaction costs and investment potential;

☐ **Knowledge transfer and technological innovation**, e.g. a defunct firm can have a spillover effect to former employees and other firms in the industry given their knowledge in research and development, and;

☐ **Knowledge and resources are 'recycled'** and economies advanced (Baumard and Starbuck, 2005; Cannon and Edmondson, 2005; Mason and Harrison, 2006; Mcgrath, 1999).

By businesses closing, a market analysis can also uncover consumer trends. This movement in consumer demand indicates where interest is declining, growing or shifting between industries. This demonstrates another area of importance in reviewing business closure: aiding in future growth of research, development and innovation (Hyytinen *et al.*, 2015). In analysing why and how businesses fail, researchers and entrepreneurs can gain advantageous knowledge on growing and sustaining a business as it can be easier to review failure over successes (Mcgrath, 1999; Singh *et al.*, 2014).

Exercise

From your own experiences of business 'births' and 'deaths' seen on a typical high street, describe a change in consumer trends. Provide an example of a particular industry.

Why do firms fail?

So why do firms fail? From Berryman's (1983) research on SMEs, many of the factors can still be applied to firms in the 21st century (Stokes and Blackburn, 2002). Business failure can be categorized by working functions both internal and external to the business. The following areas demonstrate key functions leading to failure:

10

☐ **Accounting** – it can be argued that the core reason why many firms fail is due to a lack of accurate accounting (Burke and van Stel, 2014). The working capital of the business – a healthy bank account within the business to allow fluid income and outgoings – is necessary for a successful business and stock control. Furthermore, lack of retaining earnings and maintaining profit margins can also lead to an imbalance of finances. For example, Rangers Football Club, based in Glasgow, demonstrated this with high spending on players and lack of income through both national and international game wins, so that by 2002 the football club was in £80 million debt (McDermott, 2015). This led to the Club going into administration, liquidation and revival through changes of ownerships and management in 2012 with their business model changing over time.

☐ **Marketing** – not understanding your market and poor marketing is another reason why many firms dissolve. If a firm loses sight of their target market, branding, consumer trends and marketing communication strategies, their chances of failure will increase (Keller, 2012). Failure to place your branding in line with your target market will lead to a decline in sales. Car manufacturer Volkswagen experienced a marketing failure when launching their new luxury vehicle 'Phaeton' in 2002 (Keller, 2012). Costing $1.3 billion in development costs, the car was priced at $85,000 directly competing against BMW and Mercedes-Benz. However, it was soon discovered that consumers were not willing to pay a high price for the VW brand. Only selling 2,253 units between 2004 and 2006, the vehicle was pulled from the market and relaunched with a different strategy in 2011.

☐ **Internal factors** – when a business has secured finances to start-up, an entrepreneur can underestimate the length of time this initial capital will last until the business becomes profitable. As a result much investment has been placed into the start-up costs, however not enough capital has been raised to operate. Another internal factor which can hinder the business is nepotism or negligence. Employing only within family or friendship circles can lose a work force that could be more suited for the job in skill and innovation, and also generate conflicts of interest.

☐ **External factors** – in some cases business failure is due to economic or political factors changing the environment in which a business operates. An economic down-turn can limit trust in the economy resulting in a decline in spending. This would directly affect the sales of a business due to spending cuts by both businesses and individual consumers. The recent economic crisis saw 90,000 businesses closing down in December 2008 alone, 250% more than the monthly average between 2006 – 2010 (Connolly and Duedil, 2012).

☐ **Behaviour of entrepreneur** – business failure also questions the entrepreneur's ability to run a successful business. The entrepreneur could lack skills and business acumen leading to a low level and decline in profitability. These could be in line with the inability to delegate, reluctance to seek help, excessive optimism, lack of awareness of the external and internal environments, or inability to adapt to change.

These main influential factors govern the likelihood of a business to fail, questioning the operation and functioning of a business. Table 10.1 below highlights additional factors which could also play a role as to why firms fail.

Factor	Reason
Age of business	Young firms are more likely to fail than older firms. Half of all new firms cease trading in the first 3 years (Müller and Stegmaier, 2015).
Size of business	Smaller firms are likely to fail – they have fewer assets and are unable to weather adversity in the short-term (Coad, 2014).
Past-growth	Firms that grow in a short period of time are less likely to fail (Davidsson, *et al.*, 2009).
Sector	Failure rates vary from sector to sector – but the construction and retail sectors show the highest rates of failure (Stokes and Blackburn, 2002).
Economic conditions	Smaller firms are much more likely to be vulnerable to changes in economic activity (Lai *et al.*, 2015). During the height of the economic recession – 50 businesses a day were closing in the UK.
Type of firm	Franchises are less fragile and tend to do well, but limited companies are at the most risk of closure.
Location	There are clear regional variations in failure rates – for example, London has higher rates of failure than any other region in the UK (but also has higher rates of formation because of its location) (Rhodes, 2014).
Ownership	Bigger firms with more than one plant are likely to close one plant than all the plants (Müller and Stegmaier, 2015). Ownership is less studied when it comes to failure.
Business in receipt of state subsidises	State subsidies are given to the weakest firms – this is often difficult to verify.

Table 10.1: Why firms fail

Exercise

Research and describe how the 2008/2009 UK recession affected the banking/financial industry providing examples of closures and survival.

10

Business failure and the entrepreneur

When an individual has committed resources, time and effort, a business becomes of high importance. Shepherd (2009) explains that a business is regarded highly important because it provides an entrepreneur with an income, sense of satisfaction and independence. Thus, by losing the business a sense of grief is experienced (Jenkins *et al.*, 2014; Yamakawa *et al.*, 2015). This may also mean the entrepreneur keeps a failing business going for too long, accumulating losses with wider and longer term impacts. Negative emotional reactions can be portrayed knowing that time and effort into a venture has been a wasted effort. Many entrepreneurs are passionate about their venture, thus when business begins to fail, pride is also affected (Singh, *et al.*, 2014). The self-image comes to the forefront whereby the entrepreneur would want to avoid the topic of failure arising by friends and family. Additionally, the stigma of failing can have a consequential effect of mental trauma in 'losing money'. It has been found that the majority of entrepreneurial careers that were forced into business exit were financially disappointing (Coad, 2014).

One fundamental effect of business failure on an entrepreneur is the financial strain they would undergo (Ucbasaran, *et al.*, 2012). Many times, personal savings and borrowed capital are used to start up a venture. As a business fails this debt would have to be resolved legally and/or continue to be a burden for the entrepreneur and also restrain their future ability to gain finance, as seen earlier. Both a sense of grief and financial strain can cause stress for an entrepreneur, potentially resulting in mental tension, decline in health and rise in family problems (Uy *et al.*, 2013).

Forward planning, knowledge of industry and moving in line with trends are all necessary for an entrepreneur to adopt, especially as many industries have accelerated in innovation and competition (Naldi and Davidsson, 2014). Nevertheless, the characteristics of an entrepreneur can also positively react to business failure. Many successful entrepreneurs have adopted a need for achievement and self-starter attitudes (Landstrom and Astrom, 2011) resulting in the ability to learn from a mistake and utilise what knowledge they have gained to create another venture. With a disregard to want to work for another organization, a key entrepreneurial trait is based on creativity and innovation – being able to change failed products or services into another use (Olaison and Sørensen, 2014). Previous studies in the UK have shown that serial entrepreneurs – who start several businesses – have the same level of optimism when experiencing failure as when they started (Ucbasaran, *et al.*, 2010). In line with a Schumpeterian view of 'creative destruction', entrepreneurs can see a failure as an encouragement to face competition, leading to a better idea (Müller and Stegmaier, 2014; Olaison and Sørensen, 2014). Figure 10.2 demonstrates this process of creative destruction. The creation of a business would begin by an individual taking the risk to start up a venture. For unsuccessful businesses, if an entrepreneur can overcome economic, regulatory and financial reasons of closure, their personality traits will enable them to re-organize their business or to start a completely new venture with a different strategy.

Exercise

Choose an entrepreneur who has created an innovative product or service from undergoing the process of creative destruction. Justify your choice.

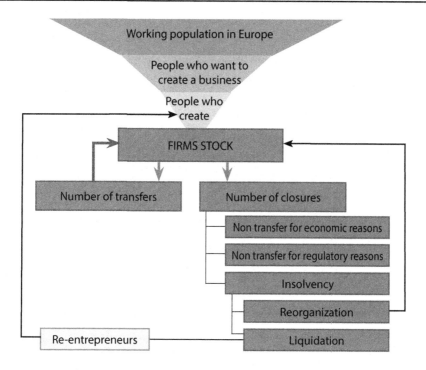

Figure 10.2: Process of creative destruction
Source: (European Commission, 2011: p.167).

Prevention of business failure

In discussing in more detail business failure and the effects upon an entrepreneur, it is useful to highlight areas of prevention for business failure. Lussier (1996) highlighted ten areas for an entrepreneur to avoid failure:

1 **Business plan and adequate capital**: when creating a business plan, it is highly necessary to establish start-up prices to attain adequate capital (Parhankangas and Ehrlich, 2014). Underestimating start-up costs can cause financial strain once set up. Starting capital should allow for operational flow with extra margin until the business gains sustainable profits. Keeping fixed costs low will also assist in keeping start-up costs low.

2 **Start your business in a boom economy**: products and services that are economically sensitive will benefit from being launched during a booming economy (Burke and van Stel, 2014). If money is not being spent in the economy, small businesses will decline in sales and profit.

3 **Close relationships with creditors**: creditors – financial lenders to your business – will provide capital and interest rates based on their assessment of the viability of how quickly the debt can be paid. Maintaining

10

a close relationship will eliminate any future problems and can assist in future necessity of a financial boost, such as expansion (Singh *et al.*, 2014).

4   **Good account receivables**: all start-up businesses will need to receive payment for their product or service in the shortest time frame. It is necessary to maintain fluid income and outgoings and to avoid organizational slack (Bradley *et al.*, 2011).

5   **Good record keeping**: this will maintain a professional business organization. Use of a reliable accountant, awareness of taxation and sight of profit and loss accounts will aid an entrepreneur towards forward planning (Lantto, 2013).

6   **Diverse customer base**: though a product or service may be aimed at a specific target market, possessing a diverse customer base will reduce a risk of decline in sales. Where consumer trends are constantly shifting, marketing your product to a variety of demographic groups will create sustainability.

Example

Harley Davidson sought to diversify their customer base because they were only attracting the traditional stereotypical bikers (Keller, 2012). To escape this niche segment, the motorcycle company began promoting merchandise to various groups and sponsoring events attracting a wider customer base. Furthermore, with an adaption in product and promotional events, Harley Davison managed to attract 27,000 women to adopt the brand in 2010 – breaking what was seen as a traditional male biker image (Keller, 2012).

---

7   **Developing management skills before starting**: many times an entrepreneur can fail due a lack of a basic business skill set and not being able to manage a team. Therefore it is necessary to gain industry capabilities which will support in both gaining managerial experience and finances.

8   **Consider use of partners**: partners can be advantageous because they can potentially increase financial capital, bring a wider skill set and share the work load. Risk is also shared between the partners. However, choosing the wrong business partner can lead to business failure due to factors such as disagreements and incapacities (Singh *et al.*, 2014). Therefore, it is wise to set clear objectives and functional roles within the business creating a good working environment and transparency.

9   **Grow slowly**: a small business is often more secure by expanding slowly. The income from the business should be able to support the growth. Thus if a business grew too fast without making enough profit, the high increase of costs (such as new infrastructure and labour) would outweigh the working capital which would lead to failure (Davidsson *et al.*, 2009).

10 Financial control: keeping a tight control of business finances will mini-mise theft and unnecessary expenditure. With due diligence, money can be spent in assets through reliable sources (Toft-Kehler *et al.*, 2014).

Exercise

You have a great idea for a business, would you have a business partner to help start the business? How would a partner be beneficial to your company?

Famous failed entrepreneurs who tried again and again

Walt Disney: A global sensation and mastermind behind the much loved Disney characters, and the businessman of the highly successful theme park Walt Disney World. Walt Disney was reportedly fired from previous editorial jobs for lacking imagination.

Thomas Edison: Having attempted 10,000 times to invent the light bulb, Thomas Edison revolutionised the world. His scientific workings only paid off through continuous determination to create something that was unimaginable at the time but now has become part of everyday life.

Steve Jobs: An exciting well know entrepreneur who showed the tech-nological world the power of resilience and innovation. Being fired from his own company in the early days, Steve Jobs turned this experience into a huge success. He went onto to create Pixar Animation Studios as well as transforming the Apple brand and Macintosh computers to what is known today as the Apple product series.

Oprah Winfrey: Known for being the 'Queen of Daytime Talk TV', Oprah Winfrey has become one of the most successful icons in talk shows. With a net worth of $3 billion Oprah Winfrey has become a global sensation. She was once fired as a new reporter for being inadequate.

10

Steven Spielberg: A global cinematic success, Steven Spielberg has been known for creating films such as Schindler's List, Jurassic Park, E.T and Saving Private Ryan. He was initially rejected 3 times from his chosen film school before rocketing to fame.

Henry Ford: Henry Ford had established two automotive businesses, which had failed before creating what is known today as the Ford Motor Company. Revolutionising the way automotive vehicles were manufac-tured, Henry Ford had created a standardization strategy, which was highly successful.

Exercise

Reading about the different entrepreneurs above, describe any common trends you may have noticed and what you could learn from their experiences.

Conclusion

This chapter has demonstrated that business exit can be viewed as both failure and success. The concept of failure arises due to the inability to reach a minimum threshold of economic viability and as a result forcing an entrepreneur to exit their venture, voluntarily or involuntary. In reviewing this, it can be conceptualised that there are different types of exit such as liquidation or bankruptcy. It was seen that several factors such as inadequte accounting and marketing gave reasoning as to why firms fail. The importance of making a business venture successful holds not only financial attachments but also emotional attachments, where grief and pride are elements the entrepreneur and others link with failure.

Further reading

Byrne, O. and Shepherd, D. (2015). Different strokes for different folks: Entrepreneurial narratives of emotion, cognition, and making sense of business failure. *Entrepreneurship: Theory and Practice,* **39** (2), 375–405

McGrath, R. G. (1999). Falling forward: Real options reasoning and entrepreneurial failure. *Academy of Management Review*, **24**(1), 13-30.

Politis, D. and J. Gabrielsson (2009). Entrepreneurs' attitudes towards failure: An experiential learning approach. *International Journal of Entrepreneurial Behaviour & Research*, **15**(4): 364-383.

References

Baumard, P. and Starbuck, W. H. (2005). Learning from failures: Why it may not happen. *Long Range Planning*, **38**(3), 281–298.

Berryman, J. (1983). Small business failure and survey of the literature. *International Small Business Journal*, **1**(4), 47 – 59.

Bhattacharya, S. (2014). *Operations Management*. Delhi: PHI Learning Private Limited.

BIS. (2013). SMEs: The key enables of business success and the economic rationale for government intervention. *BIS Analysis Paper Number 2: London*.

Bradley, S. W., Wiklund, J. and Shepherd, D. A. (2011). Swinging a double-edged sword: The effect of slack on entrepreneurial management and growth. *Journal of Business Venturing*, **26**(5), 537–554.

Burke, A. and van Stel, A. (2014). Entry and exit in disequilibrium. *Journal of Business Venturing*, **29**(1), 174–192.

Byrne, O. and Shepherd, D. A. (2015). Different strokes for different folks: Entrepreneurial narratives of emotion, cognition, and making sense of business failure. *Entrepreneurship: Theory and Practice*, **39**(2), 375–405.

Cannon, M. D. and Edmondson, A. C. (2005). Failing to learn and learning to fail (intelligently): How great organizations put failure to work to innovate and improve. *Long Range Planning*, **38**(3), 299–319.

Coad, A. (2014). Death is not a success : reflections on business exit. *International Small Business Journal*, **32**(7), 721 – 731.

Connolly, A. and Duedil. (2012). Duedil map the UK recession by region and sector. Available from: http://www.theguardian.com/news/datablog/2012/aug/20/duedil-analysis-impacts-recession-uk-business [Accessed: 22nd May 2015]

Davidsson, P., Steffens, P. and Fitzsimmons, J. (2009). Growing profitable or growing from profits: Putting the horse in front of the cart? *Journal of Business Venturing*, **24**(4), 388–406.

DeTienne, D. R. and Chirico, F. (2013). Exit strategies in family firms: How socioemotional wealth drives the threshold of performance. *Entrepreneurship: Theory and Practice*, **37**(6), 1297–1318.

DeTienne, D. R., Mckelvie, A. and Chandler, G. N. (2014). Journal of Business Venturing Making sense of entrepreneurial exit strategies : A typology and test. *Journal of Business Venturing*, **30**(2), 255–272.

European Commission. (2011). *Business Dynamics: Start-ups, Business Transfers ad Bankruptcy*. Brussels.

Hall, G. (1995). *Surviving and Prospering in the Small Firm Sector*. London: Routledge.

Headd, B. (2003). Redefining business success: Distinguishing between closure and failure. *Small Business Economics*, **21**(1), 51–61.

Hill, C. and Gareth, J. (2013). *Strategic Management Cases: An Integrated Approach* 10th ed. Mason: South-Western Cengage Learning.

Hsu, D. K., Wiklund, J. and Cotton, R. D. (2015). Success, failure, and entrepreneurial reentry: An experimental assessment of the veracity of self-efficacy and prospect theory. *Entrepreneurship Theory and Practice*, **1**(828), 1–29.

Hyytinen, A., Pajarinen, M. and Rouvinen, P. (2015). Does innovativeness reduce startup survival rates? *Journal of Business Venturing*, **30**(4), 564–581.

Jenkins, A. S., Wiklund, J. and Brundin, E. (2014). Individual responses to firm failure: Appraisals, grief, and the influence of prior failure experience. *Journal of Business Venturing*, **29**(1), 17–33.

10

Justo, R., DeTienne, D. R. and Sieger, P. (2015). Failure or voluntary exit? Reassessing the female underperformance hypothesis. *Journal of Business Venturing*. doi:10.1016/j.jbusvent.2015.04.004

Keller, K. (2012). *Strategic Brand Management: Building, Measuring, and Managing Brand Equity* 4th ed. Harrow: Pearson.

Knott, A. M. and Posen, H. E. (2005). Is failure good? *Strategic Management Journal*, **26**(7), 617 – 641.

Lai, Y., Saridakis, G., Blackburn, R. and Johnstone, S. (2015). Are the HR responses of small firms different from large firms in times of recession? *Journal of Business Venturing*. doi:10.1016/j.jbusvent.2015.04.005

Landstrom, H. and Astrom, F. (2011). Who's asking the right question? Patterns and diversity in the literature of new venture creation. In K. Hindle and K. Klyver (Eds.), *Handbook of Research on New Venture Creation* (pp. 34 – 71). Cheltenham: Edward Elgar Publishing Limited.

Lantto, A.M. (2013). Business involvement in accounting: A case study of international financial reporting standards adoption and the work of accountants. *European Accounting Review*, **23**(2), 335–356.

Levie, J. D., Don, G. and Leleux, B. (2011). The new venture mortality myth. In K. Hindle and K. Klyver (Eds.), *Handbook of Research on New Venture Creation* (pp. 194 – 215). Cheltenham: Edward Elgar.

Lofstrom, M., Bates, T. and Parker, S. C. (2014). Why are some people more likely to become small-businesses owners than others: Entrepreneurship entry and industry-specific barriers. *Journal of Business Venturing*, **29**(2), 232–251.

Lussier, R. (1996). Reasons why small businesses fail: and how to avoid failure. *The Entrepreneurial Executive*, **1**(2), 10–17.

Mason, C. M. and Harrison, R. T. (2006). After the exit: acquisitions, entrepreneurial recycling and regional economic development. *Regional Studies*, **40**(1), 55–73.

McDermott, J. (2015). Glasgow Rangers: a club in danger of losing its identity. Available from: http://www.ft.com/cms/s/2/cfbddcce-9c12-11e4-a6b6-00144feabdc0.html [Accessed: 22nd May 2015]

McDonald, M. and Ailsa, K. (2014). *MBA Marketing*. Basingstoke: Palgrave Macmillan.

Mcgrath, R. G. (1999). Falling forward: Real options reasoning and entreprenurial failure. *Academy of Management Review*, **24**(1), 13–31.

Müller, S. and Stegmaier, J. (2015). Economic failure and the role of plant age and size. *Small Business Economics*, **44**, 621–638.

Naldi, L. and Davidsson, P. (2014). Entrepreneurial growth: The role of international knowledge acquisition as moderated by firm age. *Journal of Business Venturing*,

29(5), 687–703.

Olaison, L. and Sørensen, B. M. (2014). The abject of entrepreneurship: failure, fiasco, fraud. *International Journal of Entrepreneurial Behaviour & Research,* **20**(2), 193–211.

Parhankangas, A. and Ehrlich, M. (2014). How entrepreneurs seduce business angels: An impression management approach. *Journal of Business Venturing,* **29**(4), 543–564.

Politis, D. and Gabrielsson, J. (2009). Entrepreneurs' attitudes towards failure: An experiential learning approach. *International Journal of Entrepreneurial Behaviour & Research,* **15**(4), 364 – 383.

Rhodes, C. (2014). *Business Statistics.* London: House of Commons Library.

Roper, S. and Scott, J. M. (2009). Perceived financial barriers and the start-up decision: An econometric analysis of gender differences using GEM data. *International Small Business Journal,* **27**(2), 149-171.

Sarason, Y., DeTienne, D. R. and Bentley, C. (2014). Wham-O's offer to buy Sprig Toys: Selling in or selling out? *Entrepreneurship: Theory and Practice,* **38**(4), 959–972.

Shepherd, D. (2009). Grief recovery from the loss of a family business: A multi- and meso-level theory. *Journal of Business Venturing,* **24**(1), 81–97.

Singh, S., Corner, P. D. and Pavlovich, K. (2014). Failed, not finished: A narrative approach to understanding venture failure stigmatization. *Journal of Business Venturing,* **30**(1), 150–166.

Stokes, D. and Blackburn, R. (2001). *Opening up business closures: a study of businesses that close and owners' exit routes. A research report for HSBC.*

Stokes, D. and Blackburn, R. (2002). Learning the hard way: the lessons of owner-managers who have closed their businesses. *Journal of Small Business and Enterprise Development,* **9**(1), 17 – 27.

Toft-Kehler, R., Wennberg, K. and Kim, P. H. (2014). Practice makes perfect: Entrepreneurial-experience curves and venture performance. *Journal of Business Venturing,* **29**(4), 453–470.

Ucbasaran, D., Shepherd, D. A., Lockett, A. and Lyon, S. J. (2013). Life after business failure: The process and consequences of business failure for entrepreneurs. *Journal of Management,* **39**(1), 163–202.

Ucbasaran, D., Westhead, P., Wright, M. and Flores, M. (2010). The nature of entrepreneurial experience, business failure and comparative optimism. *Journal of Business Venturing,* **25**(6), 541–555.

Uy, M. A., Foo, Der M. and Song, Z. (2013). Joint effects of prior start-up experience and coping strategies on entrepreneurs' psychological well-being. *Journal of Business Venturing,* **28**(5), 583–597.

10

Wolfe, M. T. and Shepherd, D. A. (2015). "Bouncing back" from a loss: Entrepreneurial orientation, emotions, and failure narratives. *Entrepreneurship: Theory and Practice*, **39**(3), 675–700.

Yamakawa, Y., Peng, M. W. and Deeds, D. L. (2015). Rising from the ashes: Cognitive determinants of venture growth after entrepreneurial failure. *Entrepreneurship: Theory and Practice*, **39**(2), 209–236.

11 Enterprise Policy

Norin Arshed and Mike Danson

Over the last 30 years, the importance of entrepreneurship to employment, innovation, productivity and income growth has led to an interest in enterprise policy (Shane, 2008; Blackburn and Smallbone, 2008). Enterprise policies have been seen to encourage economic growth, create jobs and generate economic development (Audretsch and Beckmann, 2007), with the aim of meeting economic and social challenges (Wright *et al.*, 2015). Acknowledging the importance of entrepreneurs and Small and Medium Enterprises (SMEs) allows an understanding of why so much attention is being paid to enterprise policy. This chapter answers the following fundamental questions in order to define, understand and review enterprise policy:

- ☐ What is enterprise policy?
- ☐ What is the economic rationale for undertaking enterprise policy?
- ☐ Why has enterprise policy become so important?
- ☐ What are the main instruments of enterprise policy?

What is enterprise policy?

As a first step it is important to understand that enterprise policy in this context includes both entrepreneurship and SME policy. It is indeed essential to understand that entrepreneurship and SME policies are seen as separate entities and are often confused and used synonymously in policy circles and by commentators. After studying numerous economies, Lundstrom and Stevenson (2005: p. 5) defined entrepreneurship policy as being:

> aimed at the pre-start, the start-up and post-start-up phases of the entrepreneurial process; designed and delivered to address the areas of motivation, opportunity and skill and; is the primary objective of encouraging more people in the population to consider entrepreneurship as an option, to move into the nascent stage of taking the steps to get started and then to proceed into the infancy and early stages of a business.

In contrast, SME policy targets the existing population of enterprises and encompasses virtually all of the support measures included in the policy portfolio which is designed to promote the viability of SMEs (Audretsch, 2004). There are four major areas of divergence between the two types of policy:

1 Entrepreneurship policy focuses on *individuals*, while SME policy focuses on *firms*.

2 Entrepreneurial policy concentrates on supporting the needs of people as they progress from one stage to the next (from awareness to pre-start-up to post-start-up); SME policy emphasises support for established firms that have already acquired sufficient capacity to benefit from SME schemes and measures.

3 Entrepreneurship policy makes greater use of 'soft' policy measures, such as mentoring, advice and entrepreneurship promotion; SME policy makes use of 'hard' policy instruments, such as financial support like grants, venture capital, etc.

4 The implementation of entrepreneurship policy includes a number of players in the makeup of its support infrastructure, such as educators, the media, and government agencies, whilst SME policy is more likely to be directly implemented through a constricted set of key players such as economic development agencies and financial intermediaries (Lundstrom and Stevenson, 2005).

However, both policies have similar long-term visions. It has been argued that "there is considerable overlap in the meanings attached to these terms and a general lack of precision regarding the differences between them" (Stevenson and Lundstrom, 2001: p. 15). Although the differences between entrepreneurship and SME policy have been outlined, the underlying proposition remains unchanged: to enhance economic prosperity in a country, be it through encouraging business start-ups or the growth of existing firms (Arshed *et al.*, 2014).

Furthermore, there is a typology of the different approaches to enterprise policy adopted by various governments, indicating considerable diversity of the policies available (Stevenson and Lundstrom, 2007). Table 11.1 illustrates the different approaches and policies towards enterprise.

A government implementing an *e-extension policy* generally embeds this policy within an existing SME policy framework. The *niche entrepreneurship policy* is often planned in conjunction with a dominant entrepreneurship policy approach where the overall entrepreneurship culture is strong but special efforts are needed to help specific groups of the population to overcome adverse effects or obstacles. There are two types: the first targets those who are under-represented amongst business owners, e.g. women, ethnic minorities, disabled and the unemployed, and tries to address specific barriers that individuals face.

Policy type	Policy objectives	Example
E-extension	Start-up programmes 'added-on' to existing SME initiatives, where they tend to be somewhat marginalised and weakly resourced.	Taiwan, USA, Australia, Canada and Sweden
'Niche' entrepreneurship	The government formulates targeted entrepreneurship around specified groups of the population.	US, Canada and Sweden
New firm creation	The aim of this policy is to reduce time and costs to a minimum so that more people will be able to start their own businesses.	Italy
Holistic entrepreneurship	National government policy objectives include reducing barriers to entry and exit, improving access to start-up resources (financing, information and assistance) and addressing the start-up needs of target groups such as the disabled, women, ethnic minorities and the young, but also promoting an entrepreneurship culture, along with attempting to embed this ideology within the educational system.	UK

Table 11.1: Types of enterprise policy

*Source***:** Adapted from Stevenson and Lundstrom (2007) and Verheul *et al.* (2009).

The second type aims to generate high growth potential businesses based on R&D, technology or knowledge inputs by targeting people with the highest potential for starting such firms e.g. scientists, inventors and university graduates. *New firm creation* policy is dominant in countries where there may be many structural and regulatory barriers to creating businesses. It involves a number of government policies and structures, including regulations and policies related to competition, social security, employment, taxation, company law and bankruptcy or insolvency rules. The *holistic entrepreneurship policy* ultimately aims to produce a more entrepreneurial society. This type of policy endeavours to establish and enhance an entrepreneurial culture and infiltrate the education system to instigate entrepreneurship at all levels of society.

11

Exercise

Choose three countries other than those discussed above and undertake some research giving examples of each type of policy within the different countries.

The economic rationale for enterprise policy?

Researchers, policy-makers, support agencies and SME groups tend to assume that there exists a strong case for the provision of government intervention for the SME sector. There has been a long-running debate as to whether or not enterprise policy should be employed by the government to provide businesses with information, support and training which is financed by central government (Johnson, 2005).

> **Tip:** A record number of small firms in the UK in 2015: some 5.2 million, an increase of 760,000 since 2010 (Young, 2015).

■ Arguments for undertaking enterprise policy

The Bolton Report (1971) increased the recognition that small firms were important and that they had to cope with an "uneven playing field" (Greene *et al.*, 2008: p. 57). This led to governments introducing numerous policies, including the provision of advice, to facilitate the formation of new firms and to offer support to SMEs to aid their survival and foster improved rates of growth (Robson and Bennett, 2000). The rationale behind publicly funded enterprise support programmes is that they benefit not only the individual firms, but also the economy as a whole (Massey, 2003). Many countries have been introducing policies aimed at stimulating entrepreneurship (OECD, 2005a) as they believe entrepreneurship is central to the sound functioning of market economies (OECD, 2005b) and in assiting in the creation of a global and knowledge-based economy (Doh and Kim, 2014). The rationale for government intervention was described by the Department of Trade and Industry (DTI) as:

> The small firms sector is recognized by government as having a vital part to play in the development of the economy. It accounts for a significant proportion of employment output and it is a source of competition, innovation, diversity and employment (Frank *et al.*, 1984: p. 257).

The key argument put forward for defending government assistance is that market failure exists as there is inefficiency in the allocation of goods and services, a scenario where individuals' pursuit of self-interest leads to bad results for society as a whole (Krugman and Wells, 2005). Thus, the market failure argument suggests that small firms in certain fields have difficulty in developing and attracting investment, therefore the government should assist them to reach optimum levels of business performance. The existence of market failure presumes that the market will not be Pareto efficient and, as a result, the need for government intervention can be advanced (Connolly and Monroe, 1999).

> **Tip:** An allocation is Pareto efficient if there is no other allocation in which some other individual is better off and no individual is worse off.

If market failures exist as a consequence of specific barriers or unequal treatment, government should then intervene on the grounds of equality (Bennett, 2008). In the case of the small business sector, several types of market failure have been identified (Table 11.2), suggesting government intervention and justifying the introduction of enterprise policies to support entrepreneurs and small businesses in the UK (Johnson *et al.*, 2000).

Type of market failure	Explanation
Monopoly	Markets are dominated by one major firm or a very small number of firms, who have sufficient control over a product or service to determine customers' access to it – higher prices and lower output than the ideal free market.
Imperfect information	A player does not know exactly what actions other players are going to take because smaller businesses may find it more difficult and expensive than larger enterprises to locate and utilise the relevant information. There is a case to provide specific assistance to small businesses in the form of free information.
Risk and uncertainty	If smaller firms are less able to absorb risk uncertainty they may need encouragement to take risks in order to benefit fully.
Financial support	The difficulties small businesses have in obtaining finance due to their size is often seen as grounds for the government to intervene with subsidised finance or loan guarantees for SMEs.
Externalities	A reason for intervention in the field of entrepreneurship stems from potential market failures resulting from three types of existing externalities (network, knowledge and learning externalities).

Table 11.2: Types of market failure
Source: Adapted from Audretsch et al. (2007) and Bennett (2008).

Furthermore, smaller firms may not be able to invest in the training development of staff, not only because of time and financial constraints but due to the risk of larger firms 'poaching' their staff. It has been suggested that government take the role of regulator (e.g. to impose specific training on all firms) or as a supplier (e.g. to provide government-financed training or subsidy for private provision) (Bennett, 2008). Advocates of laissez-faire capitalism, such as libertarians, objectivists and economists of the Austrian School argue that there is no such phenomenon as market failure. Where analysis focuses on individuals' actions towards attaining their goals or needs, inefficiency arises: means are chosen that are inconsistent with desired goals (Cordato, 1980). Hence, such government interference may take the form of taxes or subsidies which could

11

contribute to an inefficient allocation of resources, better known as government failure.

Another argument for government involvement is that SMEs have become a major part of the economy. Government assistance for SMEs provides potential benefits such as creating employment opportunities and establishing a number of growing firms, as well as improving innovation and competitiveness (Johnson *et al.*, 2000). The most frequent argument claiming the importance of small firms is that they are a major source of job creation (Storey, 2005). The view that SMEs create new jobs is based on Birch's (1979) study which concluded that small firms (those with fewer than 20 employees) in the USA generated 66% of all new jobs between 1969 and 1976. Scotland also demonstrated that public support had a positive effect on the creation of businesses, and thus lowered unemployment (Griggs and Weaver, 1997). However, a causal link between entrepreneurial prevalence and economic growth has not been conclusively established (Valliere and Peterson, 2009). The Richard Review (2007) reported that 48% of the UK workforce is employed in SMEs and 49% of UK turnover is generated by SMEs. Further statistics demonstrate that SMEs contribute to 52% of turnover and provide 60% of employment (BERR, 2009).

A final argument used to justify government intervention is that government itself creates the severest disadvantages for small firms via the cost of compliance with its regulatory and administrative requirements which burden SMEs (Bennett, 2008). By enforcing these regulations and burdening SMEs, government then volunteers to eradicate the inequalities or inefficiencies in the small business sector, creating a Catch 22 situation. Whilst others may argue that government intervention is controversial, it is justified by some as stimulating the economy by supporting SME development and reducing small firm failures.

Why should taxpayers provide support for entrepreneurs and SMEs?

1 **They contribute disproportionately to job creation:** 1970s saw a doubling of the real price of oil, high international interest rates, high rates of inflation, and unemployment levels in developed economies not seen since before the Second World War. Birch (1979) highlighted the importance of small businesses to employment creation. Every year around 200,000 to 250,000 private sector firms are born in the UK (BIS, 2013).

2 **Contributions to economic development:**

■ Technological advances

■ Increased globalization and competition

■ Changes in the workforce

- ■ Consumers increasing demand
- ■ Greater focus on innovation due to a shortening of product life-cycles and competitive pressures

3 **Sustainability benefits:**
- ■ SMEs and entrepreneurs provide choice and variety to consumers
- ■ They support local communities because of the personalized way that owners run their business
- ■ They represent an alternative outlet for people who perceive that they are not suited to employment – a shift from 'dependency' to an 'enterprise' culture

4 **A core political constituency:** the scale and focus of enterprise policy is that entrepreneurs and SMEs constitute a large group of voters in democratic countries. For example, at least 95% of all businesses in any economy are SMEs.

Exercise

Under each market failure give examples of enterprise policies which may assist in resolving such issues. You can also provide your own feasible and sustainable ideas for future enterprise policies.

■ Arguments for not undertaking enterprise policy

Nevertheless, even if entrepreneurship conceivably contributes to enhanced economic growth, this is no instinctive economic justification for government to intervene with policy (Audretsch *et al.*, 2007). Government intervention in the economy to promote business investment has not been without controversy as an existence of a market failure or 'need' in itself has been argued not to justify government action (Bennett, 2006). While government intervention may have been helpful in preventing negative business cycles and controlling inflation, it has created new kinds of problems like inefficiency, reduced growth rates, causing unproductive entrepreneurship and creating a parallel economy (the production that takes place outside of the declared and formal circular flow of income). The result of such failures is that governments can then in turn harm small firms and reduce the welfare of society through diverting resources, and deflecting or impeding businesses (Bennett, 2006).

Parker (2007) argues that there are several 'practical dangers' of government intervention where small firms are concerned:

☐ Where there is market failure, government intervention is not always justified, as it may be costly. For example, the subsidies directed towards entrepreneurs are publicly funded, but taxation crowds out private effort and capital, and distorts incentives. The government does not always

11

have superior information that is any better than the private sector, which effectively makes intervention difficult. There is an incomplete market when it comes to an 'impartial diagnosis' as most of the advice being offered is via the private sector (Hjalmarsson and Johnson, 2003). The lack of a market for impartial diagnosis would appear to be a much more solid basis for intervention.

☐ The government does not always intervene wisely, especially in the area of regulation (Parker, 2007). Seemingly endless paperwork is involved, imposing a fixed compliance cost on firms which large firms can spread over time and financially, putting their smaller competitors at a greater competitive disadvantage.

☐ It is often argued in the political economy and public finance arena that politicians and interest groups may direct subsidies in ways which primarily benefit themselves, rather than to increase social welfare (Becker, 1983). For example, it might be argued that along the lines of 'public choice' theory, politicians support policy initiatives that will maximise their chances of re-election (Johnson, 2005; Arshed *et al.*, 2014).

☐ The government is assumed to have clear objectives; however, in the UK (amongst many governments) enterprise policy aims have been difficult to pin down (Curran, 2000). Bannock and Peacock (1989) argue that politicians and bureaucrats often deliberately complicate the aims of policies to ensure everyone is satisfied; it is then less easy to identify when the policy fails. The economic objectives (e.g. high survival rates, profitability and employment creation) are often set in conjunction with social objectives (e.g. getting those people employed who are hardest to employ). These objectives frequently demonstrate blurred aims. For example, the Local Enterprise Growth Initiative gave some of England's most deprived local authorities a chance to bid for funds to support enterprise initiatives with the expectation that such approaches complement other regeneration activities in the local area (BERR, 2008).

☐ When policy objectives try to solve both economic and social problems, specific government enterprise policies become difficult to evaluate and, if and when they are evaluated, it is often in the most favourable light (Storey, 2003). Parker (2007) has argued that there should be more consistent and wide-ranging enterprise policy evaluations which take into account the different programmes that are appropriate when evaluation is done. This allows government to justify whether or not intervention is worthwhile.

Furthermore it has been argued that entrepreneurs and SMEs are not in favour of taking up such support and often favour private providers of support (Loader, 2013).

Why has enterprise policy become so important?

Over the years enterprise policy has been high on the agenda of politicians, and the aspiration to have an entrepreneurial society is seen as vital. Johnson *et al.* (2000: p. 52) recognize that:

> It is reasonable to conclude that the role of the small business sector in promoting economic growth and competitiveness is at the forefront of current government thinking on small business policy, and will continue to be so for the foreseeable future.

A rise in entrepreneurship has been a necessary response to fundamental industrial and economic restructuring, where it has become evident that there has been a shift from the 'managed economy' to the 'entrepreneurial economy' (Audretsch and Thurik, 2001). Governments in developed countries are paying more attention to enterprise policy because of the need for renewal of their economic performance (Lundstrom and Stevenson, 2005), and a global consensus has emerged viewing entrepreneurship as an engine of economic and social development (Audretsch and Beckmann, 2007). Entrepreneurs and small businesses have been seen to generate employment (Audretsch and Beckmann, 2007), contribute to the GDP, increase competition, provide stability in rural areas of the country and drive innovation (Audretsch, 1995; Dennis, 2011). It has been argued that the level and quality of entrepreneurship makes a difference in the economic vitality of communities, regions, industries and nations as a whole, and that enterprise policies can enhance an economy and the social fabric of a society (Hart, 2003).

As the perception of the benefits to be gained from increased levels of entrepreneurship has gathered momentum, governments have been quick to intervene to encourage such prosperity (Hanley and O'Gorman, 2004). Governments can see the benefits of enterprise in an economy as "raising the degree of competition in a given market, fuelling the drive for new economic opportunities and helping to meet the challenges of rapid change in a globalizing economy" (OECD, 1998: 35). The restricted expenditure available to government suggests a favourable argument and reliance on private initiative as a source of employment creation and of a preference among many policy-makers for supply-side solutions to unemployment (Hanley and O'Gorman, 2004). Promoting entrepreneurship is thus viewed as part of a formula that will bridge the economic success with social cohesion (DTI, 1998).

11

Exercise

Research a country outside of Europe and discuss the enterprise policies being delivered there and what issues they are addressing with respect to entrepreneurs and SMEs.

The main instruments of enterprise policy

With increasing interest and political attention in the promotion of enterprise, new policy instruments have been created and implemented since the mid-1990s (Audretsch and Beckmann, 2007). Policy across the European Union includes access to finance, maintaining existing jobs and/or integrating unemployed or those at risk into the labour market, facilitating cross border activities, encouraging tax breaks and financial incentives for purchases of specific sector products (Lambrecht and Pirnay, 2005).

The significance of small businesses in a country's economic and social climate has led to a range of small business support schemes and initiatives being announced. To take into account the range of objectives and the variety of the delivery instruments, the Commission of European Communities (2001: 7) advocates a relatively broad definition of business support:

> Business support services refer to these services, originating in a public policy initiative, that aim to assist enterprise or entrepreneurs to successfully develop their business activity and to respond effectively to the challenges of their business, social and physical environment.

The notion of support is most commonly used in the context of subsidised programmes of public intervention at the national and/or local level (training, loan guarantees and finance counselling) (Gibb, 2000). The level of direct government support for SMEs has increased significantly over the last couple of decades. For example, in the UK the value of support, has increased more than fivefold in the two decades after the early 1980s (Richard, 2007). There are different types of instruments employed:

☐ *Hard/direct/operational policy instruments* – these include a range of implemented financial measures such as direct grants, subsidised loans, loan guarantees and increasing initiatives to make venture capital more readily available (Lambrecht and Pirnay, 2005).

☐ *Soft/indirect/strategic policy instruments* – which are predominant in many industrialised countries utilising taxpayers' money to offer 'soft' business support to SMEs (OECD, 2000). This type of support comes in the form of advisory assistance, the dissemination of best practice and encouragement of partnerships and gateway services which endeavour to strategically address particular kinds of market failure facing small firms (Wren and Storey, 2002).

Many governments are actively working on encouraging SMEs to take part in the developmental activities on offer.

Lundstrom and Stevenson (2001) found that policy instruments used to support enterprise and entrepreneurship fell into six major categories according to what the policy (and its instruments) had been designed to address:

☐ The *regulatory environment for start-ups* - where governments are engaged in a process of examining the impact of administrative, legislative, and regulatory burdens on both existing small firms and new business entries. The main reason for this attention was to reduce the disproportionate burden of regulatory and administrative requirements on small firms in comparison to larger firms.

☐ The *promotion of entrepreneurship* – addresses how to move beyond the conventional focus of enterprise education, based upon new venture creation and management, to a broader concept based on an understanding of the way that entrepreneurs live and learn entrepreneurship (Patel, 2004). An effective strategy is to build a widespread awareness of entrepreneurship in society at large, and to increase its legitimacy and role in the economy and in the media.

☐ The *entrepreneurship education* – is important in most developed and developing countries, where it has become fashionable to view entrepreneurship and entrepreneurship education as a panacea for stagnating or declining economic activity (Matlay, 2001). Entrepreneurship education is increasingly hailed as the most effective way to facilitate the transition of a growing graduate population from education to work (Matlay and Westhead, 2005; Maritz and Donovan, 2015).

☐ The *business start-up support measures* - are of importance where SMEs appear increasingly crucial to the success of a national economy (Johnston and Loader, 2003). This support has policy objectives of improving the dynamism of economies in a number of ways: by increasing market entry and innovation, by producing a more equal spread of economic benefits, and by improving competition and increasing employment.

☐ *Access to finance and seed-capital* - is critical for entrepreneurial success, it is important that businesses have the knowledge, skills and opportunities to access the finance they need to make their enterprising ideas a reality.

☐ The *target group strategy* – entrepreneurs come from different backgrounds, experiences, motivations, behaviours, needs and demographic areas, and this motivates the government to foster policy aims and initiatives directed towards targeting certain groups. The main benefit of targeting a policy to those who fit in a particular group, e.g. women, the young, ethnic minorities and the disabled, is that it can reduce the range of expenditure as well as focus resources where they are needed. It also allows enterprise policies to increase rates of participation and productivity (Carter *et al.*, 2015).

Exercise

Are there more categories that could be added to list above? If so, explain what they are and why they are important.

Some UK enterprise policy initiatives

- **Growth vouchers** – programme which raises finance and manages cash flow, recruits and develops staff, improves leadership and management skills, attracts customers and makes the most of digital economy.

- **Sirius** – assists graduates (and international graduates) to set up businesses in the UK. Mentoring and support is given.

- **£1.1 billion package of business rates measures**, with extra relief for small businesses through the extended doubling of the Small Business Rate Relief.

- **The apprenticeship Grant for Employers** provides £1,500 to firms taking on their first apprentice. In the first year, 80% of grants went to firms employing 25 people or fewer, helping small firms train up their future workforce.

Conclusion

This chapter has introduced the importance of enterprise policy. Enterprise policies are emerging as one of the most influential and essential instruments for economic growth. Therefore, it is important to understand what is meant by enterprise policy and how governments' aim of achieving economic growth can be met by increasing skilled entrepreneurs and growing SMEs with the availability of support and advice.

Further reading

Arshed, N., Carter, S. & Mason, C. (2014). The ineffectiveness of entrepreneurship policy: is policy formulation to blame? *Small Business Economics* **43**(3), 639-659.

Blackburn, R., & Smallbone, D. (2011). Policy support for SMEs. *Environment and Planning C: Government and Policy*, **29**(4), 571-576.

Wright, M., Roper, S., Hart, M. and Carter, S. (2015). Joining the dots: Building the evidence base for SME growth policy. *International Small Business Journal 33*(1), 3-11.

References

Arshed, N., Carter, S. and Mason, C. (2014). The ineffectiveness of enterprise policy: Is policy formulation to blame? *Small Business Economics, 43*(3), 639-659.

Audretsch, D.B. (1995). *Innovation and Industry Evolution*. Cambridge: MIT Press.

Audretsch, D.B. (2004). Sustaining innovation and growth: Public policy support for entrepreneurship. *Industry & Innovation, 11*(3), 167-191.

Audretsch, D.B. and Thurik, A.R. (2001). What is new about the economy? Sources of growth in the managed and entrepreneurial economies. *Industrial and Corporate Change, 10*(1), 267-315.

Audretsch, D.B. and Beckmann, I.A.M. (2007). From small business to entrepreneurship policy. In D.B. Audretsch, I. Grilo and A.R. Thurik (Eds.), *Handbook of Research on Entrepreneurship Policy* (pp. 36-53). Great Britain: Edward Elgar.

Audretsch, D. B., Grilo, I., & Thurik, A. R. (2007). Explaining entrepreneurship and the role of policy: a framework. In D. B. Audretsch, I. Grilo & A. R. Thurik (Eds.), *Handbook of Research on Entrepreneurship Policy* (pp. 1-17).UK: Edward Elgar.

Bannock, G. and Peacock, A. (1989). *Government and Small Business*. London: Paul Chapman.

Becker, G. (1983). A theory of competition among pressure groups for political influence. *Quarterly Journal of Economics, 9*(8), 226-239.

Bennett, D. (2008). SME policy support in Britain since the 1990s: what have we learnt? *Environment and Planning C: Government and Policy, 26*(2), 375-397.

Bennett, R.J. (2006). Government and small business. In S. Carter & D. Jones-Evans (Eds.), *Enterprise and Small Business: Principles, Practice and Policy* (pp. 49-75). London: Prentice Hall.

BERR. (2008). *Enterprise: Unlocking the UK's Talent*. Retrieved August 2008, from http://www.hm-treasury.gov.uk/budget/budget_08/documents/bud_bud08_enterprise.cfm.

BERR. (2009). *Solutions for Business: Supporting Sucess* Retrieved February 2009, from http://www.berr.gov.uk/files/file50698.pdf.

Birch, D. (1979). *The Job Generation Process*. MA: MIT, Cambridge.

BIS. (2013). *SMES: The key enablers of business success and the economic rationale for government intervention*. Analysis paper 2. London.

Blackburn, R. and Smallbone, D. (2008). Researching Small Firms and Entrepreneurship in the U.K.: Developments and Distinctiveness. *Entrepreneurship Theory & Practice, 32*(2), 267-288.

11

Bolton, J.E. (1971). Report of the Committee of Inquiry on Small Firms. *In (Vol. Cmnd.4811).* London: HMSO.

Carter, S., Mwaura, S., Ram, M., Trehan, K. and Jones, T. (2015). Barriers to ethnic minority and women's enterprise: Existing evidence, policy tensions and unsettled questions. *International Small Business Journal,* **33**(1), 49-69.

Commission of European Communities. (2001). *Creating Top-Class Business Support Services (28 November).* Retrieved August 2008, from http://ec.europa.eu/enterprise/entrepreneurship/support_measures/support-services/staff_working-paper_2002_en.pdf

Connolly, S. and Monroe, A. (1999). *Economics of the Public Sector.* London: Pearson Education Ltd.

Cordato, R.E. (1980). The Austrian theory of efficiency and the role of government. *The Journal of Libertarian Studies,* **4**(4), 393-403.

Curran, J. (2000). What is small business policy in the UK for? Evaluation and assessing small business policies. *International Small Business Journal,* **18**(3), 36-50.

Dennis, W.J. (2011). Entrepreneurship, Small Business and Public Policy Levers. *Journal of Small Business Management,* **49**(1), 92-106.

DTI. (1998). *Our Competitive Future: Building the Knowledge Driven Economy, Competitiveness White Paper.* London: HMSO, Cm 4176.

Doh, S. and Kim, B. (2014). Government support for SME innovation in the regional industries: The case of government financial support program in South Korea. *Research Policy,* **43**(9): 1557-1569.

Frank, C.E.J., Miall, R.H. C. and Rees, R.D. (1984). Issues in small firms research of relevance to policy making. *Regional Studies,* **18**(3), 257-266.

Gibb, A.A. (2000). SME policy, academic research and the growth of ignorance, mythical concepts, myths, assumptions, rituals and confusions. *International Small Business Journal,* **18**(3), 13-35.

Greene, F.J., Mole, K.F. and Storey, D.J. (2008). *Three Decades of Enterprise Culture.* UK: Palgrave MacMillan.

Griggs, R. and Weaver, R. (1997). *An evaluation on the effectiveness of government intervention in developing entrepreneuship and creating new ventures: A Scottish study.* Paper presented at the Babson College. Boston.

Hanley, M. and O'Gorman, B. (2004). Local interpretation of national micro-enterprise policy: To what extent has it impacted on local enterprise development? *International Journal of Entrepreneurial Behaviour & Research,* **10**(5), 305-324.

Hart, D. M. (2003). *The Emergence of Entrepreneurship Policy. Governance, Start-ups and Growth in the US Knowledge Economy.* Cambridge: Cambridge University Press.

Hjalmarsson, D. and Johnson, A.W. (2003). Public advisory services - theory and practice. *Entrepreneurship & Regional Development*, **15**(1), 83-98.

Johnson, S. (2005). *SME Support Policy: Efficiency, Equity, Ideology or Vote-Seeking?* Paper presented at the Institute of Small Business and Entrepreneurship Conference. Blackpool.

Johnson, S., Sear, L. and Jenkins, A. (2000). Small-business policy, support and governance. In S. Carter & D. Jones-Evans (Eds.), *Enterprise and Small Business: Principles, Practice and Policy* (pp. 163-186). London: Prentice Hall.

Johnston, K. and Loader, K. (2003). Encouraging SME participation in training: identifying practical approaches. *Journal of European Industrial Training*, **27**(6), 273-280.

Loader, K. (2013). Is public procurement a successful small business support policy? A review of the evidence. *Environment and Planning C: Government and Policy*, **31**(1): 39-55.

Krugman, P. and Wells, R. (2005). *Economics*. New York: Worth Publishers.

Lambrecht, J. and Pirnay, F. (2005). An evaluation of public support for private external consultancies to SMEs in the Walloon region of Belgium. *Entrepreneurship & Regional Development*, **7**(2), 89-108.

Lundstrom, A. and Stevenson, L. (2005). *Entrepreneurship Policy – Theory and Practices (ISEN International Studies in Entrepreneurship)*. Birkhäuser: Springer.

Massey, C. (2003). Enterprise assistance: response from the public and private sectors. *Journal of Small Business and Enterprise Development*, **10**(20), 128-135.

Matlay, H. (2001). Strategic issues in vocational education and training in central and Eastern Europe. *Education and Training*, **43**(8/9), 395-404.

Matlay, H. and Westhead, P. (2005). Virtual teams and the rise of e-entrepreneurship in Europe. *International Small Business Journal*, **12**(3), 353-365.

Maritz, A. and Donovan, J. (2015). Entrepreneurship and Innovation: Setting An Agenda for Greater Discipline Contextualization. *Education + Training*, **57**(1), 74-87.

OECD. (1998). *Fostering Entrepreneurship, the OECD Jobs Strategy*. Retrieved August 2008, from http://www.ingentaconnect.com/content/oecd/16080203/1998/00001998/00000016/0498041e

OECD. (2000). *Small and Medium-sized Enterprise Outlook*. Retrieved August 2008, from http://www.ingentaconnect.com/content/oecd/16080203/2000/00002000/00000009/9200021e

OECD. (2005a). *SME and Entrepreneurship Outlook*. Retrieved August 2005, from www.oecd.org/document/15/0,3343,en_2649_34197_35096847_1_1_1_37461,00.html.

11

OECD. (2005b). *OECD Annual Report 2005; 45th Anniversary*. Paris. The Organization for Economic Co-operation and Development.

Parker, S. (2007). Policymakers beware! In D. B. Audretsch, I. Grilo & A. R. Thurik (Eds.), *Handbook of Research on Entrepreneurship Policy* (pp. 54-63). Great Britain: Edward Elgar.

Patel, R. (2004). *Creating an Enterprise Culture Understanding the National Mission; A Campaign Perspective*. London: Enterprise Insight.

Richard, D. (2007). *Richard Review on Small Business & Government*. Retrieved August 2008, from http://www.conservatives.com/pdf/document-richardreport-2008.pdf.

Robson, P.J.A. and Bennett, R.J. (2000). The use of and impact of business advice in Britian: An empirical assessment using logit and ordered logit models. *Applied Economics, 32*(13), 1675-1688.

Shane, S.A. (2008). *The Illusions of Entrepreneurship; The costly myths that entrepreneurs, investors and policy makers live by*. New Haven: Yale University Press.

Stevenson, L. and Lundstrom, A. (2001). *Patterns and Trends in Entrepreneurship Policy and Practices in Ten Economies*. Volume 3. Sweden. Swedish Foundation for Small Business Research.

Stevenson, L. and Lundstrom, A. (2007). Dressing the emperor: The fabric of entrepreneurship policy. In D. B. Audretsch, I. Grilo & A. R. Thurik (Eds.), *Handbook of Research on Entrepreneurship Policy* (pp. 94-129). Great Britain: Edward Elgar.

Storey, D.J. (2003). Entrepreneurship, small and medium sized enterprises and public policies. In Acs Z.J. and Audretsch, D.B. (Eds.), *Handbook of Entrepreneurship Research* (pp. 476–511). Dordrecht: Kluwer Academic Publishers.

Storey, D.J. (2005). *Understanding the Small Business Sector*. UK: Thomson Learning.

Valliere, D. and Peterson, R. (2009). Entrepreneurship and economic growth: Evidence from emerging and developed countries. *Entrepreneurship & Regional Development, 21*(5-6), 459-480.

Verheul, I., Carree, M. and Santarelli, E. (2009). Regional opportunities and policy initiatives for new venture creation. *International Small Business Journal, 27*(5), 608-626.

Wren, C. and Storey, D.J. (2002). Evaluating the effect of soft business support upon small firm performance. *Oxford Economics Papers, 54*, 334-365.

Wright, M., Roper, S., Hart, M. and Carter, S. (2015). Joining the dots: Building the evidence base for SME growth policy. *International Small Business Journal 33*(1), 3-11.

Young, L. (2015). *The Report on Small Firms 2010-2015*. London.

12 Business Ethics

Jane Queenan

This chapter is probably not your first encounter with the concept of business ethics; most modern business management texts consider the topic. However, as your knowledge of business management broadens, it is interesting to revisit the principles of ethical business practice and explore their application in greater depth. Business ethics offers a way of thinking about business management decision making that is substantially different from other areas of business management theory. Rather than ask what a business should do in order to achieve a particular objective, we simply ask what a business should do – what might constitute good behaviour. Of course, the aim of all businesses is to make profit and so, having asked what constitutes good behaviour, we can then examine how good ethical practice contribute to commercial success.

Defining business ethics

One challenge of engaging with business ethics is the risk of mild ridicule. Managers who are under pressure to generate profit within their business, might express wry amusement, commenting they cannot believe that the subject can possibly exist. In informal argument, opponents readily offer examples of wrong-doing to support the claim that business ethics is an oxymoron (Collins, 1994).

It is probably true that bad news attracts more attention than good; within the business pages of newspapers, or on social media, there is a constant stream of stories about alleged inefficiency, wrongdoing and corruption in commercial, sporting and political life. For example, between Monday 1 June 2015 and Friday 27 June 2015, lead stories in UK media included:

☐ The President of FIFA, Sepp Blatter, facing allegation of corruption (Halliday, 2015).

☐ Jail sentences for four bankers in the collapse of the Icelandic bank Kaupthing.

☐ A case brought again a UK MP for electoral misconduct (BBC News, 2015).

This flow of stories about bad behaviour helps explain a cynical response to the examination of business ethics; with bad behaviour so prevalent, can it ever be worthwhile trying to identify good behaviour?

As soon as you describe behaviour as 'bad', on what grounds do you make that claim? You might argue that bad behaviour leads to inefficient outcomes; in legal terms, bad behaviour might be unlawful or illegal. Yet, in the day-to-day discussion of corporate behaviour, we quickly move beyond 'lawful or illegal' – a corporation may do things which are entirely legal and yet the general population regards those actions as 'bad' or 'unethical'.

Example: Starbucks has used legal rules regarded by many as 'loopholes' to reduce or evade the payment of UK corporation tax (Hickman, 2015).

Consider when you first began your business management studies. You could probably have loosely defined terms such as 'management' and 'business'. Now, though, you should be able to define these terms much more precisely, and to recognize, for example, that there are many entities to which the tools of management might be applied. You will probably think of business management studies as the analysis of the organization and behaviour of these entities. We might use names such as 'company', 'corporation' or 'firm', to define the legal forms of particular business entities, but in everyday parlance such terms are used interchangeably. We see that precise definitions and careful use of language are already important tools in your studies. Here, we simply extend such analysis to the new field of business ethics.

Ethics is a branch of philosophy. There is a wealth of academic literature which defines and discusses business ethics from every imaginable philosophical angle. In general discussion, however, we might start with a simple dictionary definition. *Chambers Dictionary* defines ethics in two ways: as a singular noun, it is the study or the science of morals (and so the philosophical study itself); (Chambers, 2014) but as a plural noun, it is the rules or principles of behaviour (the conclusions of the study). For completeness, we note that *Chambers* defines morals as a sense of right and wrong, or a standard of behaviour based on such a sense. In speaking of ethics, then, we might mean awareness of what constitutes good or bad conduct, a set of principles allowing us to determine what might constitute good or bad behaviour, or else the systematic study and classification of behaviour as good or bad. In academic study, we shall usually rely on this last definition.

Turning now to define business ethics, here we treat it primarily as a form of academic enquiry, (Marcoux, 2008) and just one sub-field of applied ethics. For people who are engaged in business, ethics might be their own awareness that the conduct of business dealings might be seen as being right or wrong, or indeed, self-appraisal of their dealings, invoking Adam Smith's impartial spectator (Fleischacker, 2015). In addition, for people who are members of a profession, such as lawyers, accountants or doctors, we might interpret business ethics as being embodied within codes of practice that have been laid down over many years to allow members of these professions to distinguish between good and bad behaviour.

> **Example**: When new staff join a company, they are often asked to sign a confidentiality agreement, in which they undertake not to share a company's commercially confidential information with external bodies unless the employer gives permission.

de George (2012) defines the practice of business ethics as "the long tradition of applying ethical norms to business, just as it has been applied to other areas of social and personal life".

In this context, we also find it useful to refer to the definition of business ethics offered by Crane and Matten (Crane and Matten, s, activities and decisions where issues of right and wrong are addressed".

Exercise

Select three definitions of business ethics. One should be from a textbook, one from an academic journal and one from a more general journal or modern media source. Reference them in Harvard style. Identify the similarities between the definitions and the areas in which they differ.

Why are business ethics important?

Think for a moment of how our daily lives are affected by the conduct of business. Every product, every service, our food, our transport, our leisure – all are created, managed and disposed of through active businesses. We make choices about what we buy or do, but even if we actively seek to minimize our contact with the world around us, it is almost impossible to avoid commercial activity. So, since business plays such an important part in our lives, we have a legitimate interest in how that business is conducted

12

Everyday ethics example

You go into a shop to buy a can of Coke, costing, say 70p. You ask for a can of Coke and hand over a £1 coin, the shopkeeper hands you a can of Coke and 30p in change. This is a very simple everyday transaction. What are your mutual expectations, beyond a reasonable degree of good manners?

Customer	Shopkeeper
A genuine can of Coke, not a fake	Legal tender, not a fake coin
A can of Coke which is within date	You will not attempt to steal the product
The correct change	

Does this transaction have any ethical import? Well, let us consider various factors. Firstly, both customer and shopkeeper have choices. They can use intelligence and good sense to make choices about where they shop, the products they offer and so on. However, once the decision is made to undertake a transaction, we enter the field of ethics. The customer has to **trust** that the shopkeeper has the correct stock, that the price is appropriate, that the can is not out of date, is fit for purpose and so on. The shopkeeper has to **trust** that the customer is going to hand over legal tender.

Let's examine another transaction, buying a product on EBay. Purchases on this popular auction website seem much more complex than the simple purchase of a can of Coke. The most obvious difference is that buyer and seller are at a distance, they cannot meet. The buyer must rely on photographs and descriptions of the product. Both must rely on the banking system to protect financial interests. Again, what can the buyer and seller expect?

Buyer	Seller
The photo should be an accurate representation of the product	The buyer will pay promptly
The product should be sent safely and promptly	The buyer will not attempt to evade payment by false claims of non-delivery etc.

The greater complexity of this transaction is demonstrated by intricate layers of technological and legal protection. PayPal, laws on distance selling and customer feedback are all methods of protecting both buyer and seller. At base, however, we see that this transaction also depends to a large extent on mutual trust and fairness.

We can confidently assert, therefore, that business transactions are based on ethical principles – ideas such as fair price, honesty and trust.

So, at a very basic everyday level we see that our daily transactions are guided by ethical considerations. Looking at the larger corporate environment however, we can also make an argument for the examination in ethical terms of company behaviour.

☐ Companies have an influence on every aspect of our daily lives – we can therefore argue that a company's good or bad behaviour is of interest to us.

☐ Large companies are powerful. Procter and Gamble noted net sales of $83,062,000,000 in its 2014 Annual Report (Procter & Gamble, 2014). World Bank statistics for 2013 reveal that this is markedly more than the Gross Domestic Product of many countries, such as Luxembourg, (GDP $60bn) or Bolivia with GDP of $34bn (World Bank, 2015). Again, we may argue that we have an interest in the behaviour of those with financial power.

☐ Companies can act for good or ill, giving employment to the community or causing pollution. Some may do good things and bad things at the same time, for example, providing employment while polluting the atmosphere. We can argue therefore that we have a legitimate interest in holding companies to account for their behaviour.

In all these cases, we are assessing standards of ethical behaviour.

One particularly interesting area of business ethics is its relation to entrepreneurial organizations. (Harris, *et al.*, 2011) ask if such businesses may be faced with a complex range of ethical dilemmas which are specific to innovative new ventures.

Example: Pre-internet, a business manager might receive a letter and write a considered reply. Now, ready electronic communication demands an instant response. This could lead us to reply too speedily without considering all the consequences of our decision.

Exercise

If you are an internet user, you probably access Google on a daily basis. Identify three elements of Google's business model which may have ethical import.

What is the scope of business ethics?

We see that ethical business practice can affect our everyday transactions. However, we may also ask to what extent ethics are embedded in the various parts of a business. Does every business activity have an ethical dimension? Are some business activities outside of the reach of business ethics? We ask the question: "What is the scope of business ethics?"

First, let's return to our basic discussion of definitions. They address concepts of right and wrong – of morality. This relationship with moral behaviour is important. Indeed, in the older Scottish Universities, Ethics is known as Moral Philosophy. The study of ethics, therefore, can be seen as comment on personal behaviour.

12

Business ethics, however is concerned with good and bad behaviour within the sphere of business. This is not as obvious a statement as it seems.

☐ In any business a wide range of activities are undertaken on a daily basis. Some have a very obvious ethical aspect – we can easily see that issues such as fair pricing or the way we treat our employees involve us in questions of good and bad behaviour.

☐ Some decisions, however, may simply be straightforward questions of business. The design of our marketing material or the location of our shops or the choice of company vehicle may have no ethical import – they are simply decisions which help maintain or increase our business. They are ethically neutral.

☐ So, not every business action has ethical import.

We might also note that many business activities are regulated by law. Businesses have no choice but to conform to laws and regulations relating to Sale of Goods, Merchantable Quality, Consumer Credit and so on.

Take a moment to think about these rules and regulations. In most societies, bodies of law are created to capture those values and principles which that society holds dear. Business principles are included in that group. You'll know from your previous studies that historians and archaeologists have discovered evidence of trade regulations in cultures as old as the ancient Babylonians (Iseline, n.d.)

Again, some rules and regulations do not have ethical import. For example, rules about not walking on the grass, or not parking in particular places are designed to support the organization of daily life. We may object to transgression – walking on the grass may spoil the lawn for other people, poor parking may block access – but they may not have an ethical aspect. We might refer to such rules and activities as being 'morally neutral'. But the laws we are discussing relate to principles of fair trading, which do have ethical importance.

Example: Talking in the library while you are trying to study is inconsiderate. It may not break a law, but it certainly transgresses our ideas of appropriate behaviour.

So, when we talk about the scope of business ethics, we may say:

☐ When we think about business ethics we are considering ideas of right and wrong in relation to business decisions.

☐ Not all business decisions have an ethical import. Business ethics addresses only those activities which do have an ethical import.

☐ Some business decisions are governed by laws or regulation. Some of these laws and regulations reflect ethical stances.

☐ We may make a particular business decision because the law demands it, not because we choose to. Nevertheless, if that law has an ethical dimension, then the decision is also within the scope of business ethics.

Exercise

Identify three activities within a company of your choice which are morally neutral. Explain why they are so.

A current ethical dilemma – the living wage

Wage setting is considered here as an example of ethical consideration in business.

Heart of Midlothian Football Club ('Hearts') plays in the Scottish Professional Football League. Formed in 1874, the club plays at Edinburgh's Tynecastle stadium. In December 2014, Hearts became the first British football club to obtain accreditation as a living wage employer (Hearts Football Club, 2014).

In the UK, there is a statutory minimum wage – at the time of writing, £6.50 per hour for people over 21 (UK Government, 2015) Separately, the Living Wage Foundation, working with the Centre for Research in Social Policy (CRSP), recommends a 'living wage' of £7.85 per hour (CRSP, n.d.) which is just over 20% higher than the minimum wage. The living wage concept emerged in the 1990s from Joseph Rowntree Trust research (Parker, 1998) and is updated annually (David, *et al.*, 2014). The basis of its calculation is that a family of two adults and two dependent children, with both adults in full time work, should be able to achieve a 'low cost but acceptable' standard of living. The Living Wage Foundation works with employers to confirm that employment contracts meet specific standards, designed to ensure full compliance with the recommendations of the CRSP. (Werner, 2015).

Here, we see the difference between legal compliance and voluntary adherence to ethical norms. Hearts FC could have chosen to pay its lowest paid staff the minimum wage. In announcing its accreditation, a Hearts FC spokesperson claimed that, "The club feels that implementing the Living Wage is entirely in keeping with the values that we hold dear as Edinburgh's oldest football club." (Hearts Football Club, 2014) Note the reference to values: the argument does not rest on questions of efficiency, increasing ticket sales, or profits, but that this commitment was justified in and of itself.

In the UK, only Chelsea FC has followed Hearts' example. (Chelsea Football Club, 2014) Indeed, Celtic FC, the largest and wealthiest club in Scotland, announced its intention 'to consult with our employees... but our objective

12

will be to introduce a minimum hourly pay rate of £7.85 for all permanent employees.' (Celtic Football Club, 2014). This decision was widely criticised by shareholders who requested living wage accreditation at the club's annual general meeting. Their argument was that accreditation would be consistent with the club's origins and traditions. Again, this is an appeal to a set of values, against which the club's behaviour might be appraised.

The commitments into which Hearts and Celtic have entered may look similar, but there are some important differences. Hearts (and Chelsea) have agreed that their low-paid staff should receive the living wage; Celtic (and all other clubs) have declined to enter into a formal commitment. The arguments advanced by the directors of Celtic against accreditation are essentially prudent. They note the intensely competitive environment in their retail operations and suggest that it would not be possible to pay wages substantially higher than the minimum wage in this part of the business and still make profits (BBC, 2014).

The debate within Celtic FC raises some interesting questions. Celtic FC is owned by Celtic plc, a publicly limited company. The directors have a fiduciary responsibility to shareholders to maximize the value of the business. This business relies on the loyalty of supporters, some of whom have small shareholdings. So, the directors cannot simply ignore the opinions of shareholders.

Hearts FC has a similar structure. But we cannot claim that the directors of Hearts have behaved in an ethical manner, while Celtic's have behaved unethically, because both have been able to provide a rationale for their behaviour, based on consideration of what they believe to be right given the environment in which their club operates.

Exercise

Nova IT is a new technology company creating cutting edge medical hardware. A J Smith is a traditional firm of chartered accountants. Identify two ethical dilemmas which both companies might handle in the same way. Identify one dilemma which each company might treat very differently.

Corporate social responsibility and stakeholder theory: an example of ethical argument

In this section we will look at one particular area of ethical analysis – that of the relationship of corporate social responsibility and 'stakeholders' to the living wage dilemma discussed above.

Our examples demonstrate the nature of ethical argument. With any question of ethical behaviour, we should be able to advance a variety of arguments. The idea of an ethical dilemma reflects this: there is no simple right or wrong answer in a dilemma, simply justifications for each of the alternatives. The example that we have used of living wage certification demonstrates this. If paying the living wage was obviously the only ethical stance, then all businesses, not just all football clubs would pay it. That, of course would also mean that there would be no reason to have a minimum wage, since all businesses would voluntarily pay the higher level of wages.

In other areas of study you may already have encountered the concept of corporate social responsibility, Bowen interprets CSR as the responsibility which business has to pursue goals which support the aims and values of wider society (Bowen, 1953).

What this means in practice is the subject of much research and discussion, too detailed for this chapter, but such a definition suggests that organizations have responsibilities beyond simply the generation of profit. Indeed, much research has been conducted on the effect on financial performance of such responsibilities (Harrison and Wickes, 2013).

> **Example**: IKEA, the well-known furniture manufacturer has an extensive 'sustainability' agenda, reflecting its status as an important purchaser of raw materials such as wood and cotton.

The analysis of this proposition gives a good example of business ethics in action.

Let us begin with arguing **against** the concept of CSR.

The ethical question that we consider here relates to how businesses decide their objectives. In law, a company is incorporated. It has legal identity, quite separate from that of its owners. The owners appoint directors, whose task is to manage the business for the owners. The company enters into contracts in its own right. Ownership is a property right acquired through the purchase of some of the capital of the business (usually called shares). Generally, the owners of a concern will share its profits through dividend payments, usually a proportion of the market value of the capital of the business. The important point is that it is possible to identify a group of people who are the ultimate owners of the company, and who therefore have particular legal rights.

In an essay, written for the *New York Times* in 1970, Milton Friedman, an economist who subsequently won the Nobel Prize in Economics, summarized the argument of his book *Capitalism and Freedom* (Friedman, 2002) in respect of

12

the responsibilities of the directors of a business. "That responsibility is to conduct the business in accordance with [the owners'] desires, which generally will be to make as much money as possible while conforming to the basic rules of the society, both those embodied in law and those embodied in ethical custom." (Friedman, 1970). This newspaper essay is still worthy of discussion some forty five years later because it was influential in bringing ethical arguments to the forefront of popular discourse. Friedman's argument has three main elements.

☐ Corporations are legal entities, not human beings and therefore do not have moral responsibilities. Moral responsibility is assumed by human beings.

☐ The responsibility of managers is to act in the interests of shareholders and owners. Acting for any other purpose is out with the remit of the manager and the company.

☐ Social responsibility is the job of the individual and government.

His argument is therefore that a company should not be diverted from its core objectives by the demands of outside interests.

At first glance, we might assume that Friedman is suggesting that organizations need have no ethical responsibilities at all. However, this would be to misread his much more subtle argument. At no point does Friedman suggest that good ethical behaviour is unimportant. Indeed, he clearly notes that organizations must function within the constraints of the law and prevailing ethical standards.

What he does suggest is that to act in a way which does not contribute directly to the objectives of owners or shareholders is not legitimate. Since the clearly defined objectives of such owners and shareholders will probably include the generation of profit, it is not legitimate for a manager to act in a way which does not contribute to that aim.

For Friedman therefore, the purely philanthropic activities which many modern companies are asked to engage in are inappropriate. They are only permissible if they contribute to the long term objectives of the company (for example, if charitable giving increases a company's good reputation) in which case, Friedman would argue that such actions are legitimate business activities rather than philanthropy.

This provides a good defence of the actions of the directors of Celtic plc: they believed that paying the living wage to all employees would be inconsistent with the achievement of the owners' objectives of maximizing the long-run economic value of the company.

According to Friedman, the problem is quite simple. The owners of a company have rights in setting its objectives, and managers should implement those rights as far as possible. If the owners' objectives are clearly defined, and there is no uncertainty about the effects of all possible actions, then directors will never face ethical dilemmas. Yet, by referring to 'ethical custom', Friedman acknowledges that there are certain actions that would be considered wrong by so many people that no company should engage in them. For example, it is very unlikely that an oil company would simply dispose of an oil rig in the North Sea by sinking it because of the objections that environmental lobbyists would raise. Similarly, criticisms of labour standards within the production chains of fashion retailers, such as Gap, have led to the adoption of labour standards that are much higher than those required by law in many countries. (Gunther, 2015). Yet, as we noted at the start of the chapter, it is very easy to find situations in which the behaviour of businesses fails to meet the expectations of the society in they operate.

We might therefore set aside Friedman's claim that only the owners of a company have the right to set its objectives, and ask instead who has a legitimate right to be involved in that process. Going back to the example of Celtic plc, whose business is to run a football club, it seems very easy to argue that the owners of the business merely provide it with capital. Employees, notably the players are the visible identity of the organization. Supporters, who buy tickets, and travel long distances to watch the team play, create much of its identity. Television companies, paying substantial sums for recording and broadcast rights, clearly have considerable influence upon the company's activities. And all football companies will be members of an association, since without competition, the sport could not exist. Rather than declare, with Friedman, that the interests of the owners always and inevitably have priority, we might consider that an organization needs to address the interests of all groups who have an interest in its performance.

In this context, Edward Freeman argues that a company is not responsible simply to its shareholders, but has to recognize a responsibility to all people, groups and organizations that might be considered to have an interest in its activities (Freeman, 1984). He calls these **stakeholders** – we have listed some of the stakeholders of Celtic plc already. For Freeman, an organization's ethical purpose is defined by how it balances the interests of the many groups with which it has a relationship, and secures their assent to its activities.

A simple illustration of traditional stakeholders might be:

12

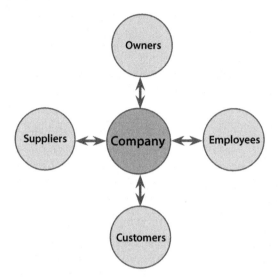

Figure 12.1: Traditional stakeholder
Source: Adapted from Crane and Matten (2010).

Note that interests are mutual and a two way process. It can easily be seen why these groups would have a close interest in the firm's behaviour and wellbeing.

A more complex view of stakeholder theory may include groups out side of the immediate circle of the firm, which may nevertheless be affected by its success or failure.

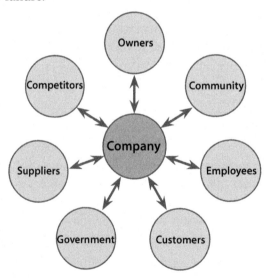

Figure 12.2: A more complex stakeholder diagram
Source: Adapted from Crane and Matten (2010).

However, just as Friedman's theory does not ignore ethical practice, so Freeman does not suggest that there are no limits on the ethical rights of stakeholders. In stakeholder theory, not all stakeholder groups have an equal right to be considered at all times. In certain circumstances the rights of one group may have a higher claim than those of others.

Example: Company A is in dispute over employee wages. It can be argued that in this discussion the interests of the employee stakeholder group have a greater claim to be considered than, for example, the stakeholder interests of a local environmental group. Later that year, however, the company is considering building some new plant, which will impinge on a local park. In such a case, the interests of the local environmental group move to the fore and may be of more immediate significance than say, a stakeholder group made up of competitors.

The need for balance follows directly from the diverging interests of stakeholders. The higher the wage rate, the more will be paid to employees, and the less will be available for distribution to the owners. The interests of employees and owners appear to be in direct conflict. Yet if the owners insist on paying wages that are lower than the market rate, the company may be unable to hire productive workers, forcing it to close. In making a decision to become an accredited living wage employer, a company is stating very publicly how it intends to take account of the interests of its employees, and is making a series of commitments that it cannot easily break.

12

Conclusion

In this chapter, we have developed our arguments using examples, many of which continue to be the subject of active debate. This reflects our preferred definition of business ethics as the process by which we analyse and justify the behaviour of businesses – or their owners and managers – rather than as some set of principles defined purely in terms of theoretical considerations. We do not use ethical analysis to attempt to score the effectiveness of a business in meeting externally-set criteria. We do, though, consider that most business managers, even those who scorn the possibility of ethical considerations informing their decision making, engage in ethical consideration, if only in a very limited way.

Of the many theoretical questions that we might have explored, we have concentrated on perhaps the most widely examined in the last fifty years of the development of business ethics: in whose interests does a business operate? Here, we have set out two opposing arguments: that a business exists to return profits to its shareholders; and that a business is a social organization that has a responsibility to a wide range of stakeholders. We have shown that the practice of corporate social responsibility may be consistent with the first of these objectives if activities that appear to serve the interest of external stakeholders enable the business to increases its profits, possibly in future. It is therefore possible that we might observe substantial agreement among business ethicists about what constitutes 'good' or 'right' or 'just' behaviour, even while the arguments that they advance in support of these conclusions differ considerably.

Business ethics arises from philosophical theory but is nevertheless a practical branch of applied ethics. Our argument is that in the rapidly developing world of modern business, a regular review of ethical practice is more relevant than ever. The proposition that businesses have no responsibilities other than to meet the objectives of their owners within the law and standard ethical norms is still popular. However, given the global reach of many corporations and the extent to which they influence our daily lives, the expectation that companies address the needs of relevant stakeholders is increasingly accepted.

References

BBC News, (2015). *Alastair Carmichael legal campaign reaches £60000 target.* Available at: http://www.bbc.co.uk/news/uk-scotland-scotland-politics-33062216 [Accessed 30 June 2015].

BBC, (2014). *Celtic have been used over living wage says Peter Lawwell.* Available at: http://www.bbc.co.uk/sport/0/football/30150594 [Accessed 30 June 2015].

Bowen, H., (1953). *Social Responsibilities of the Businessman.* New York: Harper.

Celtic Football Club, (2014). *Club reflects on Positive Year at AGM.* Available at: http://www.celticfc.net/news/7143 [Accessed 30 June 2015].

Centre for Research in Social Policy, (n.d.). *The Living Wage.* Available at: http://www.lboro.ac.uk/research/crsp/mis/thelivingwage/ [Accessed 30 June 2015].

Chambers, (2014). *Chambers Dictionary.* 13 ed. London: Chambers Harrap.

Chelsea Football Club, (2014). *Chelsea to pay Living Wage.* Available at: http://www. chelseafc.com/news/latest-news/2014/12/chelsea-to-pay-living-wage.html [Accessed 30 June 2015].

Collins, J., (1994). Is business ethics an oxymoron? *Business Horizons*, September-October, pp. 1-8.

Crane, A. &. Matten, D., (2010). *Business Ethics: Managing corporate citizenship and sustainability in the age of globalization*, 3 ed. Oxford: Oxford University Press, p. 5.

David, A., Hirsch, D. & Padley, M., (2014). *Minimum Income Standard 2014.* Available at: http://www.jrf.org.uk/publications/minimum-income-standard-2014 [Accessed 30 June 2015].

de George, R. T., (2012). A history of business ethics. In: *Values and Ethics for the 21st Century.* Buenos Aires: BBVA , pp. 337-358.

Fleischacker, S., (2015). *Adam Smith's Moral and Political Philosophy.* Available at: http://plato.stanford.edu/archives/fall2015/entries/smith-moral-political [Accessed 30 June 2015].

Freeman, E., (1984). *Strategic Management: A Stakeholder Approach.* London: Pitman Publishing.

Friedman, M., (1970). *The Social Responsibility of Business is to Increase its Profits.* Available at: http://doc.cat-v.org/economics/milton_friedman/business_social_ responsibility [Accessed 30 June 2015].

Friedman, M., (2002). *Capitalism and Freedom.* 40th Anniversary Edition ed. Chicago: University of Chicago Press.

Gunther, M., (2015). *Protecting a tangled workforce that stretches across the world.* Available at: http://www.theguardian.com/sustainable-business/2015/apr/28/ gap-kindley-lawlor-human-rights-workers-jobs-garment-industry [Accessed 30 June 2015].

Halliday, J., (2015). *Why has Sepp Blatter resigned as FIFA president?* Available at: http:// www.theguardian.com/football/2015/jun/02/why-has-sepp-blatter-resigned-as-fifa-president [Accessed 30 June 2015].

Harrison, J. S. and Wickes, A.C., (2013). Stakeholder Theory, Value and Firm Performance. *Business Ethics Quarterly*, **23**, pp. 97-124.

Hearts Football Club, (2014). *Hearts Officially Living Wage Employer.* Available at: http://www.heartsfc.co.uk/news/4026 [Accessed 30 June 2015].

Hickman, M., (2015). *Good Bean Counters? Starbucks has paid no tax in UK since 2009.* Available at: http://www.independent.co.uk/news/business/news/good-bean-counters-starbucks-has-paid-no-tax-in-uk-since-2009-8212579.html [Accessed 30 June 2015].

12

Iseline, C., (n.d.). *Code de Hammurabi, roi de Babylone.* Available at: http://www.louvre.fr/oeuvre-notices/code-de-hammurabi-roi-de-babylone# [Accessed 30 June 2015].

Marcoux, A., (2008). *Business Ethics.* Available at: http://plato.stanford.edu/archives/fall2008/entries/ethics-business [Accessed 30 June 2015].

Parker, H., (1998). *Low Cost but Acceptable: A minimum income standard for the UK: Families with young children.* Bristol: Policy Press.

Procter & Gamble, (2014). *Procter and Gamble Annual Report.* Available at: http://www.pginvestor.com/interactive/lookandfeel/4004124/PG_Annual_Report_2014.pdf

UK Government, (2015). *The National Minimum Wage Regulations 2015.* Available at: http://www.legislation.gov.uk/ukdsi/2015/9780111127964 [Accessed 30 June 2015].

Werner, A. L. M., (2015). The ethics of the living wage: a review and research agenda. *Journal of Business Ethics,* Issue forthcoming.

World Bank, (2015). *World Bank.* Available at: http://data.worldbank.org/ [Accessed 01 July 2015].

Index

Printed in the United States
By Bookmasters